Dreams and Delusions

Dreams
and
Delusions

The Drama of German History by

FRITZ STERN

ALFRED A. KNOPF NEW YORK 1987

Library of Congress Cataloging-in-Publication Data

Stern, Fritz Richard.
Dreams and delusions, the drama of German
history.

Bibliography: p.
Includes index.
1. Germany—History—20th century. I. Title.
DD232.S765 1987   943.08   87-45117
ISBN 0-394-55995-9

To Felix Gilbert
in affection and admiration

Contents

Dreams and Delusions

Drawing and Designing

Introduction

Franzosen und Russen gehört das Land,
Das Meer gehört den Briten,
Wir aber besitzen im Luftreich des Traums
Die Herrschaft unbestritten.

The land is held by Russians and French,
The sea's by the British invested,
But in the airy realm of dreams
Our sway is uncontested.

HEINRICH HEINE,
"Germany: A Winter's Tale,"
1844

The fate of democracy rests on faith in history.

ERNST REUTER, 1913

THE GERMANS HAVE TAUGHT US history as they have lived it: sublimely and cruelly. They began as teachers in the literal sense. It was Ranke, himself steeped in German thought and poetry, who, in the first half of the last century, established history as a central and autonomous discipline, and for decades thereafter German scholarship was celebrated as a model, most importantly in the United States. In our own century, the Germans have taught us—and themselves—the power, the inescapable horror, that history can visit upon its victims. The Third Reich was a lesson in history that still haunts our collective memory—in however dim and distorted a fashion.

It is part of the German paradox that while idealizing history as an essential means to self-knowledge and self-cultivation, the Germans have found it hard, indeed impossible, to grasp their own tormented past. From belated unification to unprecedented devastation, that is, from 1871 to 1945, Germans alternately exulted in triumphs and lamented defeats, suffered disasters and changed regimes—and at the very least until 1945, most of their historians wrote with nationalistic, anti-Western blinders.

To understand the German past is to remember the promise that pre-Hitler Germany represented, and never fully actualized. The achievements in science and in industry, in art, architecture, and academic scholarship, were truly prodigious and a warrant for hope. But it was never a quiet, balanced country: Even before the Great War and most especially after it, Germany was restless, fearful, aggressive, and divided.[1] It was also a country that many Germans and foreign visitors, especially in the period before 1914, regarded as appallingly rigid, militaristic, and illiberal, as demonstrated in Chapter 9 (page 243). Till Hitler, it was a country of immense contradictions, attractive and alarming, with dreams of peace colliding with a recurrent lure of power, with many Germans having dreams of great national and spiritual unity and denying at the same time the inevitability of social and political conflicts, thus turning them into principled, mortal enmity. For over a century, "the German Question," in all of its guises, has had a decisive bearing on the history of the world.

There is no denying the centrality of German history, and fascination with it requires no apology. The accident of German birth and the childhood experience of living for five years under National Socialism may have given my professional concern a personal imperative. I hope that detachment and involvement still complement each other in these essays.

The essays all deal with Germany, past and present, and with the effort of historians to come to grips with that past. They dwell on the promise and the achievement, on the costs, psychic and political, of partial triumphs. They also raise the persistent question of how so many Germans could have succumbed to National Socialism, to a regime that offered redemption, brought terror, and delivered ruin. In short, these essays touch on various aspects of what I would call the German drama, mirrored in some essays in the lives of individuals. I have tried to set promise and disaster in context; rarely in the history of Europe has so much been squandered so catastrophically.

As I acknowledged on an earlier occasion, I find essays an attractive format. They allow for tentative explorations of new themes; they allow for a personal tone that larger studies tend to inhibit, though even in the latter the austere effort of "extinguishing the self," deemed imperative by some historians, has never been my goal or style. "Disciplining the self" might be a better dictum, awareness of self a better guide.

The main reason for collecting these essays is simple: Composed over the past decade, but most of them in the last few years, they were written in the hope that they would be read. They were scattered, and some had appeared only in German. I wanted to make them more accessible, the more so as some topics (the public lives of Einstein and Haber, as well as National Socialism as temptation) took an unexpected hold on me; I intend to pursue them further.

In collecting these essays and lectures, I came to realize that accident—and a receptive unconscious—had led me to more congenial subjects in German history than I had hitherto written about. An invitation to speak at the Einstein Centenary in Jerusalem gave me a chance to study this inscrutable genius, to read in his unpublished correspondence, and to try to understand why he, who hated so much of German life, spent the happiest years of his life there. An invitation to address an Ernst Reuter Memorial in Berlin, together with Helmut Schmidt, led me to try to reconstruct the making of an extraordinary German democrat. In 1986, I was asked to speak at the seventy-fifth anniversary of the founding of what is now called the Fritz Haber Institute, and I tried to sketch the life of Haber, preeminent chemist and great organizer of German science. These were encounters that opened new doors, even as they touched on certain childhood memories.

I am drawn to studying earlier periods through individuals who are of intrinsic and representative importance. Of course there are "the broad, anonymous forces" that characterize the setting or structure of an age, but it is the interplay between these forces and actual people that allows us to recapture something of the spirit of an age. In this fashion one can hope to detect not only the rational political motives of particular actors, but perhaps something of their less conscious, more spontaneous responses as well. National Socialism epitomized what has been called projective politics—and the adaptation of particular people to the movement could only be understood if one studied the divided mind, the ambivalence, and the uncertainty of individuals confronting an unprecedented, deceptive promise.

One of the pleasures—and pitfalls—of historical study is its indeterminacy. In beginning a new topic, in finding new material, one discovers new questions, larger themes, a different context. A continuous, if sometimes unconscious, revisionism is at work: The new material is interpreted in accordance with one's general sense of the past—but that very sense is modified by new voices or new insights.

In reviewing these essays I realized afresh how much I have gained from close friendships and professional associations in Germany. They have left their mark on my work. They have also spurred my interest in contemporary life; in continuous conversations I have tried to understand the puzzlement, the changing perspectives of various Germans. At the same time, the themes of earlier work inform present efforts, and hence they perhaps deserve brief mention.

In writing *The Politics of Cultural Despair*, I discovered that the men who cried out against the deficiencies of the new world, who felt the hurts of modernity, who dreamt of a past that never was and a future that could never be, appealed to a wide German audience. I studied three generations of cultural critics who, because they vilified "Western" values such as materialism or liberalism, were hailed as prophets and who could thus invest brutal anti-Semitism or great imperialist ambition with the mantle of idealism. These men preached anti-bourgeois sermons and lamented the passing of an older Germany, characterized by true religion and a genuine community. They intuited deep and genuine grievances and blamed their pervasiveness on invidious foreign elements, most notably on Jews. They had their European analogues—in their laments, their crankiness, and their anti-Semitism. Their anti-capitalism and their anti-bourgeois anti-materialism recalled thoughts of the young Marx.[2] In short, I found in the work and the astounding reception of Lagarde, Langbehn, and Moeller van den Bruck a perverted version of a great European tradition, the noble protest against the deficiencies of modern capitalist-secular society. Here was a bridge between European idealism and Hitler's nihilism.

In *Gold and Iron* I came to see that the much-vaunted triumph of capitalism was partial and precarious—a theme I develop further in the last essay of this volume. The story of Bismarck and Bleichröder taught me the role of concealment in Germany, how reality was filtered through the expectations of decorum. Bismarck used his Jewish banker—as did the German elites generally—but without acknowledging the concern for money or the commerce with the Jew. When Bleichröder became the target of anti-Semitism in the 1870s (the term itself was a neologism of that decade), his patrons maintained an ominous silence—about which Bleichröder remained silent in turn. He had his own deep ambivalences: He was forever torn between filial piety, which included loyalty to ancestral Judaism, and an almost grotesque wish to be assimilated, accepted, and rewarded by a society that celebrated rank and demanded deference. He lived in an illiberal and hypocritical world, so that Theodor Mommsen's measured defense of Jewish rights was quickly hailed as a great clarion call of liberality. Bleichröder's life illustrated some of the traumatic effects of German mobility: For some, mobility meant a climb to the top; for many, uprootedness; for most, painful change. Materially, the nobility was declining (private bankers could shore them up, but they also bought their indebted estates), in a rank-conscious society the middle class discovered that prosperity was not enough, and the lower classes were impoverished, degraded, feared. I followed traces of that society in some fifteen years of working in diverse archives, but for context and meaning I drew as well on the great novels of the last century and on sociological observation—from Max Weber to Ralf Dahrendorf.

Some of the essays here collected complement earlier work. Einstein and Reuter represent the hope that existed in pre-Hitler Germany, and the essays on National Socialism try to understand how the latter could disguise its brutality so as to appeal to the spiritual and disinterested impulses of many Germans. They also show that the dream of peace, when disappointed, led to bitterness and hatred, just as the lure of power was often disguised in idealistic, pseudo-religious terms that promised redemption—hence peace.

Einstein, Haber, and Reuter were quite different and yet there were important links among them; each exemplified some important themes of German history. Einstein and Haber were fraternal opposites: They were good friends and colleagues, fellow scientists and fellow Nobel laureates, yet men of radically different temper and commitment. Each had a preeminent place in German life. During the Great War, their paths diverged completely; Einstein became a pacifist and Haber became Germany's chief scientific organizer, the inventor of chemical warfare. Reuter was a young, rising member of the Social Democratic Party. In November 1914, Einstein and Reuter became members of a tiny radical group, Bund Neues Vaterland, which advocated a peace without annexations—a drive for an early peace that in those days of chauvinistic frenzy was a lonely and dangerous enterprise. The Berlin authorities soon drove it underground. After Hitler, all three men went into exile: Haber died, a broken man, in 1934; Einstein remained in the United States, a critical, semi-isolated celebrity; Ernst Reuter, after his exile in Turkey, returned to Germany and became the world-famous lord mayor of Berlin during the grim, heroic days of the airlift.

In the Weimar years, all three men represented the promise, the great and unfulfilled promise, of a liberal-democratic Germany, and above all a Germany at peace. Einstein and Reuter had always cherished that dream of peace, in part because in their own private and public lives they had experienced hatred at home and war abroad. As an adolescent, Einstein was repelled by an authoritarian, militaristic style in German life, and he fled Germany to develop himself in the more peaceful climate of Switzerland. Yet he returned to Germany in 1914 because Berlin had become the preeminent center of the natural sciences. Voluntarily he had left Germany and voluntarily he returned to it—not knowing, of course, that within weeks of his return the Great War would break out, and that his colleagues and compatriots would surrender to an orgy of exultant chauvinism. From the first days of the war, Einstein recoiled, appalled by German enthusiasm. In the vengeful period after Versailles and before Hitler, he became the champion of militant pacifism. In his devotion to peace and tolerance he reckoned but partially with the forces obstructing these hopes; he saw villains and mass stupidity, but rarely the historically rooted obstacles. Peace was the ultimate dream—the more so as he saw his countrymen seduced time and again by the lure of power.

Einstein and Haber recall other aspects of German culture as well. In the fifty years before Hitler, Germany was probably the world's leader in the natural sciences. In these fields German Jews were allowed to distinguish themselves, and they worked in close cooperation with their Christian colleagues. Among humanists in German universities, there remained a suspicion of "soulless" science and a great hostility to positivism, but scientific achievement and world renown could not be gainsaid.

After 1919 Einstein became a celebrated genius—in a country suddenly depleted of heroes and very much attuned to the veneration of genius. He was probably the last of the German geniuses—before Hitler. Ever since the *Geniezeit,* the early romantic, *Sturm und Drang* period, the Germans have celebrated the mysterious and sometimes demonic creativity of the poet, the artist, the warrior-statesman, and finally the scientist. They also have a certain fear of the untamed genius. The greatest of them, Goethe, suppressed his most erotic poetry and it remained suppressed or ignored till long after his death.[3] A genius could also be seen as a public nuisance *(öffentliches Ärgernis)* and certainly Einstein encountered such hatred because of his fame and his anti-nationalistic views. As husbanders of talent, Germans were probably unsurpassed; in their veneration of the amoral genius, of the divine poet who could intuit truths accessible to no one else, they exposed themselves to great risk.[4]

Haber, a German Jew who at the age of twenty-four had converted to Protestantism, was a brilliant chemist, with an inextinguishable bent for the practical world, whether in linking scientific discovery to industrial progress or to wartime needs or, after the war, in helping German science survive economic calamity. In the 1920s he worked toward Germany's reintegration into the international community of science, trying to break simultaneously a continued Allied intellectual blockade against the former enemy and the sullen counter-blockade of German nationalistic professors who were quite willing to enjoy the pain of isolation. I have called Haber and Einstein fraternal opposites: They represented different responses to the strains of German life, and they also represented the variety of Jewish responses to success in a country that was at once hostile and hospitable.

Out of "passionate love for his fellow citizens" *(Volksgenossen)* Ernst Reuter became a socialist instead of the academically trained civil servant that his parents had expected. His choice enraged the self-righteous class egoism of his nationalistic father. A violent father-son conflict ensued—such a favorite theme in German life and literature—and the young Reuter encountered in his home all the prejudices and anxious misconceptions that the "better" classes had for socialism. For them fear of socialism took on idealistic hues: Socialism meant materialism, atheism, revolution, and above all the expropriation of all that was sacred, of property and culture. It was the fate of German social democracy to have to preach class conflict—to a society that was filled with it but refused to acknowledge it—and to be at the very same time the principal champions of democracy, the existence of which would depend on a transcending of the class conflict. The socialists had to be warriors for peace. Their rhetoric belied their revisionism and certainly belied what Reuter most wanted: a more egalitarian, a more just society that would be at peace with itself. In August 1914 when the working class rallied to the defense of Germany (Marx was quite wrong in insisting that the proletariat have no fatherland: Unlike the propertied, that is all they have!), Reuter hoped that "the truly fanatic persecution of the working class movement" would end with the war; such a result would be more profitable for Germany's strength than a victorious war. It took another war and another defeat to approximate that kind of pacification.

In his later effort to account for Hitler's triumph, Reuter lamented the apolitical character of the *Bürgertum,* the bourgeoisie, its estrangement from political reality, its absorption in money-making. He also thought that Germans were peculiarly *wirklichkeitsfremd,* remote from reality, hence particularly vulnerable to dreams, to unrealistic visions and desires. They often lived by political dreams, of peace or power, perhaps the better to survive or ignore recalcitrant reality. These notions—so unpopular among some historians today—echo the ironic epigraph from Heine.

I doubt that Heine thought Germans dreamers by nature; they were taught to dream, to shun reality. He died before his former compatriots had become the great masters of reality. Another paradox: In the second half of the last century, the Germans became virtuosos in practical life and yet clung to their earlier sense of self. Bismarck, the triumphant realist, lamented that people misunderstood him: In his deeper being he had "a dreamy, sentimental nature"; considering his psychic vulnerabilities, there was some truth as well as pretense to his remark.[5] This tough, realistic people cherished the dream of sentimental innocence, and the society in which they lived remained opaque. The great novelist-moralists—Balzac, Dickens, George Eliot, for example—illuminated French and English culture; the Germans read the rather gentle Theodor Fontane, but sharper illumination had to wait for Thomas Mann, and social criticism came with the satirical writings of Heinrich Mann at the very end of the century. Even the great process of secularization was disguised in Germany. The silent secularization, as I call it in "Germany 1933," especially of Protestant Germany, left an unacknowledged vacuum in which pseudo-religions could flourish.

If Germans were often tempted to flee to dreams and delusions, were German Jews to understand their place in German life? How were they to imagine their future? In "The Burden of Success" I suggest that until Hitler, the story of German Jewry was one of triumph—partial, embattled, vilified, but triumph nevertheless. In the new practical and mobile Germany, Jews leapt to success. And yet they too were ambivalent about their success. As Haber's life demonstrated, they were not blind to the hostility they aroused, the envy and the fear their new prominence induced. Many of them wanted to minimize giving offense; even in triumph they were vulnerable. It was Hitler who dramatically recalled their Jewishness to them, and some, like Haber, responded to the degradation of Nazi discrimination with instant dignity.

Since the Holocaust, it has become part of conventional wisdom to think of German Jews as servile, desperate in their hope for assimilation. Einstein is a witness to the quandaries of German-Jewish existence. He returned to Germany a self-conscious Jew, bitterly critical of the assimilationist yearnings of his "fellow-members of the tribe [*Stammesgenossen*]"; the very fact that he shunned the usual term "co-religionists" says a great deal about his efforts at honest self-definition. He found the collegial circle in Berlin, composed as it was of gentiles and Jews, the most harmonious and supportive group he ever encountered in his life. At the same time he experienced anti-Semitic attacks, saw anti-Semitism everywhere, and was certain that it would not die, that in fact it might be the only force that would keep Jewry alive.

Other Jews took Einstein himself (and many other eminent Jews) as warrant for hope. They knew that there remained realms from which they were excluded: In Wilhelmine Germany, the Prussian officer corps was closed to them, and so were the higher rungs of government. They also sensed the different forms of anti-Semitism, from polite disdain (in which, indeed, many Jews shared) to racial vilification. In Weimar, in many fields, Jews became more prominent, and a defeated and humiliated people resented this Jewish presence all the more: There was some kind of grim symbolism in the rise of Walther Rathenau to the post of German foreign minister and in his murder by "idealistic" youths a short time later. Einstein saw the murder as a reminder of fragility.

But most German Jews read their lot differently. The faith and hope that German Jewry had in their own future also testify to what I have called the German promise and the dream of peace. Jews, too, dreamt of peace, even as their enemies were driven frantic by the notion that Jews had somehow formed a conspiracy of secret power. Actually they had almost no political power; but as a group they were disproportionately prosperous and selectively preeminent. At any time in the century before Hitler, German Jews could look back and be astounded by the progress they had made, or look abroad and see how much better off they were than most of their fellow Jews in other countries. It was tempting to extrapolate from past success to future success; by and large, German Jewry assumed a continuity of progress, even without any comparative solace.

We know that most German Jews found Germany a congenial and life-enhancing home. Most of them *felt* German and unproblematically embraced the German ethos and the daily rhythm of life. They felt at home and safe—with whatever lingering ambivalence. Few emigrated; few became Zionists. Few doubted that there would continue to exist a rough equivalence between achievement and reward. Theirs was a rational hope for a peaceful future.

The Jews could not foresee the calamity of Hitler—the appointed victims could not believe the reality of the threat. But then, very few people anywhere could grasp Hitler's unrestrained criminality. They could not believe that he meant what he wrote and threatened. The hatred, after all, was pathological, beyond all reason. Disbelief was the rational response; one assumed that Hitler was but another rabble-rouser, only worse. Even after his accession to power, many people in Germany and outside deluded themselves into thinking that his early measures against the Jews would be his last, that they were concessions he was making to his more radical followers; in time, he would relent. His own cunning—or fearful—duality in rule, i.e., the appearance of normality interrupted by terror and selective extrusion, encouraged the hope that there would be limits to this lawlessness. Perhaps the Jews of Germany should have noted the silence with which their initial extrusion from public office was accompanied. The eminent psychologist Wolfgang Köhler did protest—and two years later concluded that if only twenty German professors had acted as he had, things would have been different. He left Germany, disillusioned by the psychologists and therapists who speedily conformed to the new regime. "Analysts without resistance" could be an essay in self-imposed conformity.[6]

I doubt that anyone in 1933 could have imagined the extermination of the Jews. One would have had to believe in the absoluteness of Hitler's murderous desires, one would have had to imagine a confluence of circumstances that would have boggled the sane mind. Was the final impulse to extermination Hitler's realization that he had lost the war in the east? Historians have recently suggested that Hitler's decision systematically to exterminate the Jews was made in the wake of the battle of Moscow, in apprehension of ultimate defeat.[7] This is a plausible hypothesis, but not a conclusive one. In any case, European Jewry would not have survived a German victory.

No one could have imagined Auschwitz before it happened. It was neither accidental nor inevitable. The Nazis themselves were conscious of the monstrous magnitude of their deed: They hounded their victims "in night and fog," they established most of the death camps outside the Reich's borders. They had learned from the uncertain response to the pogrom of November 1938 that their own people had no liking for public violence. And still the regime gave the order to carry out mass murder across all of Europe, in a remote and semi-concealed fashion. The conditions had been created by the triumph of German arms; the implementation depended on the willing cooperation of tens of thousands, Germans and non-Germans. The lower the rank, the closer to the actual murder. It was in truth an unprecedented mobilization of sadism.

In Chapters 5 and 6 I once more ask the question: How could National Socialism have triumphed in 1933, how could the German elites—with notable exceptions—have succumbed so quickly to a power that threatened to destroy what they had for so long cherished? A people humiliated and disarmed by the vengeful Treaty of Versailles, and frightened by the unprecedented unemployment that began in 1930, saw in National Socialism a great temptation. Of course Hitler's rhetorical themes struck old German chords, but the temptation was magnified by the succession of real disasters that inspired a mood of hopelessness. None of Hitler's promises could be achieved without violence—and his appeals for putative peace were always orchestrated by the presence and the exercise of terror. And yet millions of Germans embraced the movement and other millions hesitated, shrinking back into doubt and ambivalence. To understand National Socialism one must understand its subliminal, psychic appeal that either rallied or paralyzed a large segment of even the educated and certainly the propertied classes. Some of the "better" Germans excused, perhaps even admired the brutal side of Hitler and appeased their own consciences by ridiculing the cruder side of the Austrian corporal. In the months just before Hitler's accession to power and in the first years after, he appeared, I think, as a great temptation, at once a promise and a terrible danger, combining one's yearning for unity and power.

The biblical temptation appeared after forty days in the desert. Germans, humiliated by defeat, battered by inflation, and frightened by depression and by a political system that appeared to have failed, thought themselves abandoned in a desert. Of course, they were afraid for their material future, but they also longed for peace, for order, for delivery; they wanted hope restored. The uniformed thugs marching in the streets, the storm trooper battalions, seemed to promise some kind of order, even if it was an order that encompassed torture chambers. Hitler appeared to many as some kind of redeemer. He himself used Christian rhetoric unceasingly. In this mood of desperation and uncertainty, given the "silent secularization" and the concealed retreat from Christianity, many Germans believed in Hitler as the savior and redeemer.

Of course, there were many other, meticulously researched

causes of Hitler's rise. Material interests played a great role. But not all the 14 million who voted for Hitler or the untold millions who were uncertain about him had a great material stake to defend or bargain for. In those early months and years, when a measure of free choice was still possible with relative impunity, more than opportunism or fervent nationalism played a role. The promise of a charismatic liberation seduced the uncertain, the wavering. The presence of violence seemed to bolster the promise of power. The whole uncanny spectacle of Nazism allowed some to suspend their disbelief, to succumb to a temptation that had a demonic character to it. The demonic had its own attraction; the Germans had been taught that greatness, that genius, was amoral—perhaps, in reverse, amorality promised greatness. Evil in the service of frenzied patriotic fantasy appealed. There were many other reasons why Germans (and not only Germans) embraced the movement, but some did it as a kind of unconscious wager: Perhaps it was deliverance. Some came to realize that they had been wrong, that Hitler's regime, despite its many peacetime successes, was an instrument of terror, lawless, corrupt, destructive. The war and its atrocities convinced others of the regime's dangerous criminality. Some paid with their lives for what had been a world-destroying delusion on their part.

It was only after Hitler's defeat that Germans came to realize just how many of their traditions, how many of their dreams and delusions, Hitler had annexed, exploited, corrupted, and betrayed. In 1945, most Germans were dazed, overwhelmed by their own misfortune; they felt that they had been dispossessed not only of most of their material goods but of their spiritual heritage as well.* Hitler had corrupted the very language of the country. What remained was a multiple homelessness and the moral opprobrium

* In what may be the most famous of postwar German novels, *The Tin Drum*, Günter Grass tried to depict the daily devastations of Nazism, the losses incurred. But it was left to an astute English critic to pinpoint a message that most readers probably overlooked: "And hence forward," Siegbert Prawer concludes, "it will be part of Oskar's task to remind his fellow-Germans not only of their guilt but also of their loss—the loss they sustained when they so bloodily rejected the love, the service, the help, the companionship, and the enrichment of life, offered by the Jews who had settled in their midst." I have heard Germans confess such sentiments, but it would be hard to believe that even a fraction of Grass's readers have assimilated this thought into their consciousness. Siegbert Prawer, "The Death of Sigismund Markus: The Jews of Danzig in the Fiction of Günter Grass," in *Danzig, Between East and West: Aspects of Modern Jewish History*, ed. by Isadore Twersky (Cambridge, Mass., and London, 1985), p. 107.

of most of the world. No longer could Germans regard their peculiar history, their *Sonderweg*, their divergent, unique development, with "the proud melancholy" that a German sociologist recently ascribed to earlier times.[8] After 1945, the pride was gone and even the melancholy faded into a kind of numbness. The defeat was total and the country was in ruins. The response was what comes perhaps easiest to people, and what Germans had practiced for so long: work. And work they did, especially after 1948, after the currency reform provided incentives.

We are only now beginning to study the immediate postwar era. Adenauer wanted peace at home and integration abroad. At home, peace was bought by deliberate forgetfulness. Denazification had been an Allied effort which, when turned over to German authorities, was tacitly abandoned. Perhaps forgetfulness was a precondition for the establishment of a democratic polity, but it was an act of more or less willed repression—and the return of what had been repressed was all the more turbulent in the 1960s. Adenauer sought moral rehabilitation by paying restitution money to Israel; his own party objected at the very least to his secretive tactics. For him, this was a necessary moral counterpart to his chief aim, the integration of the "rump" Germany in the West—as much, I think, out of fear of what unintegrated Germans might do as out of fear of the Russians.

In the first two decades after defeat, most Germans were content to work hard, to reach out for material well-being and prosperity. They were glad that the burden of political power had been lifted from them. They contented themselves with passivity and prosperity. A new society did emerge: more open, less class-ridden, more American. At last, the obstacles to democracy seemed breached or diminished.[9] In the first two or three decades after total defeat, Germans indulged in the release from greatness: The lure of power had disappeared.[10]

My concern with the German past has led me to watch the evolution of the Federal Republic. For one thing, the treatment of the past was—and remains—a kind of seismograph for the condition of the Federal Republic, a condition inextricably linked to the fortunes of Europe and of world politics. It took a dramatic event and perhaps my "imagination of disaster" to prompt my first essay on contemporary events. In early 1974 I wrote an article, "The End of the Postwar Era," in which I argued that the Arab-

Israeli war of 1973 and the subsequent oil embargo and price inflation had marked a deep caesura with everything that had gone before. In instant—perhaps too hasty—retrospect, I argued that the period from 1948 to 1973 had marked the most spectacular leap to pacification and prosperity that Europe had ever seen; that era, which had confounded the many pessimists who assumed that the devastation of the war and the trauma of decolonization would lead to permanent stagnation, was now over. The Federal Republic had flourished in that postwar period. I was concerned lest new conflicts and a new stringency in the West would upset one of the greatest achievements of the postwar era, i.e., the willing integration of West Germany into the West. The very term "West" has lately lost some of its luster. I still believe in its reality and I still believe that a renewed distancing of a German state from the West would be disastrously debilitating for both. That is the bias that informed my concern with the German scene after 1973.

It was therefore with some worry that I considered German developments in the late 1970s. By 1979, the strains between the United States and the Federal Republic had become much greater, and in subsequent years a growing disenchantment in West Germany with the United States and with Europe developed. In the immediate postwar period, when the Germans were at the nadir of their existence and the United States at its zenith, the Germans formed an almost paradisaical picture of American society. But gradually that admiration and that trust began to dissipate at a time of Vietnam, Watergate, Jimmy Carter's vacillations, and Ronald Reagan's perceived bellicosity. At the same time the idea of Europe seemed to fade, as a great dream was more and more replaced by the reality of a Brussels bureaucracy and endless wrangling over budgets and agricultural protectionism. I thought one could detect the first signs of a new restlessness, the more so as the great work of pacification in both West and East had been accomplished. A kind of disenchantment took hold of Germans, regardless of age or party. Foreigners thought Germans were becoming more German again—whether out of a feeling "we are somebody again" or out of anger at myriad deficiencies.[11]*

---

* Ernst Reuter's son, Edzard, a leading economist, writer, and industrialist, warned in 1983 that the free part of Germany needed greater political talent and achievement than countries with older democratic institutions: "Therefore the worry that in a few years we could prove

Once again, a German question surfaced, this time not so much addressed to the past as to the future. In Chapter 8, I suggest that the country is experiencing yet another "return of the repressed." What had been repressed was a whole complex of guilt, shame, and forbidden longing. Actually, the creation of the two German states in 1949 represented a division by deception or illusion: In the early years, leaders of both states insisted that division was but a prelude to early reunification. Yet, in the first decade of Bonn's existence, West Germans were little concerned with the past or with what happened "in the zone," in the Soviet part of Germany. They were too self-absorbed, too ready to allow the East Germans to disappear behind an iron curtain or behind the rhetoric of the cold war; the much-vaunted nationalism of the Germans was so completely muted or destroyed that the country seemed to accept division—content to have ritualistic avowals of ultimate unity but for the rest to indulge in a remarkable degree of indifference. They felt safe, moreover, under American tutelage—or unsafe in questioning it. In the last few years, at a time of sometimes unacknowledged distancing from erratic American leadership, much of this has changed: The East Germans have become, what presumably they always were, "the lost brothers and sisters," and German-German relations have acquired a new and to some extent mysterious intensity. Now Germans in the Federal Republic feel that *Deutschlandpolitik* has primacy over everything except the preservation of peace—and even that cause can perhaps best be served by closer ties between the two German states. The German future has suddenly become a new national focus at the very time when a new revisionism would like to end or moderate German self-laceration about the past. Germans are tired of their "special" guilt; they point to the historic sins of others. And in the process of lifting some of their own guilt and ascribing greater culpability to others, they arouse hostile feelings abroad that have long since been buried.* "Restless Germans" inspire anxiety—though as so

to be still only a transitory, comfortable fair-weather democracy is no unseemly dark prophecy [Schwarzmalerei]." Edzard Reuter, *Vom Geist der Wirtschaft: Europa zwischen Technokraten und Mythokraten* (Stuttgart, 1986), p. 130.

* At Bitburg in 1985, Chancellor Kohl wanted a gesture of symbolic forgiveness; he wanted to have the American president acknowledge dramatically, publicly, what most people had come to feel implicitly, fuzzily: that the German present was detached from the terrible past.

often in the past, some of that restlessness, some of their criticism, say, of American leadership or, more generally, of Western industrial civilization, may be immensely valuable. The Germans have always been exceptionally prescient in intuiting the often intangible deficiencies of modern life; but their remedies, their absolutist impatience, have often been calamitous.

Many Germans are growing impatient with their own—relative—impotence, with the limits on their autonomy, even if these limits are the result of Germany's last, desperate, criminal bid for world power. They still live with the consequences of their past, and in recent years many of them have felt an ever greater political and psychological need to deal with that past; some wish to understand it, others to banish or trivialize it. The German past has assumed a new, portentous present.

In 1985, on the occasion of the fortieth anniversary of Germany's unconditional surrender, Richard von Weizsäcker, president of the Federal Republic, made the honest and forthright plea that Germans must face the truth, live with the memory of crimes committed and retribution suffered, draw lessons from it. The speech itself was historic, widely and rightly hailed. Sometime later, prominent historians of divergent views warned against an ahistorical mood, against new delusions that could ignore the lessons of the twentieth century: "In a country without memory anything is possible."[12]

One must now regretfully wonder whether Weizsäcker's speech should be seen as the authoritative and representative voice of Germany or whether in retrospect it will come to be regarded as a coda to a period of soul-searching, as a perhaps unconscious premonition of a new wave of embittered, self-pitying indifference that may now be emerging in Germany. In the last few years— more noticeable after Helmut Kohl's accession to power—a new tone can be heard. Some Germans, including some well-known historians, would like to "relativize" the crimes of the Nazi period; in their vision, these crimes must be understood in the context of other crimes that occurred in our century; perhaps German crimes were—at least in part—reactive.[13] Some right-wing politicians

---

He wanted more: Today's moral equivalence should be extended retroactively, an amnesty for the dead.

readily, crudely chime in. A metaphysicized amnesia about the
recent past could be in the making, with ominous implications for
life in the Federal Republic. For Germans more than for any other
people in the Western world, both the past and the future are
unsettled, uncertain, open.

There is also a growing realization that the two German states
with their divergent social systems and their links to opposing
blocs share a common past; and though they continue to interpret
that past differently, they do so now much less polemically than
before. The East German regime has become far more solicitous
of the national heritage, of the place, for example, of Frederick
the Great and Bismarck in German history. In 1983, both East
and West Germany held joint celebrations of the five-hundredth
anniversary of Luther's birth. Among West Germans, perhaps also
among East Germans, there is an emergent feeling that a common
past, acknowledged by both sides, could strengthen present bonds
and could somehow point to a common future. The power of
dreams, of utopian hopes, cannot be measured, but they seem
more pervasive today than at any time since 1945—perhaps because
some Germans regard the realities of power, the division of Europe,
the East-West conflict, as a kind of historical anachronism.

In a sense, *West-*, *Ost-* and *Deutschlandpolitik* have gone as far as
one could expect; at the moment there seems little room for
maneuver, let alone for dramatic accomplishment. At such a point,
and given a break in the previously existing consensus about
foreign and defense policy, it is a propitious time for dreams:
Some Germans wish for a neutralized Germany, a super-Switzer-
land, that would allow the two German states to disengage from
the two blocs, drop out from the conflict of the two superpowers
that in their imagination have reached a kind of moral equivalency,
just as they have reached an equivalency in arms. On the Right,
there is the desire for greater assertiveness, for an end to self-
laceration. The rhetoric is changing: One hears allusions to a
vanished Reich, a Reich whose lost territories in the East had once
been the base of an all-important German presence in *Mitteleuropa*.
Primitive nationalists claim that Silesia and other eastern territories—in Polish hands now for forty years—remain German. Things
are being said in Germany today that were barely thought of a
generation ago.

The West Germans are a strong and restless people with the

greatest grievance—national division—of any country in Europe. Nationalist or neutralist dreams are inimical to the true interest of the Federal Republic, as are the claims of any kind of resurgent revisionism. A disenchanted, sullen Germany would also put at risk the pacification achieved so far. Germans need to heed their own critics, warning them against utopianism, admonishing them not to forsake a policy of realism.[14] It is also a time when the Germans need friends who remember, not friends who pretend in some travesty of truth that the past can be dissolved in a kind of retroactive vague commonality. Germans deserve friends who feel the burden of the past, as so many of them do, but who have compassion for a people that have had so rich and terrifying a history.

I

The Dream of Peace

ONE

EINSTEIN'S
GERMANY

The invitation to speak at the Jerusalem Centennial celebration of Einstein's birth in 1979 made me hesitate: What
could a nonscientist contribute? Then I remembered that
a decade earlier, while at the Institute for Advanced Study
in Princeton, I had looked at the Einstein Archive and
found some extraordinary letters; later, while lecturing at
the University of Chicago, I chanced upon an exhibition
about James Franck, German physicist and exile, and saw
an exchange between him and Einstein from the year
1945: old friends fighting—in Germanic depth—about the
German character. The subject and the occasion as well
as the lure of new sources led me to accept the invitation—
with wholly unanticipated consequences for me.

The task proved far more difficult than I had imagined.
Einstein and his circle *were* formidable, and what was
central to them, their scientific work, was impenetrable
for me. But other themes emerged: the great scientific
community in pre-1933 Germany, Einstein's response to
the Great War, his pacifism, his sense of himself as a Jew,
his place among progressive thinkers of the 1920s, his
implacable hatred of everything German after 1933. Com-
plexities abounded.

In the archives I also found new material about my
parents' involvement in this world. I gave the lecture, here

reproduced in slightly revised form, and subsequently had the privilege of repeating it in places that had touched Einstein's life intimately—at the University of Leiden, at the ETH (Federal Institute of Technology) in Zurich, and, most memorably for me, at the Niels Bohr Institute in Copenhagen. In 1984, I was asked to join the Editorial Committee of the Collected Papers of Einstein. Gradually I came to realize that I could not abandon the subject; I am now working on a book, *Genius and the Germans: Einstein, Haber, and the Passions of Their Time.*

THERE WAS NOTHING SIMPLE about Einstein, ever. His simplicity concealed an impenetrable complexity. Even the links to his native Germany were prematurely ambiguous. At a time when most Germans thought their country a hospitable home, a perfect training ground for their talents, Einstein was repelled; in 1894, as a fifteen-year-old, he left Germany and became a Swiss citizen. Twenty years later, a few weeks before the outbreak of the Great War, he returned to Germany and remained for eighteen years of troubled renown, years in which he appreciated what was congenial and opposed what was antipathetic in Germany. Long before Hitler, he felt unease. He could joke about his multiple, if uncertain, loyalties—the better perhaps to hide his feelings. In 1919, at the moment when fame first engulfed him, he explained in a letter to the London *Times*: "Here is yet another application of the principle of relativity for the delectation of the reader: today I am described in Germany as a 'German savant,' and in England as a 'Swiss Jew.' Should it ever be my fate to be represented as a *bête noire*, I should, on the contrary, become a 'Swiss Jew' for the Germans and a 'German savant' for the English."[1]

His fame, his capacity for homelessness, and the degradation of his country made Einstein a citizen of the world, seemingly detached from Germany. But I believe that his early encounters with Germany, his hostility to its official culture, shaped his public stance. My deliberately ambiguous title is meant to suggest that Einstein's Germany was both real and imaginary—that he had his own perception of reality. The German experience haunted Einstein to the very end, as it haunted so many of his generation later. It was the text of his political-moral education, the background against which he came to mold his unorthodox views and play his controversial public role.

In Einstein's time, Germany was the promise and later the nemesis of the world, the country that had a decisive bearing on world politics and where, for a moment that seemed a lifetime, the moral drama of our era was enacted. At certain critical moments, Einstein and even his closest colleagues described radically different responses. I believe this diversity will help to complicate our understanding of Germany, and this will be desirable, because Germany's past has often been treated with didactic simplicity. Einstein and Germany: they illuminate each other.

Before turning to my proper subject, however, I would like to express my unease. The writing of this essay posed special difficulties. Historians have a right to feel awe—a right perhaps rarely exercised these days—and I felt awe at my subject.

It is generally said of Einstein that he revolutionized modern physics and natural philosophy and that his genius had no equal save that of Newton's. But I shall not—and I could not—deal with what was central to him. I shall deal with the public figure, with the first scientist-hero to appear in the Western world. I shall concentrate on the thoughts that were important to this public figure who placed his scientific fame at the service of his moral indignation. The genius hovers in the background, and the occasional partisan in the foreground. In doing this, I was mindful of what Lionel Trilling has said:

> Physical science in our day lies beyond the intellectual grasp of most men. . . . This exclusion of most of us from the mode of thought which is habitually said to be the characteristic achievement of the modern age is bound to be experienced as a wound given to our intellectual self-esteem. About this humiliation we all agree to be silent; but can we doubt that it has its consequences, that it introduces into the life of mind a significant element of dubiety and alienation which must be taken into account in any estimate that is made of the present fortunes of mind?[2]

I felt this exclusion the more as I came to realize the intensity of the aesthetic joy that Einstein and his colleagues found in their discoveries, as their correspondence exemplifies. We are shut out from that knowledge and from that particular beauty. Lionel Trilling was abundantly right in calling this exclusion an unacknowledged wound.

Exclusion from substance was compounded by my more or less accidental familiarity with some of the men around Einstein and, as a child, with the fringes of that milieu. From time to time I shall allude to some of these personal ties, which added puzzlement and poignancy to my efforts to understand even a part of Einstein's world. I read in Einstein's unpublished correspondence with the historian's habitual hope that the archives would yield some nuggets to shock or prod the mind; the letters were marvelously human, but Einstein remained elusive and enigmatic. The search has been fascinating and disheartening—and has fully borne out what a friend said at the very beginning: Einstein is the hardest person to say anything about. His own friends found him inscrutable, and not even their love of him offered a firm bridge of understanding.

In analyzing the scientific ideal that some historians cherished, Richard Hofstadter once said: "The historian is quickly driven to a kind of agnostic modesty about his own achievement. He may not disparage science, but he despairs of it."[3] Einstein would have agreed with this judgment, though drawn different conclusions from it. The one time I met him—in 1944, while an undergraduate at Columbia—he inquired after my plans, and I told him I was in a quandary, not knowing whether to continue my original purpose, which was to study medicine and thus follow in the footsteps of a father, two grandfathers, and four great-grandfathers, or to switch to history, an old interest turned into a new passion by the power of my teachers. To Einstein this was no quandary. Medicine, he said, was a science (which I doubt) and history was not—though it is significant that I cannot remember his rather harsh words about history. I chose not to follow his advice, but I will confirm his view that history is not a science, that it is an approximation of a time and space that we knew not.

At the risk of risible compression, let me recall some of the characteristics of modern Germany, particularly those that would have impinged on Einstein's life and thought. He was born in the decade of Germany's unification, and he died a decade after its dissolution. The 1870s were a heady and extravagant time for a country whose historic experience had been defeat and division.

For centuries, Germany had been a geographic expression, everybody's battlefield, Europe's anvil on which other nations forged their destinies. In the unbroken annals of defeat, Prussia had been the sole exception; and Prussia had evolved its own ethos of frugal duty, rectitude, and obedience. It was also, as Mirabeau had pointed out at the end of the eighteenth century, not as other countries, a state with an army, but an army with a state. In the Napoleonic era, even Prussia collapsed, but political impotence had its compensations: In the shadow of defeat, the Germans created a great literary and philosophical culture and a national identity based initially on intellectual-aesthetic, not political, achievement. That culture enshrined as a moral imperative the cultivation of the self and education—at least for the elite—as the prescribed path to self-formation. There were always two strains to this conception: the ideal of the harmonious being, the rational, aesthetically literate humanist on the one hand, and the demonic, inexplicable, mysteriously creative genius on the other. Einstein fitted both categories. By piously and pedantically trying to inculcate the rational, German schools often encouraged the yearning for the irrational. By the mid-nineteenth century, it was widely believed that Germany had a special vocation for learning.

Unification under Prussian aegis, achieved in battle, directed by Bismarck, codified in a constitution that preserved the privileges of a governing elite—that kind of unification was a celebration of force and a denial of earlier hopes of freedom. As Nietzsche warned, this triumph could destroy the German spirit, drown it by the worship of practicality and power. The new Reich, rapidly industrializing, exuded power. But the country became still harder to govern; new social cleavages appeared next to old regional and religious divisions. Nationalism and militarism were a means of providing cohesion, of overcoming a sense of *unfulfilled* unity. Bismarck's Germany was an authoritarian state of uncertain viability, but it was also a government of laws, a haven of constitutionality as compared with primitive, autocratic Russia, a country without torture, callous and sentimental, rigid, efficient, hardworking, bent on achievement.

Whatever the shortcomings of the new Reich, Bismarck's generation had seen the fulfillment of the great national ideal. The next generation—epitomized by the young emperor, with his dreams and delusions that could never banish his anxieties—

thirsted for its own glory, for its own imprint on history. Germany had become a giant in the center of Europe: It had the best army, the strongest economy, the most efficient industry. But what was its vocation, its purpose? In a celebrated phrase, Max Weber warned that unification would be "little else than a piece of folly which was committed by the nation in her old days, and which, in view of its costly nature," should not have been embarked upon at all unless Germany would now take the next step and become a world power.[4]

What was it that Germany sought after 1890? It sought what every aspiring nation in Europe had sought before: recognized greatness, a measure of hegemony. Perhaps the Germans were more frantic in their search for greatness, but then their day had come late. They wanted grandeur, as others had wanted it before; they needed to exorcise centuries of dependency. Europe's competition for greatness, which involved more than political dominion, its ethos of heroic striving, was the very hallmark of its exacting and triumphant civilization. Europe had always been a crucible of genius. Should the Germans—the originators of the Faustian myth—restrain their will and not try for collective preeminence?

Let me cite one more example of this exhortation to greatness. Few scholars in Germany were as critical of the nation's development and of Bismarck's character as was the great historian Theodor Mommsen; few railed as much against the servility and political nonage of their fellow citizens, few combatted anti-Semitism as vigorously as he did. But he too felt the grip of greatness, and he too preached sermons of duty, as did the professoriate throughout Europe. I believe the call to greatness gnawed at Germans more deeply than at others. Witness Mommsen's rectorial speech:

> Of course we are proud of being Germans and we do not disguise it. Of all the boasts none is more empty and less true than the boast about German modesty. We are not at all modest and we do not want to be modest or appear to be. On the contrary, we want to continue to reach for the highest in art and science, in state and church, in all aspects of life and striving, and we want to reach for the highest in everything and all at once. There is no laurel wreath which would be too magnificent or too ordinary for us . . . we think it normal that

our diplomats as our soldiers, our physiologists as our sailors
stand everywhere in the front rank. . . . But even if we content
ourselves in no way to be content, we are not therefore blind
. . . in research and instruction . . . there is no standing still
. . . if you don't go forward, you stay back and fall behind.[5]

Even in Mommsen, then, we find this call for greatness as the only
alternative to decline.

The contradictions of imperial Germany have often been noted.
Economic giant, master of the disciplined society, model of technical proficiency, nurturer of talent—and yet a nation that recklessly defied prudence in dealing with foreign nations, a governing
class that suffered from the paranoid fear that Germany was
threatened by subversion at home and encirclement abroad. This
alternation between presumption and anxiety grated heavily on
some Germans and on many foreigners.

In Germany as elsewhere, the generation before 1914 was
prodigious in talent and achievement; it was then that Germany
attained a preeminent place in the natural sciences. German
universities, which had long thought scientific studies a secondary
concern, suddenly discovered that their scientists had won world
renown. Universities had not been inhospitable to talent—provided
it came in politically respectable, male, preferably Protestant guise.
Any deviation from the norm had to be paid for by a superabundance of talent and, on the whole, was admissible only in the
newer and politically neutral fields, such as medicine and the
natural sciences. In those fields, achievement was more easily
measurable and more immediately useful. In medicine and physics,
in particular, the barriers against Jews began to be breached early.

It is notoriously hard to account for creativity. Was the German
flowering a result of Germany's having the highest rate of literacy
and the highest per capita expenditure for public education? Was
it that German industry decided early on to support scientific
research with particular largesse? Was the system of the master
and the apprentices, the professor and his school, productive not
only of dependency and exploitation but also of a special bond?
Did success have anything to do with the fact that German scientists
had a particularly austere view of their profession, so much so that
one of the early Nobel laureates, Wilhelm Ostwald, spoke of all
the grief and loneliness that a true scientist must endure, "because

every important discovery must be paid for by a human life. . . ."[6] No doubt there was much suffering, acknowledged and unacknowledged, but there was also an extraordinary measure of camaraderie and high spirits.

In our century, scientific achievement, whatever its causes, can be measured by the incidence of Nobel Prizes won. From the inception of that prize to the rise of Hitler, Germans garnered a larger share of prizes than any other nationality, about 30 percent. In some fields the share was higher still; of these German Nobel Prizes, German Jews won nearly 30 percent; in medicine, 50 percent. Germans and Jews collected a disproportionate share; and although Harriet Zuckerman has recently demonstrated how complicated the notion of disproportionateness is, it does seem clear that Germans and Jews shared a certain immodesty in talent.

The prominence of German Jews also says something about their place in culture, about the milieu in which they worked, which mixed, perhaps uniquely, hospitality and hostility—and perhaps both were needed for this extraordinary achievement. I have said that Germans had a veneration for learning, a yearning for greatness, a lingering insecurity. German Jews shared these traits and found further sustenance for them in their own distinct past. Jews did not foster talent; they hovered over it, they hoarded it, they nearly smothered it. Elsewhere I have pointed out that the rise of German Jewry is one of the most spectacular leaps of a minority in the social history of Europe, but their new prominence was painfully precarious and recalled Disraeli's desperate boast to young Montefiore: "You and I belong to a race that can do everything but fail." It is impossible to talk about Einstein's Germany without talking of German-Jewish relations, and to this theme I shall return later.

I have tried to suggest some of the contradictory aspects of German culture. At this point we may be more familiar with the darker sides, with possible portents of later disaster. Einstein seemed peculiarly attuned to these portents; his friends, as we shall see, relished the virtues of German life. Perhaps the Nobel laureate I. I. Rabi said it all when he remarked to me the other day that he had found German culture "brutal and brilliant," that he had come to post-1918 Hamburg "knowing the libretto but learning the tune." In the first third of this century German institutes of learning and research orchestrated many voices into one tune of discovery. The German contribution to our civilization was immense, and the greatness that eluded Germans in politics they realized in the realms of science and of art.

Einstein grew up in southern Germany. We know little of his early life. He was no child prodigy; rather, his reticence in speaking for the first three years, his difficulty with learning foreign languages, and his mistakes in computation have been a source of endless comfort to the similarly afflicted or to their parents, though affinity in failure may not suffice for later success. He went through a brief but intense religious phase, the end of which, he said, left him suspicious of all authorities. His parents, secularized Jews, had little to do with his intellectual development; an uncle fed his mathematical curiosity. His father was an amiable failure, mildly inept at all the businesses he started. In 1894, his parents went to Italy to start yet another venture, leaving the fifteen-year-old Albert behind in a well-known Munich gymnasium. The authoritarian atmosphere and the mindless teaching appalled him. There is more than a hint of arrogance about the young Einstein, and hence it does not strain credulity to believe that one of his teachers exclaimed: "Your mere presence spoils the respect of the class for me." He was a rebel from the start.

Encouraged by his teachers' hostility, he decided to quit school and leave Germany. His unsuccessful career facilitated his later fame in Germany. Erik Erikson has rightly referred to "the German habit of gilding school failure with the suspicion of hidden genius."[7] It is often said that Einstein left school because he objected to its militarism. I find this unpersuasive: Bavarian militarism? I would suppose that there might have been stifling Catholicism, insolent, thoughtless authoritarianism, a repulsive tone—all of which would have sufficed to discourage a youth like Einstein. I suspect Einstein left so precipitously in order to escape serving in the German army; by obtaining Swiss citizenship in time, he could do so without incurring the charge of desertion. His first adult decision, then, was to escape the clutches of compulsion—and the image of Einstein as a recruit in a field-gray uniform does boggle the mind. He left Germany without regrets. His first encounters with that country had not been happy.

There followed the obscure and difficult years in Switzerland, the failures, the marginal existence, the Zurich Polytechnic, and, finally, the security of the patent office in Berne. From there in 1905 emerged the four papers destined to revolutionize modern physics and cosmology. They were published in the *Annalen der Physik*, and Max Planck was the first man to recognize the genius of the unknown author. The international scientific community took note as well, and Einstein finally received his first academic appointments. In 1913, while he was a professor at the Zurich Polytechnic, two German scientists appeared, Walter Nernst and Max Planck, in order to offer him an unprecedented position: salaried membership in the Prussian Academy of Sciences, so that he would not have to teach, though he would have a chair at the university as well. When Nernst and Planck left, Einstein turned to his assistant, Otto Stern, and said: "The two of them were like men looking for a rare postage stamp." The remark was perhaps an early instance of that self-depreciatory humor, that modesty of genius.

As a native Swabian, Einstein found Prussian stiffness uncongenial; the gentler, less strident rhythm of southern Germany or Switzerland was more to his taste. He began his new German life in April 1914 with some trepidation at his "Berlinization," as he called it. Berlin was the world's preeminent center of the natural sciences, and Planck, Fritz Haber, and a dazzling array of talent rejoiced at having this young genius at the head of their circle. Three months later the war shattered the idyllic community. Einstein had returned to Germany in time to see the country seized by the exaltation of August 1914, when almost all Germans were gripped by an orgy of nationalism, by a joyful feeling that a common danger had at last united and ennobled the people.

The intoxication passed; the business of killing was too grim to sustain the unbridled enthusiasm of August 1914. The elite rallied to the nation—as it did elsewhere too. In the fall of 1914, ninety-three of Germany's best-known scientists and artists, including Planck, Haber, Richard Willstätter, and Max Liebermann, signed a manifesto that was meant to repudiate Allied charges of German atrocities, but by tone and perhaps unconscious intent argued Germany's complete innocence and blamed all misfortunes and wrongdoing on Germany's enemies. The Manifesto of the Ninety-three has often been seen as a warrant for aggression, as a declaration of unrestrained chauvinism. I suspect it was as well the outcry of people to whom the outside world mattered and who intuitively sensed that the Allies would come to cast Germans as pariahs again. Some of the ninety-three probably hoped for continued respect across the trenches—and signed a document that had the opposite effect. It was not the last time Germans confirmed the sentiments they set out to deny. With but few exceptions, intellectuals everywhere joined in this chorus of hatred and in the cry for blood. So did the guardians of morality and the servants of God, the priests who sanctified the killing as an act of mythical purification. In time, some of the ninety-three turned moderate—or perhaps they remained the patriots they had been— but others passed them on the right, in the nation's wild leap to pan-German madness.

Einstein was alone and disbelieving.* The war that was to politicize everyone as the cause of universal grief politicized him as well. Before 1914 he had never concerned himself with politics; his very departure from Germany had been a youthful withdrawal from the claims of the state. Now, for the first time, he ventured forth from his study, convinced of the insanity of the war, shocked by the ease with which people had broken ties of international friendship and mutual respect. A pacifist physician and fellow-professor, Georg Friedrich Nicolai, asked him to sign a counter-manifesto addressed to Europeans, demanding an immediate, just peace, a peace without annexations. It was the very first appeal he ever signed. It was published only in 1917 and abroad. In November 1914, he joined nine other like-minded democrats and pacifists to found Bund Neues Vaterland—a reformist organization, a German Fabian Society; the Bund gradually grew, but was effectively silenced in 1916. In November 1915 the Berlin Goethebund asked for his opinion about the war, and he sent a message with this rather special ending: "But why many words when I can say everything in one sentence and moreover in a sentence which is particularly fitting for me as a Jew: Honor Your Master Jesus Christ not in words and hymns, but above all through your deeds."[8]

His work remained his central passion. But intermittently he forsook it to bear witness in an unpopular cause for what he took

---

* Less than three weeks after the outbreak of the war, Einstein wrote his good friend Paul Ehrenfest in Leiden: "Europe, in her madness, has now started something incredible. At such a time we see what a wretched species of beast we belong to. I am going on quietly with my peaceful meditations, and feel only a mixture of pity and disgust." Martin J. Klein, *Paul Ehrenfest*, vol. 1, *The Making of a Theoretical Physicist* (Amsterdam, 1970), p. 300.

36   THE DREAM OF PEACE

to be right. He had been a pacifist and a European of the first
hour, never touched by the frenzy that ravaged nearly all. Convinced of Germany's special responsibility for the outbreak and
the continuation of the war, he hoped for its defeat.

To understand Einstein's isolation, one must look at the responses of his friends and colleagues. Fritz Haber, for example,
became the very antithesis of Einstein. Haber, Einstein's senior by
eleven years, was a chemist of genius, a born organizer, and in
wartime an ardent patriot. Without Haber's process for fixing
nitrogen from the air, discovered just before the war, Germany
would have run out of explosives and fertilizers by the end of
1914. During the war, he came to direct Germany's scientific effort;
in 1915 he experimented with poison gas and supervised the
introduction of the new weapon at the western front. In order to
operate within a military machine that had no understanding of
the need for a scientist, he received the assimilated rank of captain.
He relished his new role; the marshaling of all one's talents and
energies in a cause one believes in and in the shadow of danger—
that is a heady experience. Einstein, the lonely pacifist who had
come to feel his solidarity with Jews, and Haber, the restless
organizer of wartime science and a converted Jew—the contrast is
obvious.* For all their antithetical responses, Haber and Einstein
remained exceptionally close and, on Haber's side, loving friends.
Haber's life was a kind of foil to Einstein's, and it encompassed
the triumphs and the tragedy of German Jewry. I shall return to
him because his relations with Einstein were so important—and
because he happens to have been my godfather and a paternal
friend of my parents.[9]

Einstein had been horrified at the beginning of the war, but I
doubt that even he could have imagined the full measure of
disaster: the senseless killing and maiming of millions, the starving
of children, the mortgaging of Europe's future, the tearing of a
civilization that appeared ever more fragile. For what? Why?

* As a 24-year-old, Haber converted to Protestantism—to the dismay of his father. Many
converted Jews retained a sense of special affinity for Jews; Haber did, but he also felt intensely
German. According to Nazi dogma, anyone with two or more Jewish grandparents was Non-
Aryan, hence subject to the same discriminations as Jews. For many Jews, the convert was an
object of suspicion. Chaim Weizmann wrote of Haber, "Unlike Willstätter, Haber was lacking
in any Jewish self-respect. He had converted to Christianity and had pulled all his family with
him along the road to apostasy." In 1933–34, the two men became good friends, as we will
see. Chaim Weizmann, Trial and Error (New York, 1949), p. 352.

Einstein blamed it on an epidemic of madness and of greed that had suddenly overwhelmed Europe—and Germany most especially. The old German dream of greatness had turned into a nightmare of blind and brutal greed. During the later phases of the war, Einstein was again totally absorbed in his work, but whiffs of hysteria would reach him—and always from the German side. I doubt that he knew of the excesses on the other side.

Einstein had been right about the war. At its end, many felt as he had at the beginning. The war was a great radicalizing experience, pushing most people to the left and some to a new, frantic right. If there had been no war, bolshevism and fascism would not have afflicted Europe. The war discredited the old order and the old rulers; antagonism to capitalism, imperialism, and militarism appeared everywhere. Lenin's Bolsheviks offered themselves as the receivers of a bankrupt system; bolshevism was a speculation in Europe's downfall. Liberal Europeans pinned their hopes on Woodrow Wilson, but that hope faded in the vengeful spirit of Versailles. The logic of events had brought many Europeans to share Einstein's radical-liberal, faintly socialist, thoroughly internationalist views.

For a short time Einstein had hopes for Germany. Defeat had brought the collapse of the old and the rise of a new, democratic regime, as he had expected. He supported the new republic, and in November 1918, at the height of the German Revolution, cautioned radical students who had just deposed the university rector: "All true democrats must stand guard lest the old class tyranny of the right be replaced by a new class tyranny of the left." He warned against force, which "breeds only bitterness, hatred and reaction," and he condemned the dictatorship of the proletariat in what was the first of his occasional bitter denunciations of the Soviet Union as the enemy of freedom.[10] At other times and in different contexts, he would sign appeals for what we have come to call "front organizations."

We now come to a fateful coincidence in the rise of the public Einstein. In March 1919 a British expedition headed by Arthur Stanley Eddington had observed a solar eclipse. In November it was announced that the results confirmed the predictions of the general theory of relativity. It was in London that the president of the Royal Society, the Nobel Laureate J. J. Thomson, hailed Einstein's work, now confirmed, as "one of the greatest—perhaps *the* greatest of achievements in the history of human thought." Somehow it seemed as if Einstein's achievement would revive the old international community of science. The world listened. Almost overnight Einstein became a celebrated hero—the scientific genius, untainted by war, of dubious nationality, who had revolutionized man's conception of the universe, newly defined the fundamentals of time and space, and done so in a fashion so recondite that only a handful of scientists could grasp the new mysterious truth.

The new hero appeared, as if by divine design, at the very moment when the old heroes had been buried in the rubble of the war. Soldiers, monarchs, statesmen, priests, captains of industry—all had failed. The old superior class had been found inferior; *Disenchantment* was the proper title for one of the finest books written about the war. "Before 1914," Noel Annan has asserted, "intellectuals counted for little";[11] after the war, and in a sense in the wake of Einstein, they counted for more. Einstein now became a force, or at least a celebrity, in the world.

After 1919, he appeared more and more often as a public figure. His views were continually solicited, and he obliged with his ideas about life, education, politics, and culture. He had a special kinship with other dissenters from the Great War; like Bertrand Russell, Romain Rolland, and John Dewey, he became what the French call *un homme de bonne volonté*. His views—rational, progressive, liberal, in favor of international cooperation, condemnatory of the evils of militarism, nationalism, tyranny, and exploitation—these views described as well a cast of mind characteristic of Weimar intelligentsia.

The intellectuals of Weimar—and this needs to be said at a time when Weimar is often portrayed as some sort of Paradise Lost—were a shallow lot in their moralizing politics. Their views often seemed utopian and simplistic, pious and fiercely polemical by turns. They were cynical, as Herbert Marcuse once put it to me about himself, because they knew how beautiful the world could be. They lived in a world peopled by George Grosz caricatures and three-penny indictments of bourgeois falsehood. It is perhaps too simple to say that they lived off the bankruptcy of the old order, but they did rather revel in the crudity of their opponents. It is not good for the mind to have dumb, discredited enemies. The real strength of Weimar were clusters of talent: Heidelberg around Max and later Alfred Weber; Göttingen in mathematics; the Bauhaus and the Berlin circles.

Einstein stood above these progressive intellectuals, in consonance with them, but usually more complicated, less predictable, and always more independent than they. But he too was a theorist without a touch of practical experience. Einstein offered his prescriptions the more readily because he had been so overwhelmingly right when the multitudes had been wrong. By 1919 he had not only overthrown the scientific canons of centuries; he had also defied conventional wisdom and mass hysteria in wartime. His views were often deceptively simple; they were not so naive as has often been alleged nor quite so profound as admirers thought. There was no reason to think that a scientific genius would have special insights into other realms. He had reflected on some issues and felt strongly on others; for the rest, it became clear that genius is divisible and can be compartmentalized.

Einstein's views and prescriptions were unassailably, conventionally well intended, but they often lacked a certain *gravitas*, a certain reality—in part, I think, because he approached the problems of the world distantly, unhistorically, not overly impressed by the nature or intractability of the obstacles to ideal solutions. He was not a political thinker; he was a philosopher, moralist, and prophet, and the travails of the world would prompt him to propose or support social remedies. Sometimes these remedies would be blueprints of utopia addressed to people who had lost their footing in a swamp and were sinking fast.

At a much later time, in fact at a moment when Einstein had attacked the Nazi government, Max von Laue questioned whether the scientist should deal with political issues. Einstein rejected such considerations: "you see especially in the circumstances of Germany where such self-restraint leads. It means leaving leadership to the blind and the irresponsible, without resistance. Where would we be if Giordano Bruno, Spinoza, Voltaire, and Humboldt had thought and acted this way?" Einstein's models were instructive, and Laue pointed out that they were not exact natural scientists and that physics was so remote as not to prepare its practitioners for politics in the same way that law or history did. On that letter, Einstein simply scribbled, "don't answer."[12]

Like so many thinkers of the 1920s, Einstein underestimated

the force of the irrational, of what the Germans call the demonic, in public affairs. That is what so ill-prepared them for an understanding of fascism. In their innocence they thought that men were bribed to be fascists, that fascism was but frightened capitalism. In its essence, it was something much more sinister and elemental. In his social commentary, Einstein left out the very thing he once called "the most beautiful experience we can have: the mysterious."[13]

What gave his views exceptional resonance was the magic of his person and his incomparable achievement. He was taken by many as a sage and a saint. In fact, as I have said before, he was an unfathomably complex person. In the complexity of nature he found simplicity; in the complexity of his own nature, the principle of simplicity ranked high. Indeed, it was his simplicity, his otherworldliness, that impressed people. His clothes were simple, his tastes were simple, his appearance was meticulously simple. His modesty was celebrated—and genuine—as was his unselfishness. He was a lonely man, indifferent to honors, homeless by his own admission, solicitous of humanity, and diffident about his relations with those closest to him. At times he appeared like a latter-day St. Francis of Assisi, a solitary saint, innocently sailing, those melancholy eyes gazing distractedly into the distance. At other times he was playing with the press, finding himself in the company of the famous and the powerful despite himself.

In some ways, I believe, he came to invest in his own fame, perhaps unconsciously to groom himself for his new role. He lectured in distant lands, "a traveller in relativity." In 1921, after his first visit to the United States, he said: "The cult of individuals is always, in my view, unjustified. . . . It strikes me as unfair, and even in bad taste, to select a few [individuals] for boundless admiration, attributing superhuman powers of mind and character to them. This has been my fate, and the contrast between the popular estimate of my powers and achievements and the reality is simply grotesque." This admiration would be unbearable except that "it is a welcome symptom in an age which is commonly denounced as materialistic, that it makes heroes of men whose goals lie wholly in the intellectual and moral sphere. . . . My experience teaches me that this idealistic outlook is particularly prevalent in America. . . ."[14] He knew that he had become a hero— and was endlessly surprised by it. In 1929 he described himself as a saint of the Jews. He played many roles by turns, each, I think, completely genuinely; he was a simple man of complex roles.

In the simplicity and goodness that were his, I detect, perhaps wrongly, a distant echo of his encounters with German life. Could one imagine a greater contrast between his German surroundings and himself, between people so formal in their bearing, so attentive to appearance, so solicitous of titles, honors, externals, and himself? Did the insolence of office, the arrogance of the uniform, push him into ever greater idiosyncratic informality? Was not his appearance a democratic rebuke to authority?

In the immediate postwar era, Einstein was friendly to the governments of Weimar and appalled by the vindictiveness of the Allies, who seemed to have caught what he had thought was a German disease. In all his public stands he had what Gerald Holton has called a "vulnerability to pity," and in the early 1920s he had a fleeting moment of pity for Germany.[15] He refused to leave it at the time of trial. For years he was an uncertain member of the League of Nations' International Commission on Intellectual Cooperation, intermittently resigning when he thought the commission too pro-French, too *Allied.* He hoped to restore an international community, Germans included. In the end he asked Fritz Haber to take his place. Successive German governments regarded him as a national asset, perhaps the sole asset in a morally and materially empty treasury. They saw in his travels and in his fame the promise of some reflected glory. But his own hopes gradually faded. He had warned Walther Rathenau against assuming the foreign ministry; Jews should not play so prominent a role. When right-wing assassins—widely hailed in Germany as true patriots—killed Rathenau, Einstein had reason to fear for his own life. The inborn servility of the Germans, he thought, had survived the successive shocks of 1918.

Immediately after the war and at the beginning of his popular fame, Einstein embraced several causes. Having embraced them, he would often embarrass and repudiate them as well. He was the antithesis of an organization man. Unstintingly he would help individuals and chosen causes, but I doubt that he would listen to them. He remained a detached theorist who saw the nature of the world wantonly violated. But at times his commandments contained visionary practicality. A pacifist during the war, he now became Germany's most prominent champion of organized pacifism. He hated militarism—blindly, as its defender loved it—blindly. He condemned "the worst outgrowth of herd life, the military system. . . . I feel only contempt for those who take pleasure marching in rank and file to the strains of a band. . . . Heroism on command, senseless violence and all the loathsome nonsense that goes by the name of patriotism—how passionately I despise them!"[16] This, surely, is exemplary of the spirit of the 1920s, formed by the experience of the first war and soaked in the we-they antithesis that precluded understanding. It precluded the understanding that had led William James to plead for a moral equivalent of war, for something practical that would make peaceful use of the old martial virtues. Einstein insisted that "the advance of modern science has made the delivery of mankind from the menace of war . . . a matter of life and death for civilization as we know it." But Einstein did not grapple with the psychological issues, with people's desire for danger and comradeship. In his exchange with Freud about the nature of war he acknowledged that "the normal objective of my thought affords no insight into the dark places of human feeling and will."[17] For Einstein, war was a disease, a disorder planted by men of greed, to be abolished by men of good will through the creation of international sovereignty or through a revolutionary pacifism, that is, through the refusal of men to bear arms in peace or war. He called for resistance to war; but in 1933, almost immediately after Hitler's assumption of power, he renounced pacifism altogether—to the fury of his doctrinaire followers. In fact, he urged the Western powers to prepare themselves against another German onslaught.

His second great cause was Zionism, which he seems to have embraced during the war. By November 1919 the *Times* of London referred to him as an "ardent Zionist . . . keenly interested in the projected Hebrew University at Jerusalem, and [he] has offered to collaborate."[18] By the early 1920s he became a public advocate of Zionism—to the surprise and likely dismay of many of his colleagues. Assimilated Jews must have found this reminder of Jewish apartness painful; internationalists would have boggled at the implied argument for a new national community. But Einstein had come to feel a sense of solidarity with Jews, especially with Jewish victims of discrimination, and he seemed to believe in the existence of an ineradicable antagonism between gentiles and Jews, especially between Germans and Jews—with the fault by no means all on one side. Hence his view that Jews needed a spiritual home and a possible haven. He specifically cited the discrimination that talented Jews from Eastern Europe and from Germany suffered at German universities.

In 1921 Chaim Weizmann persuaded Einstein to join him on a trip to the United States to raise money for the projected Hebrew University in Jerusalem. For Weizmann, Einstein's support was critical; for Einstein, his visit to Jerusalem in 1923 was a deeply moving experience. Still, there were conflicts. Einstein railed against the mediocrity of the American head of the university; he saw him as a creature of the crass American-Jewish plutocrats for whom Einstein had contempt even as he helped to lighten their financial burden. He quarreled publicly with Weizmann over the policies of the Hebrew University and repeatedly threatened to withdraw his sponsorship. He urged a Jewish presence in Palestine that would promote, not injure, Arab interests. In 1929, at the time of major attacks on Jewish settlements, he again pleaded with Weizmann for Jewish-Arab cooperation and warned against a "nationalism à la prussienne," by which he meant a policy of toughness and a reliance on force:

> If we do not find the path to honest cooperation and honest negotiations with the Arabs, then we have learned nothing from our 2000 years of suffering, and we deserve the fate that will befall us. Above all, we should be careful not to rely too heavily on the English. For if we don't get to a real cooperation with the leading Arabs, then the English will drop us, if not officially, then de facto. And they will lament our debacle with traditional, pious glances toward heaven, with assurances of their innocence, and without lifting a finger for us.[19]

Weizmann replied instantly, at the height of the Palestinian violence, with a four-page handwritten letter. He expounded his views, which were somewhere between Zionist extremists and the irenic Einstein—who, in the meantime, had criticized the Jewish stance publicly. Weizmann pointed to the recalcitrance of the Arab leaders, their fanaticism, their inability to understand anything but firmness. He pleaded with Einstein to cease his injurious attacks on the Zionists. Of course they would negotiate in time, Weizmann insisted, but "we do not want to negotiate with the murderers at the open grave of the Hebron and Safed victims."[20] Einstein remained skeptical. Weizmann, desperate to retain his support, had written to Felix Warburg a year earlier: "There is really no length to which I would not go to bring back to our work the wonderful and lovable personality—perhaps the greatest genius the Jews have produced in recent centuries and withal so fine and noble a character."[21]

At the time of the greatest need for a Jewish home in Palestine, immediately after Hitler's seizure of power, Einstein formally broke with the Hebrew University and with Weizmann. The correspondence between the two men suggests all the intractable issues about Jewish-Arab relations, all the differences between the safe outsider and the practical statesman. In April 1938, Einstein resigned his position and again warned against a "narrow nationalism." Once again Weizmann explained that at the moment when 5 million Jews faced, as he put it, "a war of extermination," they needed the support of the intellectual elite of Jewry, and not, by implication, public criticism. Einstein was not an easy ally. To some he must have appeared as a man of conscience and of unshakable principle; to others, as an uncompromising fanatic in purity, impervious to practical exigencies. As Robert Oppenheimer put it in his memorial lecture: "He was almost wholly without sophistication and wholly without worldliness. . . . There was always with him a wonderful purity at once childlike and profoundly stubborn."[22]

It would be hard to imagine three causes less pleasing to the bulk of the German professoriat than liberal internationalism, pacifism, and Zionism. Unlike many academics, Einstein took education with the utmost seriousness—and academics with magnificent irreverence. He had great faith in the possibilities of primary and secondary education; at one point he said that if the League of Nations could improve primary education, it would have fulfilled its mission. His ironic contemplation of universities found expression in private letters. He once complimented his close friend Max Wertheimer, the Gestalt psychologist: "I really believe there are very few who have been so little harmed by learning as yourself." In 1924 he wrote: "In truth, the University is generally a machine of poor efficacy and still irreplaceable and not in any essential way improvable. Here the community must take the point of view that the biblical God took towards Sodom and Gomorrah. For the sake of a very few, the great effort must be made—and it is worth it!"[23]

Einstein's success—the enormous acclaim, especially abroad, at a time when most German scientists were still banished from international meetings—caused much ill will at home. His opinions enraged the superpatriots. Some physicists condemned the fanfare surrounding the dubious theory of relativity; one fellow-laureate attacked it as "a Jewish fraud." To anti-Semites, Einstein became a favorite and obvious target. The waves of hatred spilled from the streets into the lecture halls, and Einstein's occasional and sometimes ill-considered deprecations made things worse.

Germany frightened him again. His hopes for the Weimar Republic had dimmed. As early as 1922, his life was threatened. He traveled even more than before, but still he refused handsome offers from Leiden and Zurich, universities with which he had the closest ties.* He stayed despite his misgivings about Germany; he stayed because Berlin in the 1920s was the golden center of physics; he stayed because, as he wrote Ehrenfest in September 1919, before the results of the Eddington expedition were known, he could not "walk out . . . on the very people who have surrounded me with love and friendship. . . . You have no idea with what affection I am surrounded here. . . ." He stayed because proximity to Planck, Laue, Haber, and others was a unique professional gift, as he wrote Laue in 1928: "I see at every occasion how fortunate I can call myself for having you and Planck as my colleagues." In 1934 he wrote Laue that "the small circle of men who earlier was

* An American university also dispatched a letter of invitation, until now buried in the archives, dated 26 February 1923; the timing was delicately perfect because Germany found itself in the throes of foreign occupation and rampant inflation.

Dear Professor Einstein:
The duties and occupations of the professorship will be precisely what you wish to have them. Our aim will be to make it easy and convenient for you to pursue your personal studies and course of reflection without onerous academic or public burdens of any kind. The annual salary of the Professorship is $10,000 or about 40,000 gold marks. I wish to put this invitation before you on behalf of [Columbia] University with all possible urgency, and to beg you to accept it in the interest of science, of international comity, and, I trust, of the most successful prosecution of your own personal work.
Nicholas Murray Butler

Alas for Columbia, Einstein declined, though pleased to have been asked "by your magnificent university."

bound together harmoniously was really unique and in its human decency something I scarcely encountered again." In 1947 he wrote Planck's widow that his time with Planck "will remain among the happiest memories for the rest of my life."[24]

The unpublished correspondence among these men suggests even more than a professional tie. The letters bespeak a degree of humane collegiality, a shared pleasure in work, as well as a delicacy of sentiment, a candid avowal of affection, which in turn would allow for confessions of anguish and self-doubt, of melancholy as well as high spirits. They spoke of joys and torment, in close or distant friendship, in an enviable style. The letters also breathe a kind of innocence, as if science was their insulated realm, nature the great, enticing mystery, and one's labors of understanding exclusively an intellectual pursuit, remote from social consequences. Such clusters of collaboration and of friendship have always existed, I suppose, and they have made life better and infinitely richer. Germany may have had a special knack for breeding them.*

Einstein's Germany included gentiles and Jews, working together in extraordinary harmony. And still it can be stated categorically that none of the Jewish scientists escaped the ambiguity, the intermittent hostility, that Jewishness produced in Imperial and Weimar Germany. Neither fame nor achievement, neither the Nobel Prize nor baptism, offered immunity. Passions were fiercer in Weimar, in that cauldron of resentments. Most official barriers against Jews had been lowered, but new fears and hatreds came to supplement old prejudices. Three incidents may illustrate the uncertain temper of the time. In 1921, Haber begged Einstein not to go to America with Weizmann, on the ground that Germans would take amiss his travels in Allied countries with Allied nationals at the very time when the Allies were once again tightening the

---

* Einstein never forgot what such clusters signified. In 1952, at the graveside of Rudolf Ladenburg, a German-born physicist at Princeton, he said: "Brief is this existence, as a fleeting visit in a strange house. The path to be pursued is poorly lit by a flickering consciousness, the center of which is the limiting and separating I.

"The limitation to the I is for the likes of our nature unthinkable, considering both our naked existence and our deeper feeling for life. The I leads to the Thou and to the We—a step which alone makes us what we are. And yet the bridge which leads from the I to the Thou is subtle and uncertain, as is life's entire adventure.

"When a group of individuals becomes a We, a harmonious whole, then the highest is reached that humans as creatures can reach." Copy in the Einstein Papers, Boston.

screws against Germany. To persuade Einstein, Haber warned that German anti-Semites would capitalize on his seeming desertion and that innocent Jewish students would be made to suffer. Anti-Semitism, rampant as it was, need not be goaded; Einstein's warning to Rathenau originated in a similar apprehension. Or take another incident. In 1920, a well-known physicist opposed the appointment of the later laureate Otto Stern: "I have high regard for Stern, but he has such a corrosive Jewish intellect."[25]

Or consider this last example. In 1915 the king of Bavaria, confirming the Nobel laureate Richard Willstätter's appointment to a professorship, admonished his minister: "This is the last time I will let you have a Jew." Ten years later, discussing with his colleagues a new academic appointment, Willstätter proposed a candidate. A murmur arose: "another Jew." Willstätter walked out, resigned his post, and never entered the university again, the unanimous pleas of his students notwithstanding. For the next fourteen years he had daily, hour-long telephone calls with his assistant so that she could conduct the experiments in a laboratory that he would no longer enter. A man of conscience and of courage, someone who did not blink at the reality of anti-Semitism. But his stand in 1924 was his undoing a decade later. A devoted German, but now no longer a civil servant, he assumed that the Nazis would leave untouched a private scholar. He believed that some Jews had contributed to this new storm. He could not comprehend the radical newness of the phenomenon. In February 1938 he wrote my mother urging her that one ought not to leave Germany without the most careful reflection. He himself refused exile until the aftermath of the pogrom of November 1938 forced him into it.[26]

I cite Willstätter's example among many precisely because of its contradictory nature: Awareness of anti-Semitism could cloud one's perception of Nazism. If anti-Semitism had always existed, then perhaps Nazism was but an intensification of it. It is not uncommon these days to hear summary judgments about German Jewry, about their putative self-surrender, their cravenness, or their opportunism. These judgments often have a polemical edge; they are likely to do violence to the past and to the future: The myth of yesterday's self-surrender could feed the delusion of tomorrow's intransigence. If our aim is to understand a past culture, we must note that German-Jewish scientists thought Germany their only and their best home, despite the anti-Semitism that crawled all around them. They may have loved not wisely but too well, and yet their sentiments are perhaps not so much an indictment of themselves as a tribute to the appeals of Germany. We owe that past no less than what we owe any past—a sense of its integrity.

In 1932 Einstein left Germany provisionally, with the intention of returning to Berlin for one semester each year. Hitler's accession to power the next year changed all that. Einstein immediately denounced the new regime, and in response he was extruded from the Prussian Academy, his books were burned, his property seized. The first Nazi decrees for the purification of the universities would have allowed some Jews to maintain their positions. Einstein's non-Aryan friends spurned such sufferance and resigned. German physics was decimated, and a few remaining masters battled to defend some shreds of decency, some measure of autonomy. Laue once wrote Einstein that in teaching the theory of relativity he had sarcastically added that it had of course been translated from the Hebrew. Even such jokes—to say nothing of Laue's eulogies of Jewish colleagues—aroused Nazi wrath. The Nazis proscribed the very mention of Einstein, even in scientific discussions. They wished him to be an unperson.

For most, exile was hard; the habits of a lifetime are not easily shaken. For others, as the physicist Max Born put it, "a disaster turned out to be a blessing. For there is nothing more wholesome and refreshing for a man than to be uprooted and replanted in completely different surroundings."[27] Resiliency was a function of age and temperament. For Haber, exile was a crushing blow and led to a final irony in his relations with Einstein. By mid-1933 he wrote to Einstein that as soon as his health would allow it, he would go to Palestine, but in the meantime he begged Einstein to patch up his public quarrel with Weizmann. Einstein replied at length: "pleased . . . that your former love for the blond beast has cooled off a bit. Who would have thought that my dear Haber would appear before me as defender of the Jewish, yes even the Palestinian cause. The old fox [Weizmann] did not pick a bad defender." He then lashed out against Weizmann and concluded:

> I hope you won't return to Germany. It's no bargain to work for an intellectual group that consists of men who lie on their

bellies in front of common criminals and even sympathize to a degree with these criminals. They could not disappoint me, for I never had any respect or sympathy for them—aside from a few fine personalities (Planck 60% noble, and Laue 100%). I want nothing so much for you as a truly humane atmosphere in which you could regain your happy spirits (France or England). For me the most beautiful thing is to be in contact with a few fine Jews—a few millennia of civilized past do mean something after all.[28]

The German patriot Haber died a few months later in Basel, en route to Palestine. And Einstein found a refuge at the Princeton Institute under conditions not dissimilar to what the Prussian Academy had offered him twenty years earlier. For as Erwin Panofsky has said of the Institute for Advanced Study, it "owes its reputation to the fact that its members do their research work openly and their teaching surreptitiously, whereas the opposite is true of so many other institutions of learning."[29]

Einstein's public life continued to be dominated by his fear of Germany. He warned the West against a new German onslaught. He abandoned the pacifism he had so fervently espoused and in 1939 signed the famous letter to President Franklin D. Roosevelt urging the administration to prepare the United States because Germany might develop nuclear fission for military purposes. In the winter of 1945, when Germany was desolate in defeat and when the Morgenthau spirit, if not the plan, had a considerable grip on American thinking, a fellow-laureate and old friend, James Franck, asked Einstein to sign a manifesto of exiles that would appeal to the United States not to starve the German people. Einstein vowed that he would publicly attack such a plea. The German police—and he said this eleven months after the war— were still killing Jews in the streets of Germany; Germans had no remorse, they would start another war. Franck pleaded with him that to give up all hope for a moral position in politics would be tantamount to a Nazi victory after all. But Einstein, who had signed so many appeals that he himself once said he was not a hero in no-saying, scathingly rejected Franck's plea.[30] For him, genocide was Germany at its most demonic; after Auschwitz he could muster no magnanimity. Even the righteous could not redeem the "country of mass murderers," as he called Germany.

He rebuffed Laue's plea to help a young German physicist. He knew that Planck, who lost one son in the first war, had lost another whom the Nazis murdered because of his participation in the plot against Hitler. The serene Einstein, always the champion of the rights of the individual against the collectivity, now proclaimed the principle of collective guilt. At that moment, of course, the world shared Einstein's horror at German inhumanity. But in him the violence of sentiment, the total absence of that vulnerability to pity, puzzles, for it shows how desperately deep and all-consuming had been his antipathy to Germany.

Even his postwar laments about America, his horror at McCarthyism, were shaped by his image of Germany. America, he believed, was somehow following the path of Germany. The world of politics he saw through German eyes—always.

Greatness in any guise is not in vogue today, not in my discipline and not in our culture. Historians feel that it is now the turn of the forgotten, both for reasons of retroactive justice and for heuristic purposes. The argument is compelling, the feeling comprehensible, though there is an implicit deprivation involved; for as Einstein, in a rather German formulation, put it: "the example of great and pure individuals is the only thing that can lead us to noble thoughts and deeds."[31] We are uncomfortable even with the rhetoric of greatness, devalued as it so often has been. I would simply say that I find it inspiriting to look upon great peaks, as from an alpine village, and contemplate the distant mountains—cold, awesome, unattained and unattainable, mysterious.

It is often asserted that a culture must be judged by its treatment of minorities and deviants; a student of the German past would find this a cogent and, indeed, irrefutable argument. It is a necessary, but not a sufficient criterion. A culture must also recognize, recruit, and, in a sense, form talent; it must know how to coax talent into achievement. This too is a test of its virtue and of its instinct for survival. These are responsibilities that speak most directly to our universities, to every university.

T W O

FRITZ HABER: THE SCIENTIST IN POWER AND IN EXILE

In 1911, at the age of forty-two, Fritz Haber was appointed the first director of the newly founded Kaiser Wilhelm Institute for Physical Chemistry and Electrochemistry. He had already achieved international eminence, principally for his discovery of a process by which nitrogen could be fixed from the air. The task of building up the institute was interrupted by the Great War, during which Haber placed himself and the institute at the service of the state. He developed and introduced a new weapon, poison gas, and supervised its first—and devastating—use at Ypres in April 1915. After the war, Haber's institute became one of the world's greatest scientific centers. In 1933, the anti-Jewish decrees of the Nazi regime made his position untenable, and he resigned. A year later, he died in exile.

In October 1986, the present institute, after World War II renamed the Fritz Haber Institute for Physical Chemistry and Electrochemistry, celebrated its seventy-fifth anniversary and asked me to give the principal lecture on Haber's life. A week before the celebration in the Auditorium Maximum of the Free University, members of the institute published a critical, indeed a polemical, brochure about the institute's involvement with military-industrial enterprises, focusing with particular hostility on Fritz Haber himself. I first saw this pamphlet a few hours before my scheduled lecture and interpolated some comments in my prepared speech.

I had not planned to include this lecture in the present volume; in fact, the lecture was written after the manuscript had been submitted to the publisher. But the reception of the lecture and the wish of the Max Planck Society to publish it forthwith made me reconsider, with lingering misgivings.

A few days after my return from Berlin, I happened to come across a letter from Herbert Freundlich to my father, dated December 14, 1940, and pertaining *inter alia* to the unwillingness of James Franck and several other scientists to help Morris Goran with his projected biography of Haber. (For many years, Freundlich had headed the Institute section on colloidal chemistry, and from 1921 to 1923, my father had worked in his department.) The objection was that Goran was not a scientist (nor was he an historian):

> The three men are essentially savants [*Gelehrte*]. For them [J. E.] Coates's excellent "Memorial Lecture," which indeed does full justice to Haber as scientist, suffices entirely. Not for me: I could not give this lecture to my wife or daughter so that she would know Haber as a human being and historical personality; but neither [could I give it] to an English-speaking historian, politician or military person. All of them would find the lecture too narrowly chemical. Therefore I would be pleased still to see a book in which Haber would be presented from a more general point of view, also perhaps as the greatest representative of Jewry, as it has lived in and for Germany since the Napoleonic wars. I am also very much aware how later times would miss such a book, if it is not written soon. . . . There is little likelihood that such a book would be written later. The Nazis are destroying the sources as far as possible. The number of people who experienced these things in a conscious way is small. None of them is likely to write such a book; everything is too close and too difficult for them.

I took the accidental discovery of this letter as a sign, as a warrant for my continued effort to write about Haber and Einstein. The lecture was originally written in German; I have translated and revised it.

IT HAS ONLY BEEN in the twentieth century that a few great scientists have attained positions of power and public responsibility; Fritz Haber was among the first of them. He belonged to that succession of men and women who by their scientific knowledge, their ambition and energy, became, to paraphrase Carlyle, whom Haber much admired, captains of science, men of multiple public roles, statesmen in mufti.

Haber's life and career paralleled the course of German history with an almost uncanny closeness. He was always open to the world, sought to contribute to it—in some sense, to impose himself upon it. His life and work mirrored Germany's exceptional rise and devastating decline.

Haber was born in 1868, three years before Germany's unification; he died in exile on January 29, 1934, a day before the first anniversary of Hitler's rise to power. The ascendancy which Germany experienced in his lifetime was partly based on its rise to scientific preeminence; Haber's own contributions enhanced its prosperity and world renown. He exemplified the all-important close relations between German industry and German science. His career also demonstrated that some of the rivalries and antagonisms within the new empire, though debilitating, also had compensatory qualities: The several German states, Prussia, Baden, Bavaria, for example, vied for outstanding talent and thus promoted and rewarded it. Jews discovered that in many fields careers *were* open to talent—even to them, while lingering prejudice demanded maximum exertion.

Haber was representative of his times: the German Jew who out of a sense of ambitious Germanness converted to Protestantism; the scientist who, in the first war in which science played a major role, put his knowledge, his energy, and his capacity for leadership at the service of the country, and in the process invented a new and terrible weapon, poison gas; the patriot who, like millions of Germans, committed his whole strength to the hope of victory, only to have to face new hardships after an unforeseen defeat. Haber did not quarrel with his fate (as did so many of his less talented colleagues), but in public penury and during an unprecedented inflation he succeeded in sustaining his own institute, with ever-rising international prestige and participation. He was also "the spiritual father" of a postwar German foundation that financed scientific research and, in the face of economic catastrophe, nurtured a successor generation of scientists.*

He was an indefatigable worker for his country; he, too, believed that science had a special mission to promote a nation's welfare. In the 1920s he sought to free his country from the bondage of reparations by finding a process of extracting gold from the world's oceans, just as he had extracted nitrogen from the air. In this effort he failed, but he succeeded in establishing new international ties, especially with Japan and the United States; he was principally involved in overcoming the boycott that Allied scientists maintained against their German colleagues after the end of the war.

He helped his country in its ascendancy and in its trials, just as he benefited from the discipline and devotion of his collaborators and from the ethos of his society. For his dedication he was amply rewarded by all the insignia of recognition. In the last year of his life—the Nazis' first year—he had to endure their initial anti-Jewish measures, the mean-spiritedness which had seized his people, and the great silence which accompanied it. German in every fiber of his being, in his restless, thorough striving, in his devotion to friends and students, in his very soul and spirit, Haber died an involuntary exile, a broken man, alone: a fate tragically prophetic for German Jewry, for German history. What he experienced in his life, in good and evil days, recalls Goethe's remark to Boisserée: "The world is an organ whose bellows the devil pushes."

Haber was born in Breslau; his mother died two days after his

---

* In 1920 Haber wrote the official announcement of the founding of the Notgemeinschaft der deutschen Wissenschaft (Emergency Association of German Science), a national foundation soliciting and distributing funds for the continued support of scientific research. He was the moving spirit behind this new and important organization; it was headed by a former Prussian state minister of education, Friedrich Schmitt-Ott, and the founding committee comprised the great in German scholarship, including Max Planck and Adolf von Harnack. It was hoped that the government, though burdened by unimaginable debts at home and still unspecified reparations abroad, would contribute 20 million marks; in the 1920s, additional funds were collected from private and corporate sources, both German and foreign, especially American and Japanese. Haber's announcement emphasized: "The destruction of our country as a great political power will remain what it is today, i.e., an incontrovertible admonition that our existence as a people depends on the maintenance of our intellectual great power position, which is inseparable from our scientific enterprise." Published by Reichsdruckerei; a copy is included in the Fritz Haber collection of the Archive of the Max Planck Gesellschaft, Berlin.

birth. That death cast a shadow over his entire life; work, success, and warm friendships could overpower a melancholic streak, as could his own high spirits, but with age, public and private griefs, and deteriorating health that streak became harder and harder to contend with, despite his ever-active intelligence. His father, who remarried nine years later, was a prosperous die manufacturer, a much-respected and devoted city councillor, who hoped that his son would follow in his footsteps. After Haber's military training and early studies, he tried to work in his father's business, but abandoned the effort and followed his own passion for science. Forty years later, in a famous memorial speech for Justus von Liebig, the renowned pioneer chemist, he said—probably unaware of the autobiographical implication—"There is hardly anything more impressive than the passionate will of an outstanding young person who directs his life toward an idealistic, idiosyncratic goal."[1] By not bowing to the will of his father, by following his own bent, the young Haber did just that.

Various failures were his initial lot. Haber's conversion to Protestantism at the age of twenty-four led to a new conflict with his father, who was alternately pleased and troubled by his son. An ambitious young man, bent on an academic or a scientific career, he must have known that there were practical advantages in conversion. For much of his life Haber felt that need for justification which comes through work and success. He had to prove himself right in breaking with his father's wishes. Neither childhood nor youth was easy for him: The becoming, as he himself called the early stage of life, before one had attained the being, was difficult.[2]

From childhood on, Haber lived in historically dramatic times. His formative years coincided with the exaltation occasioned by Germany's unification, that belated achievement which gave the Reich its fatal militaristic-authoritarian character that even Bismarck at times regretted. As a good patriot, Haber's father was undoubtedly closer to the national intoxication than to the premonitions of contemporary thinkers like Jakob Burckhardt or Nietzsche, the latter seeing in the victory over the French a great danger for the new nation. It would be foolish to draw too close a parallel between the development of the nation and young Haber, but the triumphs of both had something to do with feelings of inferiority which so many Germans wanted to exorcise. How many Germans transposed their feelings of discontent of whatever origin in ceaseless work!*

There were many elements that would account for the rapid rise of Germany, for that first economic miracle in which the new Reich began to surpass the old British imperium. The work ethic and the relentless pressure for achievement, drilled into Germans at every stage of their lives, must be reckoned one such element. The fact that state and industry considered basic research essential to the country's collective welfare was another. In the second half of the nineteenth century, the German chemical industry attained world preeminence and its products were the single most important item in Germany's ever-expanding exports. As I suggested in the previous chapter, Germans had a special knack for supporting clusters of scientists, but the sustaining fiscal and moral support was essential as well.[3]

In Haber's life the untiring devotion to science was dominant not only in regard to his own work but in his eagerness to help students and colleagues to realize their full potential. His closest friend, Richard Willstätter, spoke of the "selflessness" which characterized a truly great teacher like Haber. In his late thirties, Haber wrote Willstätter: "I am glad about everything that exceeds my ability and rejoice when I can admire."[4] Selflessness, the capacity for unenvious admiration, self-criticism: these are qualities that do not burden very many academics.

After studying organic chemistry at various universities and after his brief interlude in the paternal business, Haber was appointed assistant to the chemist Hans Bunte at the Technical Institute (Hochschule) in Karlsruhe in 1894. Accident had brought him to Germany's most liberal state, and Haber's human and scientific talents quickly converted associates into colleagues and friends. In 1906, at the relatively young age of thirty-seven, he was appointed full professor for physical chemistry and electrochemistry. In those years he taught himself physical chemistry, entirely as an autodidact. (In writing of this phase of Haber's life,

---

* As Nietzsche put it, with characteristic extravagance: "And you, too, for whom life is furious work and unrest—are you not very weary of life? Are you not very ripe for the preaching of death? All of you to whom furious work is dear, and whatever is fast, new, and strange—you find it hard to bear yourselves; your industry is escape and the will to forget yourselves. If you believed more in life you would fling yourselves less to the moment. But you do not have contents enough in yourselves for waiting—and not even for idleness." *Also Sprach Zarathustra: Werke in drei Bänden*, vol. 2, ed. Karl Schlechta (Munich, 1955), p. 311.

Willstätter noted: "Thus we are all autodidacts who have attained anything in our work."[5]) It was in Karlsruhe that he established his laboratory for physical chemistry, and researchers from all over the world flocked to it. He quickly developed his gift as mentor. During his years in Karlsruhe he wrote three basic works, one of which was on electrochemistry, of which an eminent chemist said much later: "Technical and theoretical electrochemistry had made rapid strides, but to a large extent independently of each other. His purpose was to promote progress by discussing technical aims and methods *in the light of the modern theoretical knowledge*. This highly original and suggestive book, the first of its kind, was remarkable in that it brought out the essential problems and pointed the way for fundamental research."[6]

In Karlsruhe he made his most celebrated discovery: the process of fixing nitrogen from the air, a process that was perfected and gradually established as a major industrial product by the leading chemical firm BASF. The Haber-Bosch process (as it came to be known, Bosch having been the major collaborator from BASF) exemplified the extraordinarily close relations in Germany between science and industry, a combine of efficiency, vital and enriching for both sides. The process—in its essence still used today—was the clearest proof of Haber's practical bent, of which his loyal student, Karl Friedrich Bonhoeffer, wrote later: "Free of all academic narrowness, he cherished in his work the close reciprocal relationship of technology and pure science. In this way he developed into a scientific personality whose intellectual concern was always devoted to preserving the ties between scientific progress and practical life."[7]

The two decades before the Great War were prodigious in scientific creativity. It was still a small world of natural scientists who knew each other across national boundaries, who thought of themselves as "the happy few," as "a small band of brothers." By virtue of his books, his great discovery, and his mentorship, Haber established himself in that world with astonishing rapidity, a world that shared a great faith in science.*

---

* At Max Planck's sixtieth birthday in April 1918, Einstein spoke of the motives of scientific research—and did so in his own way and yet, I believe, expressive of feelings others had as well: "It is a many-mansioned building, this temple of science." If one of God's angels were to cast out the merely ambitious and the merely practical from this temple there would remain "somewhat peculiar, reserved, lonely fellows . . . who despite these common characteristics

In turn, Haber had a boundless interest in the world; he was a patriotic cosmopolite. In 1902, on the initiative of the chemist van't Hoff and with a personal subvention by him, the German Bunsen Society sent Haber as a delegate to the annual meeting of the American Electrochemical Society, and for nearly four months he traveled across the United States, studying the American system of chemical education. His report attested to his intellectual acuity and precision as well as his unusual command of language and his power of observation: "Today there is no country in the world to which we devote more attention and concern." He planned to give "a picture of the technical development in that wonderful country." He already grasped the connection among social mores, scientific development, and technology, and therefore emphasized the peculiarities of American life and of the American character: "The self-confidence . . . of the individual as well as of the people is perhaps the most important trait of the American spirit. It is documented in the most various forms: in the early independence which the young demand, in the hypersensitivity of the mass of the people which we note with great surprise as it is mirrored in the daily press. . . ." The American and German systems of education were very different: "The position of the [American] faculty is on the whole less favorable than that in Germany. The salaries, which oscillate between two and six thousand dollars, certainly exceed the regular compensation at home. But the purchasing power of the dollar is low for the needs of a socially eminent class, retirement pay does not exist, the heavy burden of teaching inhibits the opportunity for research, and the traditionally high regard for academics, by which we compensate university teachers for a lower material income, is missing in America." He criticized much about the American system and also defined his own idea of the task of the teacher: "The achievement of the teacher can be measured by the capacity for independent thought which he develops in the student."

would resemble each other less than do those who were expelled from the crowd." What led the true followers to the temple? Einstein cites Schopenhauer that one of the strongest motives that lead to art and science is "a flight . . . from everyday life with its painful rawness and desolate emptiness, away from the chains of one's own ever-changing desires." Planck's "inexhaustible endurance and patience" he attributed to: "an emotional state, which makes possible such achievements [and which] resembles the state of a religious person or a lover: the daily striving does not spring from a precept or a program, but from an immediate need." Albert Einstein, *Mein Weltbild*, ed. Carl Seelig (Zurich, 1953), pp. 141–144.

Haber sketched the ever-closer relations between the United States and Germany and noted, for example, that Germany imported more from the United States than from any other country—and still the two countries knew little about each other: "We all know the caricature of the American, who tirelessly runs after the dollar and who because of his wish for self-enrichment loses the sense for law and order as well as the interest in any kind of intellectual culture." But Americans also have a caricature of the Germans: "We are looked upon as a people that are good at military parades and bad at lyrical poetry, that bow to the top and are rough to the people below, that regard medals and civil service positions as most devoutly wished-for goals, that are comfortable in voluntary political nonage and that pass on the pressure which they gladly accept from officialdom to their wives and daughters, whom in marriage as in life they shortchange when it comes to freedom and educational rights."* A last remark from this report strikes perhaps a poignant note as America, deficit-ridden, clings to its lead in high technology: "The American [economic] challenge has become a common slogan, and Bismarck's sentence about the Germans who fear no one but God would seem in business circles gradually to be seriously amended: 'and a little the United States.' "[8]

Willstätter thought that Karlsruhe had been the happiest time in Haber's life. Certainly as far as students, laboratory, and proximity to industry were concerned, his existence had been ideal. But duty and ambition, not happiness, determined life in Wilhelmine Germany; scientists in particular had an austere ethos, an almost devout sense of calling. Haber was willingly caught up in the dynamic and expanding world—the center of which was Berlin.

In 1911 the Kaiser Wilhelm Gesellschaft was founded, an umbrella organization which through the establishment of research institutions in diverse fields was to promote German science and learning. (The society continues to operate today in undiminished importance—having changed its name, after the Second World War, to the Max Planck Society.)[9] The leaders of German learning, including Adolf von Harnack, had drafted the plan for such a

---

* It is a sad irony that Haber's first wife, Clara Immerwahr, a talented chemist in her own right with a doctorate, felt that because of her marriage and her husband's distinction and inconsiderateness she had to sacrifice her own interests and possible career. She committed suicide in 1915.

society, and the Kaiser—in commemoration of the hundredth anniversary of the founding of the University of Berlin—announced its creation and readily accepted the proposed protectorship. From the beginning the society enjoyed an imperial nimbus. The role fitted that curious figure, in some sense the very model of the insecure modern man: anxious, impulsive, fitfully aggressive, simultaneously emperor by divine right and desperately yearning for popularity, with his alarming arrogance and his very un-Prussian preference for appearance over reality—and for all his feudal allures still an enthusiast for modern science and technology. William II recognized science as an element of national power.

The society solicited endowments from industry and rich individuals; the state made some contributions, direct and indirect. The institutes were to do for Germany what foreign models—the Pasteur Institute and the Rockefeller institutes—did abroad; the aim was to give preeminent scientists the time and the facilities to conduct basic research which, while freely chosen, would ultimately redound to the national interest, would keep Germany strong and preeminent. In this enterprise the Kaiser happily availed himself of Jewish money and of Jewish talent. In fact, the Kaiser Wilhelm Society was sometimes attacked for its philo-Semitic character; it was evidence that some common endeavors could be pursued in an atmosphere where old prejudices could be suspended or were considered irrelevant, perhaps even forgotten by some.*

Leopold Koppel, the most active benefactor-founder of the society, insisted that Haber be named the director of the first institute to be established, one for physical chemistry and electrochemistry.† Ambition and the lure of companionship made Haber

---

* For many years, the president of the society was Adolf von Harnack, scholar and senior academic statesman, the treasurer was Franz von Mendelssohn, an eminent financier, and the secretary Eduard Arnhold, a coal magnate and art collector. Both were of Jewish descent.

† Leopold Koppel was one of the richest bankers in Berlin, and a Jew. In 1905 he had already created a Koppel Foundation for the promotion of international research; to the Kaiser Wilhelm Society he contributed over a million marks—a huge amount in those days. Only Gustav Krupp von Bohlen contributed more, while the Prussian state appropriated a mere 70,000 marks and the Crown contributed royal terrain in Dahlem, an unsettled, attractive tract in a then outlying area of Berlin. Koppel's benefaction was rewarded in various ways, including his appointment as senator of the new society, and with that honor came participation in an annual reception at William's court. Many other Jewish families contributed heavily as well, including, of course, the Bleichröder family. Jewish wealth promoted Jewish and Christian talent—and in turn earned imperial recognition. See Lothar Burchardt, *Wissenschaftspolitik im Wilhelminischen Deutschland* (Göttingen, 1975), pp. 155–158.

accept instantly. Berlin was an irresistible magnet for every scientist, as Einstein's arrival three years later would prove again. For Haber, Berlin was not only the acknowledged world center of the natural sciences, but, given the presence of Planck, Nernst, Laue, and others, it was a community of mutually supportive geniuses. Berlin was also the capital of the new Reich, where the imperial court, the seat of the Prussian and Reich governments, economic, artistic, and intellectual life—all came together. Haber, installed by the Kaiser in his directorship, given at the same time an honorary professorship at the university and membership in the Prussian Academy of Sciences, had every reason to assume that he would have a preeminent place in that extraordinary world. Almost at once, he became a member of what we would call the interlocking directorship of the great academic and scientific institutions of Berlin. The new title of "Geheimrat," inadequately translated as "privy councillor," was yet another indication of rank and distinction. Haber had arrived in a Berlin that signified power, glamour, wealth, learning, and ever new discoveries.

For the forty-two-year-old Haber it was a dazzling move. In 1912, the Kaiser opened the institute, and it was Haber's instant ambition to lead it to world preeminence. From the very beginning he had an uncommon gift for recruiting the most talented collaborators. The institute mirrored the larger community of scientists in Berlin. The human bonds of those days were of immeasurable importance, providing stimulation and sustenance. Even so critical a person as Einstein, who as an ardent pacifist stood almost alone during the Great War, could nevertheless acknowledge during that war that he could not leave Berlin because of "the beautiful relations which have been formed between my closest colleagues and myself (especially Planck) and how here everybody has been and is forthcoming; if you remember that my work became truly effective only through the understanding it found here, then you will grasp why I cannot decide to turn my back on this place. . . . Here, everybody approaches, closely and yet with a certain distance, so that life runs its course almost without irritation; I learned that in life."[10] Haber was also always particularly solicitous of Einstein, who greatly needed his help.

Two years later, the outbreak of the war cut short Haber's efforts on behalf of the institute. Life changed instantly. Haber was a patriot, as were almost all of his colleagues, though he was

free of Wilhelmine chauvinism and parochialism. At the beginning
of the war, he shared in that remarkable exaltation of August
1914. It was an historic moment, often described, and became a
legend for Germans; it was a sudden outpouring of patriotism
and of some deep repressed yearnings: for sacrifice, for community, for release, even for redemption.* (Many Germans felt a
similar enthusiasm and collective hope when Hitler became chancellor, as I discuss in Chapter 5.) A great common surge seized
the country, an all-embracing feeling of unity that sent tens of
thousands of young men to volunteer and millions to wave them
on. For a moment, class differences seemed obliterated, as did
confessional divisions: workers, socialists, Jews—all joined in the
national cause, the last with particular fervor. Einstein's immunity
was exceptional, Haber's immediate and continuing commitment
exemplary.

Haber was one of those who signed the Manifesto of the Ninety-
three (discussed in the previous chapter), which became one of
the chief causes—and excuses—for Allied hatred of German
academics. Haber himself later suffered from that hatred—and
not only because of his signature on the manifesto. At the outbreak
of the war, Haber dedicated himself completely to military service,
convinced after the first few weeks of the war that Germany could
be victorious only if it survived the British blockade, only if science
and industry could solve the problems brought about by the war—
a fact the military, still deluded by the victories in the Franco-
Prussian War, had little sense of. He put his institute on a war
footing, and after its initial depletion because of military conscription, he gradually built up a very much larger staff of scientific
workers than he had ever had in peacetime.

At first Haber and the institute tackled problems associated
with the all-important production of nitrates: the need to produce
large amounts of nitrogen in order to compensate for the loss of
Chilean saltpeter. Other tasks followed, and the Kaiser himself
had to insist to the skeptical military that Haber be promoted from

* Nietzsche—so often and so erroneously depicted as a great glorifier of physical violence—
once wrote that men "throw themselves with delight into the new danger of death because
they think that in the sacrifice for the fatherland they have at long last that long-sought
permission—the permission to dodge their goal: War is for them a detour to suicide, but a
detour with a good conscience." *Die fröhliche Wissenschaft: Werke in drei Bänden*, vol. 2, ed. Karl
Schlechta (Munich, 1955), p. 200.

an insignificant post in the army reserve to the rank of captain; eventually he became the head of the chemical division in the war ministry.

By the winter of 1914, Haber was encouraged to develop a new weapon: some form of poison gas. In a few months he succeeded in producing his most bitterly controversial innovation. Supreme Headquarters (OHL) of course fostered his efforts, and Haber's son, who has described his father's work and the subsequent history of chemical warfare most thoroughly and with admirable fairness, wondered whether OHL had made the right choice: "In Haber the OHL found a brilliant mind and an extremely energetic organizer, determined, and possibly also unscrupulous."[11] With courage and with injury to his own health, he experimented with the new weapon himself—the first ingredient was chlorine; later other compounds were used—just as he asked Willstätter to develop a gas mask that would protect German soldiers, just as the most irenic of men, James Franck, organized the chemical assault on the western front itself. In April 1915, near Ypres, the Germans launched their first gas attack—with considerable success. At other times, and especially on the eastern front, the weapon proved more efficacious; as Haber reported at the time: "The panic which the first attack at Ypres caused among the enemy could be observed in the East with the Russians only after repeated attacks at the same place, then, however, regularly."[12]

In this endeavor, too, Haber had a paradigmatic importance: Like others later, he was a scientist who under the pressures of war developed a new weapon, untroubled by its consequences, anticipatable and unanticipatable. Haber was above all concerned with the effectiveness of the new weapon; science, he once said, belonged to humanity in peacetime and to the fatherland in war. He looked for a weapon that would break the decimating stalemate, that would bring about an early, victorious end. For the rest of the war, he experimented with other forms of gas and other means of delivery; the Allies learned to retaliate, and both sides came to be better shielded by the production of ever more efficient respirators or gas masks. Haber had to contend with military authorities who, he thought, did not comprehend and seize the possibilities of gas warfare. And so it remained a brutal weapon without fulfilling his hope of forcing a decision.

Haber had a technical-practical mind; higher questions, such as the legality of the new weapon, given the prohibitions against poisonous weapons in successive Hague conventions, he left to his military superiors. He probably thought that the use of gas was more humane than the mowing down of troops by machine guns and the endless, senseless killing in trench warfare. Victims were incapacitated and the resulting panic disorganized enemy ranks; in the course of the war, however, it became clear that the actual fatalities from gas warfare were comparatively low.

And still there was a special horror that attached to gas warfare. The sense of outrage grew in time; during the war, with its far greater daily horrors, the new weapon was not regarded as something uniquely baleful.* And yet it was a weapon that inflicted exceptional torment; long after the war a British officer described the horror to Haber's British counterpart, Sir Harold Hartley: "It is a hateful and terrible sensation to be *choked* and suffocated and unable to get breath: a casualty from gun fire may be dying from his wounds, but they don't give him the sensation that his life is being strangled out of him."[13]

There were later acts of horror, unanticipated, unintended, and in some sense unconnected, that nevertheless need to be acknowledged. In 1914, Haber could not envision that thirty years later, the Germans for whom he produced poison gas would use another kind of gas for the killing of millions of his own people, not in warfare, but because of an infinitely charged racial fanaticism. It is true, of course, that once the National Socialists had resolved to exterminate all Jews, they would have found the technical means to do so. Perhaps it deserves mention as well that Hitler claimed his sense of mission as savior of Germany first came to him

* There were of course immediate Allied protests at German illegality and inhumanity. A few Germans were also instantly appalled, having some sense of the portentousness of the new weapon. Kurt Riezler, Chancellor Bethmann-Hollweg's confidant, noted in his diary a few days after the attack at Ypres: "Our principal anxiety must concern the insane political unreason [caused by] the domination of blind affects. Poor Germany. Naive country. Ideologists of power and those of modesty. . . . The destruction of international law—the chlorine clouds never again to be banished from warfare. From this direction come the greatest transformations of all aspects of man and world." Kurt Riezler, *Tagebücher, Aufsätze, Dokumente*, ed. Karl-Dietrich Erdmann (Göttingen, 1972), p. 270.

In the late 1920s, George Grosz drew a picture of Christ on the cross, with a gas mask and soldier's boots, for which he was tried for blasphemy. Grosz sensed that gas warfare had become a special symbol of the bestiality of war, the depravity of man, and pacifist writers and artists sought to convey that same message.

when he lay blinded from Allied gas in a wartime hospital; some scholars have given credence to this claim. Still, it would be morally and historically senseless to seek connections where none existed.

The links between Haber, his institute, and the military became steadily closer. Haber's ever-expanding organization became a kind of Manhattan Project before its time. He may have been the first scientist to have developed such a gigantic undertaking. In the lives and sufferings of Haber and of J. Robert Oppenheimer, the director of the Manhattan Project, there were remarkable similarities—and the differences are in part reflective of the differences between the two countries. Both men were great scientists; Haber had rare leadership talents, Oppenheimer developed his only in Los Alamos, but then superbly; both helped to fashion new weapons for war; both were essentially peaceful men of the world; both were of Jewish origin; both had a poetic strain, though Oppenheimer had a visionary quality and Haber a severely practical bent; both were directors of institutes which in their best times were suffused with collegiality; both experienced much that was tragic in their private lives. At the end of their lives—and quite independent of their scientific work—both were persecuted and denounced by some of their countrymen. With only this one difference: President Kennedy decided to rehabilitate Oppenheimer by awarding him the Fermi Prize, a high presidential distinction.*

During the war, Haber's responsibilities intersected with those

---

* A recently published polemic on Haber and on the institute that now bears his name indicates that he is not forgotten, that in fact he has become a new target of attack, now no longer from right-wing, anti-Semitic circles, but from progressive, pacifistically inclined purists. See the pamphlet published by a collective from the present Haber Institute, Gerd Chmiel, et al., ". . . *Im Frieden der Menschheit, im Kriege dem Vaterlande* . . ." 75 Jahre Fritz-Haber Institut der Max-Planck-Gesellschaft, Bemerkungen zur Geschichte und Gegenwart (Berlin, 1986). The focus of the pamphlet is Haber's wartime role and the institute's continuous closeness to "the military-industrial complex." After Hiroshima, the motivation is clear, but to indict an individual—decades later—without considering context and intentionality is facile or at least problematical. Haber acted at a time of chauvinistic psychosis, when academics and clergy poisoned the minds of people. It was a time when service to one's country was a universal imperative, and most scientists had not yet learned—or had not even been warned—that theirs was a moral responsibility as well. Of course it is with sorrow that one recalls that Haber apparently never acknowledged to himself the ambiguity of his wartime work—or at least he never publicly acknowledged any misgiving, a fact that his son, not implausibly, suggests may have sprung from a reluctance to seem to be groveling. In time, Allied scientists came to understand his role much better than did German pacifists of the 1920s or later. Einstein, pacifist of the first hour, remained his close friend; perhaps latter-day followers of that apostle of peace should ponder his example.

of Walther Rathenau, whom he had previously known. Like Haber, Rathenau had offered his services at once; he, too, believed that Germany faced a long war and that the military had no sense of the economic prerequisites for survival. Rathenau, a prominent industrialist, was made head of the raw material allocation section of the war ministry, an entirely new department, which aroused suspicions among the military as well as among his erstwhile fellow-industrialists. Haber's close friend Wichard von Moellendorff was Rathenau's associate; having set up the indispensable new section, Rathenau resigned in March 1915.*

Haber certainly had a sense of the magnitude of the stakes; he understood that this was not a conventional war to be fought by conventional means and for conventional ends. He, too, believed in far-reaching war aims. In the beginning of 1916, he wrote to Rudolf von Valentini, chief of the imperial civil cabinet and his most direct contact with the Kaiser: "I hope peace will come in the next few months, even though I would not want to see a peace in which France and Belgium would remain militarily capable enemies. Leaving ethical and political questions aside, a peace that would require us to arm with the same intensity as hitherto, against an estimable foe on the western border, would impose on us material burdens, which, it would seem, are not yet recognized."[14] This was not an ideologue's or a Pan-German version of an all-out victory; it was nevertheless a cold, calculating version of a practical man concerned with the economic consequences of the peace.

But the war demanded ever greater exactions. By midsummer 1916, the new OHL recognized the need for still greater mobilization efforts, and Haber, given his experience and temperament, favored a centrally planned economy. The immediate need was for a better allocation of manpower; in early September, Haber discussed the problem with Moellendorff, who prepared a memorandum on the need for and functions of an *Arbeitsamt* (labor office) within the war ministry. Haber forwarded the letter to Colonel Bauer, who in turn submitted it to Hindenburg and

---

* A year later he wrote to Emil Ludwig: "That as a private person and a Jew I offered, unasked, my services to the state, neither of the two involved groups [the state and the industrialists?] can forgive me, and I do not believe that in my lifetime they will change their attitude." Walther Rathenau, *Tagebuch 1907–1922*, ed. Hartmut Pogge-v. Strandmann (Düsseldorf, 1967), p. 43.

Ludendorff—by that time, the supreme dictators of the German war effort. Eventually a labor office was established, and the original plan corresponded to Moellendorff's conception of a corporate state in which labor and industry would collaborate, with the state as an active partner and sometime arbiter.[15]

For a long time, despite the intermittent gloom that afflicted many in responsible positions, Haber believed in a final victory. All the more bitter the defeat. He took leave from his post in the war ministry; a great chapter of his life had ended. He too had loved the (self-styled) uniform, the authority it conferred, the responsibilities which had steadily grown; even the farewell letter of War Minister Heinrich Scheüch offered little consolation: "During the long duration of the war you put your broad knowledge and your energy in the service of the Fatherland—beyond all measure. Thanks to the high esteem which you enjoy among your colleagues, you were able to mobilize German chemistry. It was not given to Germany to emerge victorious from this war. That it did not succumb to the supremacy of its enemies after the first few months because of lack of powder, explosives and other chemical combinations of nitrogen, is in the first instance your achievement. . . . Your splendid successes . . . will always live on in history and will remain unforgotten."[16] Fifteen years later, and by decree, they were forgotten or denied.

After his immense effort, the end of the war brought him close to a physical collapse; he also had reason to be afraid that the Allies would include him among German "war criminals" who were to be extradited to Allied lands. Illness and depression took their toll.[17] Though in time, work and new demands proved capable of giving him ever fresh impetus, his health never fully recovered. In 1920, in recognition of his prewar discovery, he received the Nobel Prize for 1918—a distinction which in many of the Allied countries was sharply attacked, precisely because it signified something like a rehabilitation from a neutral side.

Even in periods of depression, Haber's concern with immediate political issues did not cease. A month after the signing of the armistice, he wrote his friend Moellendorff about the latter's plans to establish a planned corporate economy, an enterprise he undertook together with the socialist minister Rudolf Wissel. Haber was affectionately skeptical: "I don't believe that it is in any way possible to spare our people, for whom we labor, a harsh, renun-

ciatory, depressed unhappy period after the war. The people don't
want to see this and it will require a rough, strict kind of coercion.
Assuredly that would come if the enemy occupies us. If we remain
free from occupation, then we must achieve deeds of self-discipline
which in the broad masses would not succeed. . . . I think that the
condition of today's world has as much affinity with and divergence
from the original Christian ideas as the future condition of the
economy will have with the ideas which you now propagate. . . .
The [November] Revolution was a summary judgment against the
system of government, not against capitalism. The nation is 'bourgeois' to its very marrow . . ." and hence will reject the idealistic,
communal vision which Moellendorff and Wissel sought to realize.[18]
A few months later, the Wissel-Moellendorff scheme was dead.
Haber had been right in his pessimism: The nation was bourgeois,
egotistical, not ready for the sacrifices that Moellendorff's "Germanic Socialism" would have imposed. But Haber also felt that
the prewar disharmony, which had put workers at a disadvantage
and in conflict with society, had enfeebled the imperial regime
and had to be overcome if Germany were to recover at all.[19]

Haber belonged to a small group of men who instantly rallied
to the new Republic; he had come to see the bankruptcy of the
old order, however much he had once been attached to it. The
bulk of the German professoriat remained sullenly loyal to the old
order and to old prejudices; they came to be mired in resentment.
In fact, Haber proved a great asset to the new German state.

He now undertook new responsibilities. As mentioned earlier,
he became the spiritual father of the all-important Emergency
Association of German Science. He was probably the first German
scientist to obtain grants for German needs from the Rockefeller
Foundation. He visited Japan, where he was given a royal welcome,
and upon his return helped to found a German-Japanese Institute
for intellectual and scientific collaboration. When formally inter-
viewed by a British expert on gas warfare, he turned suspicion
into near-amity. In countless ways he helped to reknit old and
begin new ties.

At Einstein's suggestion, Haber took over Einstein's duties as
delegate to the League of Nations' International Commission on
Intellectual Cooperation. Both men worked hard to end the boycott
that Allied scientists continued to impose on their German colleagues; Einstein thought the boycott detrimental to science, hence

irrational; Haber also thought it detrimental to the fatherland. The defeated country needed rehabilitation; its scientists needed renewed acceptance in the international community of scientists.

In his efforts to have German scientists readmitted on equal terms to international professional organizations, he worked closely with the German Foreign Office and with Foreign Minister Gustav Stresemann. Here, too, his efforts were persistent, passionate, and skillful. Like the great foreign minister himself, Haber simultaneously faced the revanchist sentiments of foreigners (many of whom were quite glad to get rid of their often overbearing German colleagues), and the sullen resentment, the *Trotzigkeit*, of the Germans themselves who rejected all compromises with the former enemies. If foreigners did not want to deal with Germans, Germans did not want to deal with them either—and a fortiori. Haber on one level and Stresemann on another had the unenviable task of navigating between antagonists abroad and at home, whose responses were usually dictated by injured pride and envy rather than by reason or interest.

In his work, whether in scientific bodies or in public life, Haber encountered manifestations of anti-Jewish prejudices or anti-Semitic demagoguery. In Weimar, in some fields—in government, in the bureaucracy, in universities—Jews made further progress, and embittered survivors of the old order could view them as beneficiaries of the new order. At the annual meeting of natural scientists in 1920, Haber was made to feel the anti-Semitic sentiments of some of his colleagues. At another time he was afraid that Einstein, the victim of much greater agitation, would accept a post abroad; he pleaded with him not to consider the anti-Semites, "that entente of trashy nullities . . . as equivalent to the collective admiration which all serious natural scientists accord you."[20] As we saw in the previous chapter, anti-Jewish feelings led his friend Willstätter to resign; he commiserated that Willstätter had faced "more Hitlerism" [in 1924!] than he could endure.[21] But Haber's own experiences or those of his friends or the murder of Rathenau probably never made him think that the collegial bonds, to say nothing of the basic rights of Jews, would be altered. On any kind of unconscious psychic balance sheet, the good would incomparably have outweighed the bad.

Haber devoted immense effort to his postwar scheme of extracting gold from the oceans. But his hope that scientific ingenuity would help Germany free itself from the heavy reparation payments failed, to his deep disappointment.

His principal passion, of course, remained his institute; he had successfully converted it to peacetime activity and continued to recruit outstanding talent in his own and in many related fields. The institute became world-famous, as did the colloquium which he conducted every two weeks, where young students and established masters met. By his scientific empathy and his rapid grasp of scientific problems he dominated the meetings. Erwin Chargaff, himself a great scientist-humanist, recalled the specialness of those occasions: "Fritz Haber had a marvelously Socratic skill of drawing the best out of speaker and audience." Or consider the testimony of J. E. Coates: "In the Colloquium Haber was at his best. Here came out one of his most brilliant qualities, the capacity to grasp quickly the essentials of subjects not his own, to perceive their true bearings beyond the details, to discover errors, to indicate lines of advance. He had a genius for guiding discussion into the most profitable channels, for resolving obscurities and bringing the essential things into a clear light." The colloquium, truly interdisciplinary, gave new impulses to various fields, including the biological sciences. In his obituary note, Willstätter, who knew him best, recalled: "It was the uniqueness of Fritz Haber to concentrate and magnify energies for high purposes, to penetrate to the very depths of problems, to comprehend connections and consequences: He was characterized by a superabundance of insights, by the breadth of perspective, by integrity and clarity." His name was synonymous with all the institutes that the Kaiser Wilhelm Society had established in Dahlem. He was part of Weimar's glory, of what made Berlin, in Chargaff's words, "the very empyrean of science."[22] And in that empyrean, Einstein was the solitary master, the genius of theoretical creation, Haber the impresario of collective greatness, the genius of practical achievement.

He formed the character of his institute, but his influence ranged far beyond. Although a driven and ambitious man, he was still molded by the old humanistic education, with a rare talent for language and an enviable poetic gift by which he often illuminated human depths. For all his passion for science, for work generally—and there were probably few people who worked as much as he did—he saw in friends and in the life of the soul the higher meaning of existence. He who was so often in conflict with his father became a paternal and indispensable friend to many—even if his occasional eruptions of rage frightened him and his victims. Haber had a rare sense of the potential of individuals; it was his self-assigned task to push them, to push them as hard as he pushed himself. To sustain others was probably also a way of sustaining himself.

At the end of the 1920s, for a fleeting moment, it seemed as if Haber, and Germany, were to move to quieter times. What Gustav Stresemann accomplished in the political realm—the wresting of concessions from the Allies, exemplified by the early withdrawal of Allied troops from the Rhineland or the more favorable provisions for reparations under the Young Plan—Haber accomplished in the international-scientific world. Gradually German scientists were readmitted on a basis of equality. But in 1929, Stresemann died, and the great economic collapse, the worldwide depression, began.

Haber grasped the full dimensions of the crisis: He saw the breakdown of the economy, the massive unemployment, a threatened paralysis of authority brought on by political polarization and loss of hope. Never passive in moments of decision, he wrote in May 1931 to the then minister of finance, Hermann Dietrich, that Germany's situation was no less dismal than it had been in the last year of the Great War. At that time "the connection between the leaders and the people was lost . . . and in the fall of 1918 we were presented with the bill." The same gap was opening up between the captains of the economy—who swore by the need for private enterprise while praising Soviet achievements—and the increasingly hard-pressed masses.

Regretfully, he advocated draconian—and presumably, temporary—measures. The government should anticipate now what later it would have to do under duress: "to detach the power of the state from the parliamentary system and the power of the economy from private leadership and to adopt a dictatorship and a planned economy as its own program. . . ." He explicitly recalled Moellendorff's earlier plans, now more timely: "The new generation is here! It fills the streets and pushes aside the old parties. . . . It looks for a German form for what in different character has already been realized in Russia and in Italy. It no longer has faith in the liberalism of the grandfathers and in the slow evolutionary path of trade-union social democracy."[23]

Unlike so many of his friends and party people, Haber saw the depth of the crisis and the profound change of mood; he demanded a radical-authoritarian solution, an end to the rule of the market economy. The crisis required drastic action—the Nazi danger was growing daily—but there was no man, no de Gaulle, who could transform a decaying democratic system into a more or less popular and legitimate—and presumably, timebound—dictatorship. To call for an authoritarian solution was consonant with Haber's basic attitude, his *Lebensauffassung:* he had a special weakness for strength, for authority, for leadership. In his many sketches of friends or colleagues he would often speak of their heroic leadership qualities, in Carlylean tones.

All too easily he transferred his notion of leadership from the scientific realms in which he had functioned to the political world. He had rendered the Weimar Republic great services and at its end he hoped that it could be saved through a dictatorship—the dream of a democratic Caesar, of a *Führerdemokratie,* probably ran strong in him. He hoped for a leader or at least a strong political authority that would rescue Germany from chaos and from threatened radical tyranny. He probably never had much faith in "the invisible hand," in the automatic processes of capitalism. He probably also had little patience for the laborious processes of democracy, for endless parliamentary wrangling, which by 1930 or 1931 had reached a virtual breakdown in any case.

In the following months, millions of Germans believed that they had found such a leader, and thus Hitler came to power. A vulnerable society was destroyed. After Hitler, the possibility even to talk uninhibitedly about the place of a *Führer* was gone. That concept, too, was destroyed.

In early 1933 a tiny cabal persuaded President Hindenburg to appoint Hitler, the leader of the largest party, as chancellor. Many Germans had already succumbed to the temptation of National Socialism. The elites, as well as millions of ordinary people, believed in the pseudo-religious promise of Hitler; they willingly surrendered to the orgy of national passions. With a rapidity that even now is hard to comprehend, Hitler succeeded in consolidating his power. He imposed conformity—and was immeasurably helped by self-imposed conformity, especially in the universities. In April 1933, Hitler's government—still made up of a majority of old conservatives—issued a decree "for the restoration of the professional civil service"; it was the "legal" basis for the purging of Jewish and politically unreliable civil servants, including, of course, university professors. (Put in current academic parlance, the decree broke tenure.) The law would have allowed Haber, as a veteran of the war, to remain in his office; he would have had to dismiss his Jewish colleagues who did not qualify for an exemption. After some hesitation, he chose premature retirement. James Franck in Göttingen was in the same situation and wrote Haber that he had resigned from his post, officially citing as reason "the attitude of the government toward German Jewry. . . . Nor will I make use of the scrap of charity which the government offers veterans of the Jewish race."[24]

Haber's retirement took effect on October 1, 1933, after twenty-two years of unique achievement. He could hardly bear the disappointment and wrote Willstätter: "I am bitter as never before. I was German to an extent that I feel fully only now and I find it odious in the extreme that I can no longer work enough to begin confidently a new post in a different country. . . . From the circle of the I. G. Farben [with which he had had the closest connections] there has been no one who has talked to me, or visited me, concerning my offer of resignation. . . . Planck makes every effort to show me respect and affection."[25] Of course there were exceptions, aside from Planck, exceptions that suggest that the great silence surrounding Haber's last months marked callous or embarrassed indifference; in those days, a private letter of solidarity would not have required particular courage. Thus Karl Friedrich Bonhoeffer wrote him of his sorrow: "but at least I want to assure you—what I hope you would know of me in any case—that I will always proudly and gratefully acknowledge that you have been my teacher and that I shall tell the future generation of your achievements on behalf of German science and technology."[26] And still the silence of colleagues, the betrayal by the elites, was devastating. From exile, Einstein wrote Haber a letter full of compassion for his fate: "I can imagine your inner conflict. It is as if one must give up a theory which one has worked on all one's life. It is not the same for me because I never believed in it in the least."[27] The theory was faith in German decency, in a future in which Jews and Christians could live and work together.

For Haber the end was not only crushing psychologically but materially as well. In Cambridge, among former enemies, he found

a home and an unpaid position; there was an endless legal tangle
over whether he could transfer his German capital without having
to surrender most of it to a special German emigration tax. He
still had heavy obligations to his young children. He thought of
following Chaim Weizmann's invitation to settle in Palestine: A
small two-room apartment in Jerusalem would suffice for him and
his sister. "In my whole life I have never been so Jewish as now,"
he wrote Einstein in the summer of 1933.[28]

Haber, who had always helped others, now stood entirely alone.
Two weeks before his death he wrote Willstätter from Cambridge:
"I have fallen into a state of decline here. . . . The capacity for
building up a new life in one's mid-sixties is a rare gift and for me
in any case a most uncertain one." At the same time he wrote my
father: "Lucky the person who did not grow up in the German
world and does not grow up there now! But the people on the
other side of the Rhine will have greater difficulty in getting rid
of the debts against humanity which they are now incurring than
they imagine, and your children and their children will profit more
from the sufferings of their parents than we profited from the
well-being of our own forebears."[29]

On January 29, 1934, Haber died in transit in Basel, in the
foreign city closest to Germany. His friends recognized that this
death was a peculiarly tragic one. From his exile in America, James
Franck wrote: "It is simply an inextinguishable shame that this
man was morally forced into exile. . . . Much of what happened
and is happening at home [in Germany] I am able to forgive and
try to see what is good, even if that is sparse, but in my whole life
I will not be able to forgive that one has forced a man like Fritz
Haber who did more for his country than is almost imaginable to
end his life in exile. I wish that since it was not given to your
father to survive the harsh time that he would never even have
seen it in the first place."[30] A year later, Max Planck and Max von
Laue organized a memorial service for Haber, sponsored by the
Kaiser Wilhelm Society, a courageous act at that time, perhaps the
only one of its kind in the Third Reich.

At the end of his memorial speech for Liebig, Haber said: "Before
we take leave of him—having talked so much of his will power
and intellectual strength—we must ask, what was his soul like? For

nobody deserves a place among the immortals—however great his strength or luminous his mind—if he lacks magnanimity, greatness of soul. All who knew him praised that from the depth of his soul he was truthful, upright, and loyal, and at the same time proud and of a capacious spirit. . . . A man of strength [*Kampfnatur*]. The soul of a person is measured by the love which he won in his life and which remains his even beyond his death. Well, I know no one among the fighters of our field, indeed no one in the whole realm of the natural sciences, who had won more grateful love in his life and took more grateful love with him to eternity."[31]

Fritz Haber garnered abundant, grateful love in his life; he also had to endure disappointments and the recurrent, ever-gnawing dissatisfaction with himself, this tormenting feeling which in part was compensated for or at least dulled by his unceasing work, by his austere and loving help to others.

I am closely tied to him. He was my godfather and I was barely seven years old when he died. I remember the day. In my study is a picture of him with a dedication to my father:

> *If you want to give every day*
> *Its proper meaning,*
> *You must strive contentedly*
> *And in striving find contentment!**

Haber himself did not always find that contentment—and his end described a tragedy that seemed to belie the good fortune of so much of his life. But the hope that striving and contentment could and must be fused, that, too, is part of Haber's legacy, an echo of an older time when striving and contentment were expected to be in harmony, and where mediating between the two stood compassion, or, put differently, decency and kindness. We are considering a man who was not only an important historical figure, not only a great scientist, but a man who valued the intellectual

---

* Willst Du immer gleichen Tagen
  Einen rechten Inhalt geben,
  Musst Du mit Behagen streben
  Und im Streben Dich behagen!

and the spiritual with equal fervor. He left a rich legacy—the darker sides of which our darker age can better ponder. But if in his devotion to the scientific ideal and to collegiality he were to be a model for future scientists, a sustaining inspiration for them, this would be a proper memorial for him.

T H R E E

ERNST REUTER:
THE MAKING OF A
DEMOCRATIC
SOCIALIST

To celebrate the appearance of the fourth and last volume
of Ernst Reuter's collected works, the city of Berlin organized a commemorative assembly in April 1976; the
publisher of the collected works, Wolf Jobst Siedler, asked
me to give the *Festvortrag*. Like most people, I knew Reuter
only from his heroic days as Lord Mayor of Berlin, when
the city—or its Western parts—successfully defended its
freedom. He had been the first postwar official, even
before Konrad Adenauer, to impress the Western world.
He helped to allay American suspicions of Germans and
socialist suspicions of America—with its antisocialist bias.

The collected works made it possible to retrace the less
familiar, but no less dramatic, development of Reuter: his
commitment to the workers' party, to social democracy, a
commitment of a religious character; the break which that
commitment entailed with his uncomprehending father;
the brief immersion in communism; the astounding clarity
with which Reuter thereafter analyzed every great turning
point in German history. His career recalled that of the
younger, decisive figure in post-1945 Social Democracy,
Herbert Wehner, who had also been a communist, who
had also fought Hitler openly, and, after 1933, in the
underground, at the risk of his life—until he, too, went
into exile. A recent sympathetic critic noted that Wehner

possessed "that old idealism, that yearning for a better
world," which now had disappeared from the party. Reuter
exemplified it. (The German worker has often found such
idealistic champions among the young. In May 1848, the
young Rudolf Virchow, later the eminent physician-
scientist and opponent of Bismarck, avowed his radical
republican commitment to his father: "I understand how
difficult it must be for you as an old estate owner [Grund-
besitzer] and Bürger, to honor completely the importance
of the workers in this revolution. . . . If these fellows [the
landowners and the other gentlemen driven from their
monopolies] do not think the people have come of age,
should we wait to pronounce this coming-of-age till some
time [when] it is convenient for these gentlemen? That
time is gone, and we are not willing to let it come back
ever.")

Ernst Reuter belonged to a great tradition; he was one
of the last practical statesmen with this iron moral bent.
He was a passionate, rational democrat and one of the
true democratic leaders of twentieth-century Germany.
Thinking about Reuter brought back certain echoes from
my childhood, during which I had known some of the
leaders of Silesian social democracy, some of whom I had
seen after they had been tortured in the notorious cellars
of the SA (storm troopers).

I wrote the lecture in German; Robert and Rita Kimber
translated it, and I subsequently revised the text.

E RNST R EUTER WAS a rare phenomenon in German and
modern history, the phenomenon of the democratic leader.
With passion and conviction, he devoted himself to the well-being
of those entrusted to him. With tough-minded clarity, he saw the
means for accomplishing what needed to be done. By his work
and character he earned his people's trust, and he spoke to them
in words that were apt and without pathos. He felt respect and
responsibility for people. In this relationship of mutual understanding and trust, Reuter and his Berliners found renewed strength
time and again. In 1948, during the Berlin blockade, Reuter asked
his citizens to recall the example of Churchill and England in
1940. In the decisive battle for the freedom of the city, he exerted
a force of personality similar to that of Churchill in that summer
of 1940.

Perhaps we can better appreciate Reuter's historical achievement if we recall the problems of political and, particularly, of democratic leadership and then ask how his own inner struggles and his hard life prepared him for his historic role. We have to remember that in Reuter's youth a politically immature and socially divided nation was well administered but badly governed, so much so that in 1909 a well-known jurist, Hugo Preuss, remarked: "There is only *one* point in our public life about which there is complete unanimity, and that is the staggering *lack of political leaders of great stature* in Germany."[1]

We need only recall the catastrophic failure of German leadership before 1918, the complaints of Chancellor Bethmann-Hollweg and his confidant that during World War I, Germany "had been governed by insane political unreason and [by] the dominance of blind passion." Bethmann did not know "how the new Germany of power and finance supremacy could find its harmony with Goethe"; he despaired of a future with the Thyssens, the small-time Junkers, and the Hohenzollerns, in whom "the intellectual decline of the day finds its most rapid expression."[2] In a land characterized by social divisiveness, one that was leery of liberal and democratic traditions, hostile toward them, it was no easy task to establish a democracy on the heels of a military defeat. It was even harder to find democratic leaders. Ernst Reuter became a model of just what it was the German society so desperately needed.

The question of leadership and authority is one of the principal problems of politics. Democratic mistrust of authority and the necessity for authority, particularly in a democratic state, are the well-recognized components of this issue. In Germany's history, given the country's great power and its lack of inner unity, this problem became especially acute. Up until 1945, German history recorded one experience after another of leadership that failed or degenerated into seduction. But perhaps a brief look at history can cast some light both on the historical experience of Germany and on our present concerns for the governability of democratic states.

The tension, indeed the occasional opposition, between democracy and leadership is nothing new. Democracy does mistrust authority, not only class or hereditary authority, but also the authority of the unusual individual who is called to leadership.

Tocqueville already recognized this tension when he remarked in the early 1830s, "On my arrival in the United States I was surprised to find so much distinguished talent among the citizens and so little among the heads of the government. . . . Democratic institutions awaken and foster a passion for equality which they can never entirely satisfy. . . . While the natural instincts of democracy induce the people to reject distinguished citizens as their rulers, an instinct not less strong induces able men to retire from the political arena, in which it is so difficult to retain their independence, or to advance without becoming servile."

In his analysis of democratic American conditions, Tocqueville adds that in times of danger genius (to use his term) does in fact step forward, and that at such times "great names may then be drawn from the ballot box."[3] Tocqueville's recognition of this problem, like his recognition of all the weaknesses of democracy, did not, however, diminish his faith in democracy as the only just form of human society for the future.

In the long, hard struggle for democracy in Germany, in which Ernst Reuter played a symptomatic and then later a leading role, the convinced antidemocrats constantly misused arguments of this kind, as if predemocratic government in Germany had not offered enough frightful examples of blind parochialism. But precisely because German reality was so unsatisfactory, the most diverse elements of the population in the nineteenth century felt a great yearning for a leader, a Caesar, who in great enthusiasm would liberate a sullen, bellicose people. Even Heine dreamed of Emperor Barbarossa as the savior:

> *The quarrel I had with the Kaiser was just*
> *A dream—let's not forget it.*
> *When awake you don't talk back to a prince,*
> *Or if you do you regret it. . . .*

> *The real Middle Ages—the genuine thing—*
> *I'd endure, though nobody missed 'em;*
> *But deliver us from this bastard state,*
> *This kind of mongrel system,*

> *This mishmash aristocracy,*
> *This sickening stew of erring*

Gothic fancies and modern lies—
Not fish, flesh or red herring.

Chase out these clowns, and close the show,
Be their critic and chastiser;
Shut down this parody of the past—
Come soon, come soon, O Kaiser.[4]

This "Come soon, O Kaiser," this hope for a savior that Heine presents with poetic playfulness and irony, grew into a great yearning in Germany. Two generations after Tocqueville, Max Weber also recognized the question of political leadership as a central problem. For him, the limits of leadership were dictated not by the general tendencies of a democracy—which did not yet exist in Germany—but by the basic conditions of modern society. His gloomy view of the future derived from his conviction that the rationalization and bureaucratization of the modern world would, for all the technological advances, condemn human beings to living in an iron "cage of bondage."[5] In 1909, when the young Ernst Reuter, influenced by the neo-Kantian philosopher Hermann Cohen in Marburg, turned to neo-Kantianism and at the same time was taking his first steps in the direction of social democracy, Max Weber warned against a future that lacked both freedom and leadership:

We gladly acknowledge that there are honorable and gifted people in the highest ranks of our civil service, also that such people, despite all the exceptions, have a chance to rise in the hierarchy of the civil service. And we grant further, as the universities claim, for example, that despite all the exceptions found there, they offer a chance, a testing ground, for the gifted. But frightful as the idea of a world full of nothing but professors may seem—we would flee to the desert if such a thing were to come to pass—more frightful still is the idea of a world full of nothing but those little cogs in the machinery, a world full, that is, with people who cling to their little jobs like glue and who are striving only for the next higher little job. This is a condition . . . that you will find on the increase in the spirit of today's civil service and, even more so, in the *aspirants* to that service, that is, in our present-day students.

This passion for bureaucratization . . . fills one with despair. It seems as if in politics it is the overzealous janitor [Scheuerteufel] alone, with whose intellectual horizons the Germans have always seemed most comfortable, who will be permitted to take the helm, as if we, with our own knowledge and consent, are to become people who need "order" and nothing but order, who become nervous and cowardly if this order slackens for even a moment and sink into helplessness if we are wrenched out of our addiction to this order. If the world does not know anything but such order addicts—and like it or not we are already caught in this process—then the central question is not how to promote and accelerate this process but rather what do we have to *set against* this machinery so that some portion of humanity will be spared from this parcelling out of the soul, from this total domination of the bureaucratic ideal.[6]

Weber thought it possible that a charismatic leader could suddenly emerge, one who, for a brief period, could liberate the world from its path into bureaucratization. We also know how he excoriated the lack of political education of the Germans and how, in his consideration of "Politics as Vocation" after World War I, he defined a kind of leader that the Weimar period produced only rarely and then could not place in the top realm. What came at the end of the Weimar Republic was then—to use Ernst Reuter's phrase—a nationwide yowling for a leader. Yet even in those years there were men deeply concerned with the question of that all-essential authority. In Sigmund Freud's *Civilization and Its Discontents,* written in 1930, we find this startling observation that is reminiscent of Tocqueville:

But perhaps we may also familiarize ourselves with the idea that there are difficulties attaching to the nature of civilization which will not yield to any attempt at reform. Over and above the task of restricting the instincts, which we are prepared for, there forces itself on our notice the danger of a state of things which might be termed "the psychological poverty of groups." This danger is most threatening where the bonds of a society are chiefly constituted by the identification of its members with one another, while individuals of the leader type do not acquire the importance that should fall to them in the formation of a group. The present cultural state of America would give us a good opportunity for studying the damage to civilization which is thus to be feared.[7]

I have cited Tocqueville, the political moralist, to raise the old question of democracy's mistrust of its indispensable leaders. I have cited Weber to remind us of the sociological fear that men in modern society, unled, would find themselves coerced and violated, dispossessed of their humanity. And, finally, I have mentioned Freud to remind us of the psychological necessity for exemplary authority. These considerations are relevant not only in the context of intellectual history. They raise an issue of burning actuality: the governability of our society. This question too has to be seen not only in the light of theoretical considerations but also in terms of a practical example as offered to us by a great democratic leader of our time, such as Ernst Reuter. Reuter demonstrated that under certain circumstances it is both necessary and possible to assume the tasks of the responsible, democratic leader; he also proved Tocqueville and Freud correct by showing that people in distress will cling to a great figure and that this momentary attachment—and this rising above oneself—is psychologically feasible and inspiriting.

In his foreword to volume one of Ernst Reuter's writings, Willy Brandt stresses that Reuter's life was "a good example of how a man's capabilities find their time and how the times find their man." This is a great theme and a rare occurrence: The times normally want a man of that particular season, while most true leaders are not altogether of their age. Only when the times catch up with the exceptional people, so to speak, can they make use of their capabilities. It is often a crisis that forces the times to find their great and, as a rule, exacting men.

That the postwar period in Berlin found their man in Ernst Reuter is an historical fact. His capabilities were desperately needed—and they had been forged in the long interplay between Reuter and his time. Reuter did not only shape and make German history; he also experienced it, suffered it, and, with astounding clarity, understood it. More than that: In some critical aspects he anticipated German history. In his own life he experienced his country's most important social and political antagonisms before these actually erupted into German political life. His decision to become a Social Democrat was not an easy one, and it was made all the more difficult because it elicited from his conservative and nationalistic parents, whom he loved and respected, total rejection, a kind of spiritual and material disinheritance. In this struggle, especially with his father, he anticipated social democracy's struggle for moral recognition by the German bourgeoisie. His decision was a moral one, in a certain sense a religious one, by which he traded a relatively secure academic career for an insecure existence in an outcast party.

In 1913, as a twenty-three-year-old, he wrote to his parents:

I cannot help being a socialist, that is a conviction that has become firmly rooted in me through long and far-from-easy labor, and I have fought my way clear to that conviction in the harshest and most difficult of struggles. You will understand that a conviction of that kind that one has struggled to achieve cannot be put aside and that with it I could become a government functionary only with the vivid sense that I was nothing but a common hypocrite and liar. . . . It is a passionate and burning love for my comrades [Volksgenossen] and for what I have come to see as right, and it would seem natural to me that you should understand that and respect it as fully as I respect your feelings. But I am convinced that you do not do that, that you do not reciprocate the respect I have always felt for you, without any reservations and as a matter of course, far more than you realize.[8]

But for Reuter's parents, steeped in a conventional rigid Lutheranism, social democracy was a betrayal of the fatherland and of Christianity, of the most sacred values of their lives; and so, not wanting to encourage their son in his beliefs, they denied him any support whatsoever. The religious element in this conflict is unmistakable. Reuter himself used Luther's celebrated "I can do no other," and he tried time and again to make clear to his father "that if I have to leave you for the sake of my conviction it is not because I bear you no filial love but rather because you want to make my remaining with you dependent on a lie. I know very well that the base lies of [social democracy's] enemies have conjured up in your mind a totally false picture of our intentions, but even if that picture were correct, you should at least be able to separate it from my person. . . . I stand alone with my conscience and I will not allow that others try to take it upon themselves, not even if they are my parents." He hoped that the money that once had been designated for him and which, in his impecunious state, he could have used, should ease the lives of his brothers; it was futile for his father to hold it in abeyance, hoping that his son would recant.[9]

He suffered particularly from his father's mistrust, which apparently dated from before their political disagreement and extended to the son's person and convictions, things that were, for Reuter himself, identical. (Seen psychologically, this paternal mistrust may have played no minor role in Reuter's successful political career. He sought the trust of his fellows; he solicited it, without compromising his principles; and in his letters he repeatedly spoke of attaining this trust as the most satisfying aspect of the politician's calling.) The passionate debate between father and son, Reuter's "I can do no other" and his repeated references to the obligations his conviction imposed on him—all these things remind one of Fontane's novel *Der Stechlin*, where he says of an old Junker " . . . he has in him what all real Junkers have: a bit of social democracy. If you provoke them, they'll admit it themselves."[10] Did Reuter not have something of the enlightened, genuine Junker about him, a simple idealism and an unostentatious sense of duty? He was surely not the only Social Democrat of that stamp. Junkers and Social Democrats: This affinity, so embarrassing for both parties, perhaps deserves some historical attention, too. Reuter fought for the moral recognition of the workers' movement, for the recognition also by opponents as well as within the party itself, that the Social Democrats had neither invented the class struggle nor sought to incite it but wanted—in a democratic way—to attenuate it, in order to remove this burden from the nation, to which the Social Democrats were so deeply attached.

On August 7, 1914, a week after the outbreak of the war, Reuter wrote to his parents: "This last week was full of powerful and, in their way, unforgettable impressions, and I have the faint hope that after the war the persecution of the workers' movement, which has been downright fanatic in recent times, will come to an end . . . and that we will perhaps arrive at a time after all when people will stop referring to us as 'unpatriotic rabble.' That would be of greater benefit to Germany's strength than the winning of the war." He was, nonetheless, of the opinion "that Germany must emerge victorious. Our defeat would mean the end of true culture for a long time and, worse still, of socialism."[11]*

But Reuter belonged to those relatively few Germans who already in the fall of 1914 realized that a victory which would establish German hegemony or world power was neither possible nor desirable. He became an organizer of the Bund Neues Vaterland, which ten members formally established in November 1914. Albert Einstein belonged to the founding group as well; both men—so different in every other respect—hoped that the ever-growing horror of the war would lead eventually to a more reasonable world order. The Bund's goals were to bring about a world in which foreign and domestic policies would be in harmony; the real aim, somewhat disguised for fear of censorship, was a peace without annexation and the establishment of a European federation. In an anonymous broadsheet for the Bund, Reuter attacked the annexationists of the day; measured by Bismarck's policies of moderation, they had to be adjudged as sinners against the future of the German nation. In early 1915, Reuter wrote a memorandum for the Bund about the causes of the war and the need for a thoroughgoing reform of the international situation. The memorandum, careful in its tone but unmistakable in its criticism of German policies before and during the war, was distributed to two hundred influential individuals. A few days later Reuter was drafted, and by February 1916 the military authorities forbade all further activities of the Bund.[12]

Reuter had been forced to experience in his parental home a conflict that would then repeat itself in Germany—especially during the Weimar Republic—on a world-historical level. I think he understood this conflict better and actually conceived of it differently from the way many of his party comrades did because he had already been through it in his private life. He grasped the portentousness of the bourgeois rejection of the SPD, the magnitude of the implications of this estrangement; he realized that not

---

* The young Reuter had his own ideas of "true culture." As a twenty-year-old, he devoured Ibsen, "who loved the truth and expressed it, at least as he saw it." At the same time, while afflicted with a "sickly pessimism" about himself and others, he sent his brother this iconoclastic message: "Hamlet I saw twice . . . in Max Reinhardt's production. Hamlet is worth more than Faust and all of Goethe's dramas put together. It is the drama of man himself, so great and powerful, that everything else sinks before it." *Ernst Reuter: Schriften Reden*, ed. Hans E. Hirschfeldt and Hans J. Reichhardt, vol. 1 (Berlin, 1972), p. 88.

only economic ideas and interests were at the root of this estrangement but—perhaps more importantly—misunderstood ideals. This
accounts for his hope, even faith, in the educability of the bourgeoisie and his struggle to win them over. He had respect for his
bourgeois opponents because he had developed that respect in his
parents' home. In his prewar educational efforts in the SPD, he
hoped to bring "true culture," including of course German history
and traditions, closer to the workers. His dream was the reconciliation of moral antagonists.

Reuter had another early encounter with a political force that
was destined to play a major role in German life: the victorious
Bolshevism of the Russian Revolution. As a German prisoner of
war in Russia, he learned Russian, as he would later learn Turkish
in exile; and he experienced the Russian Revolution firsthand. He
offered his services to Lenin, was appointed commissar of the
Volga Germans, and later became a functionary of the KPD, the
German Communist Party.

This brief chapter in Reuter's life needs to be understood, too.
Like Einstein, like so many others, Reuter had been radicalized by
the war. But for him it was not only the utter disillusionment with
Germany's ruling classes; he was caught by the power and the
vision of the Russian Revolution: the liberation of oppressed
peoples, the end of poverty and exploitation, the realization of
social equality and of Marxism, the hope of international peace,
and the abolition of imperialism and annexationism. In its beginnings, the appeal of Bolshevism was great—and the instant fear
of it even greater. The appeal of Bolshevism at that time has to
be understood as an historical fact. For people on the Left, the
revolution was an intellectual and political challenge. All at once
Marx was dramatically confirmed and denied: A seemingly pro-
letarian revolution had swept away the old society and did so in
the most backward country. Most socialists saw the attraction, felt
the temptation, but, clinging to their faith in democracy, rejected
Lenin's demands for loyalty and subservience. The process by
which the leftist intelligentsia of Europe and North America came
to terms with Bolshevism was a long one. Every new wave of
fellow-travelers, it seemed, had to fight its own way through to the
realization that communism was an abhorrent negation of its
promise. To underestimate the attractiveness of communism,
however, is also to underestimate its power and its danger. Enthu-

siasm for communism was always strongest in those circles that
were at the farthest remove from Russia and the real world of
politics. The last traces of this Soviet infatuation, incomprehensible
as it is to us, still linger today in areas far from Russia, even after
sixty years of almost uninterrupted terror. The appeal of revolutionary Russia and the confusion it occasioned were important
elements in Western debility.

Rudolf Hilferding, who was himself hated and persecuted by
the communists (and murdered by the Nazis), once wrote:

> Conservative, bourgeois circles were not able to appreciate even
> the idealistic aims of the Russian Revolution. For them the
> revolution was merely an opportunity to give their old enmity
> for democratic socialism a new face. They claimed that Bolshe-
> vism and Social Democracy were really the same thing. And so
> from the very beginning Bolshevism both strengthened and
> confounded the right-wing circles, a disastrous mixture that
> served neither the western nor the Bolshevist world.
>
> There is something tragic in the fate of the Russian Revo-
> lution as a whole and in that of the Bolsheviks in particular.
> One's heart is on their side (heartless as they themselves have
> been in every sense of the word), but one's mind just will not
> go along.[13]

Ernst Reuter broke with the KPD in December 1921 because he
was repelled by the party's divisive and dictatorial goals. He saw
the KPD as a "branch" of Moscow, an instrument in the hands of
inexperienced Russian commissars who wanted to use it for the
benefit of the new Russian regime, not of the German working
class. From that moment on, neither Reuter's heart nor his mind
stood on the Bolshevist side. The path to and away from communism had been a hard school for him, but even this school
shaped and enriched his life. I do not think there were many
politicians or intellectuals who recognized the true character of
Bolshevism as early, as clearly, and with such relentlessness as
Reuter did in the early 1920s. He warned against the "deterring
example of Communism, [which] has established in Russia not a
dictatorship of the proletariat but a dictatorship over the proletariat."[14] On Lenin's death, Reuter wrote: "Lenin was no more than
the iron broom of the great peasants' revolution that swept aside

the rubble of feudalism. . . . Beyond that . . . his dictatorial methods destroyed the promising beginnings of the Russian workers' movement, and his hate-ridden campaign against international social democracy weakened the front of the political and union-based workers' movement in all the western countries."[15]

Reuter noted, too, that with Lenin the Bolsheviks had instigated a new "worship of saints," and from Leninism they had developed a new "doctrine of salvation."[16] As early as 1923 Reuter was seriously worried about the danger of a Communist and National Socialist alliance; nine years later such an alliance sealed the fate of the Weimar Republic and then, in 1939, pushed Europe into the Second World War. Quite early he wrote of the continuity between Russian and Soviet imperialism. But despite his passionate rejection of communism, he remained objective and never yielded to the clichés of anticommunism that were such common currency among former communists. This discriminating understanding of the nature of communism—removed from all anxious exaggeration—made it possible for him after 1945 to coexist for a short time and on a rational footing with the Soviets. It also sharpened the insight with which he grasped in 1948 that Berliners were in the midst of a struggle to determine "whether we want to bend under the yoke of a power that wants to exploit us for ends that are alien and irrelevant to us, or whether we want to claim our rights as a free people and conduct our own affairs and govern ourselves independently according to our own will and our own laws."[17] Reuter's bitter fight against that alien yoke inspired many a hesitant politician, even some from the Western powers, to side with him. And yet even at that time he repeatedly called for reconciliation with the Russian and Polish peoples.

Both these experiences—the struggle to win acknowledgment of a socialist ethic from his parents and his personal encounter with the temptation and reality of communism—made Ernst Reuter a passionate democrat and defender of freedom. He knew both the Right and the Left from close up. He did not assess the Weimar Republic from the perspective of party politics; he hoped it would rebuild the nation after a defeat the people did not understand, after a harsh peace treaty, and in the midst of a cold civil war that the Bolsheviks had started, consciously or unconsciously. Quite early on he recognized the danger that extremists might overpower what they thought was the "rotten center."[18] In this center there was a strongly developed entrepreneurial egoism that by its very nature opposed the interests of the workers' movement. But Reuter realized that antidemocratic attitudes went far deeper and that in Germany the problem was not only and not primarily one of class interests but of class insularity, of an inculcated blindness to other classes:

> To the German bourgeois the psychic constitution of the German workers seems to be a book with seven seals. . . . The general thinking of the indifferent bourgeois takes the most primitive directions in social questions. The workers should work more! The workers should make us fat again by starving themselves! . . . This oppression of the workers which is taken for granted, the condescension inherent in such thinking—that is truly the spirit of social reaction at work, the spirit that is even more reactionary than the entrepreneur's brutal will to exploit. It is less clearly defined and therefore more conservative; it stems from unconscious, unexamined, and traditional class feeling.[19]

Reuter never saw political reality from a purely Marxist perspective. His main concern was the creation of a just and secure democracy, not a class struggle between two antagonistic classes that could end only with the victory of one class over the other. For him the struggle was against class rule itself, against the blindness of a class society, a summons to bridge the abyss between the classes. In his practical work in municipal government, his constant goal was to make cooperation among different parties and interests possible and to bring that cooperation about. This approach stemmed from his humanistic sense of responsibility and from his view of practical politics. Social democracy, as the bearer of the democratic idea, had to liberate itself from its class base and free itself from its parochial mentality. At a time of increasing nationalistic demagogy, Reuter was a true patriot, concerned for the the social and spiritual unity of the nation.

The basis of Reuter's character and effectiveness was his moral power, his moral view of life and of politics. That involved not only the dissemination of his own moral convictions, his sense of duty, and his practical idealism, but also his awareness that the idealistic element in human beings had to be addressed, that people have their intellectual and psychic needs, and that the satisfying of economic needs alone, crucial as it is, is not enough. These basic assumptions of Reuter's are a welcome contrast to Bismarck's, and with them in mind we can easily understand why Reuter was moved to call out during a food shortage in postwar Berlin: "No sentence is more dangerous than [Brecht's] sentence: 'First comes the grub, then come the morals.' "[20]

Reuter's steady commitment to practical work also sprang from that moral base. Despite all the suffering and disappointment he had experienced, he remained a yea-sayer at heart, a yea-sayer in an age of complaining, vacillating nay-sayers—or as he once expressed it himself in 1922—in a time "of the demagogy of nay-sayers."[21] Yea-saying called for constant critical assessment and even for criticism of his own party. Shortly before his death he reproached his party for failing to define clear goals for the people. He believed that genuine leadership, particularly in times of danger, could call forth the masses' latent energies and willingness to sacrifice. If we look back on the high point of his historical achievements—that is, on the defense of Berlin—then we can say that that defense was made possible by the airlift from above and by an iron will from below, a will which Reuter constantly expressed and exhorted.

Reuter's thoughts and deeds embodied his special relationship to history. His sense of history was like a link between his convictions and his practical politics. As early as 1913 he wrote, "The fate of democracy depends on a faith in history."[22] His first task in the party was educational work, and for him that meant instruction in history. German history, as Reuter understood it, passed down to social democracy a democratic mission, the mission to turn into reality old national traditions from the wars for liberation in 1813 and from 1848. His historical consciousness also enabled him to comprehend his own time with astounding clarity. There were only a few politicians in the 1920s who saw their world as sharply as he did and who therefore understood so clearly the imperatives of the moment. It was no coincidence that in a major speech he gave on Constitution Day in 1931 he evoked the figure of the great reformer Baron vom Stein, "the born leader of his people," as Reuter called him, whose ideas had found expression in the Weimar constitution: "What the constitution expresses and declares to be the inviolable basic principle of our national development is nothing other than the freedom and coming-of-age, the self-rule of the people. . . . [But] a constitution is not only a gift; it is also a task entrusted to us, and much of this task remains to be completed. We are called to complete this task, and in order to complete it we will have to call upon the great masses of our people more than ever before."[23]

Reuter thought history offered enlightenment and imposed duties. Even before the catastrophe of 1933 he was fully aware of the obstacles that stood in the way of Germany's evolution toward democracy. And with what conciseness and penetrating insight he grasped the reasons for the German disaster. In 1947 he wrote to his brother, who had succumbed to the *völkisch* or racial beliefs of the prewar period: "Where has this arrogance brought us, this total ignorance of the forces that truly move the world, this political emasculation that was the very point of Bismarck's horse cure, this lack of real moral principles and of respect for the rights of others? The German catastrophe did not begin with the yowling [of the Nazis]; its roots run deep, very deep."[24]

In the same year he described some of those roots:

> The depoliticizing of a bourgeoisie that had previously had a strong yearning for freedom, Bismarck's disastrous legacy, the insulation of the universities, the institution of the reserve officer, the caste system within the civil service, the turning of the bourgeoisie to nothing but money making and of the intellectuals to an apolitical detachment from real life—a thousand sources fed into the catastrophic basic attitude of the German middle classes, an attitude that made them so susceptible to unpolitical and purely emotional suggestion and that made the victory of fascism possible through a total absorption of virtually every bourgeois constituency.[25]

Those are harsh words, to which at times he added strictures against his own party, but on the whole they present a concise and accurate sketch of Germany's development, one that, with numerous additions and shadings, approximates the view of current research. Or to put it more precisely, I should say that undogmatic historians from all over the world who have studied the German question have gradually arrived at Ernst Reuter's conclusions and supplied the details to support them.

History as challenge and responsibility—that is not a view currently in vogue. This is not the occasion to lament the crisis of historical consciousness, but it would be an inadequate discussion of Reuter that failed to observe that a lessening of a sense of history is dangerous for a free nation. History as a mirror of the past, as life recounted and reflected upon, conveys an awareness and grasp of complicated realities. For decades historiography in Germany had clearly been colored and distorted by nationalistic bias. Ernst Reuter developed his own picture of history. To live in the political world without historical awareness is an invitation to drift and disaster. All of us who experienced the terror of National Socialism were formed by it. We know terror, naked terror and terror transfigured by idealism. We can remember the systematic oppression of human beings made into a principle of government. For us, the survivors, that was an exacting education, such as I hope no later generation will ever experience. Will the memory of that time—of the years of fascist and bolshevist terror—be lost with us, or will it be somehow possible to pass that memory on to coming generations? It is worrisome to see how historians often turn away from the general public, how some are attempting to subsume history under the social sciences, how pedagogues and professional educationists deny the essential function of history and how therefore the younger generations feel estranged from history. Reuter showed that history is at once a liberating and a demanding force in political life: A respect for history is also a part of his legacy to us.

In the last years of the Weimar Republic municipal politics was Reuter's primary field of endeavor; and if we recall the long German tradition of independent city administration, we will see that his focus there is not without historical roots. Politics at the national level had always drawn him, first in Berlin and later in Magdeburg, and all the more so when he realized instantly the devastating danger that National Socialism represented, a danger that had to be fought courageously, with all the power at one's disposal. Yet his field of concentration remained city politics, and he saw his task there as one of improving life in the big cities, making it more humane. Here, too, he anticipated our own time and grasped complicated realities with astonishing clarity. When he returned from a study tour in America in 1929, he said that in the areas of industry and mass transport, America, and especially New York, were mirrors of Europe's future. Note that he said "mirrors of" and not "models for" Europe's future. The problems of the metropolis, indeed in America the very survival of the metropolis, have become a more burning issue today than ever before.[26]

Ernst Reuter's work in the Weimar Republic was his intellectual and practical preparation for his great postwar achievements. As a convinced democrat, a fighter for freedom, and a German patriot, he fought National Socialism for what it truly was: an uprising of the lowest instincts, a horrible collusion of old traditions and new resentments. The National Socialists realized he was a special enemy, and they tormented him with special brutality. In exile in Turkey, despite the joy and satisfaction he found in his work, his thoughts were always with Germany; and he remained a hopeful patriot, free of all the hatred that so many exiles understandably felt. In his passionate devotion to his country and its democratic future, in his attachment to history, and especially in his impulse to act and to achieve democratic leadership, he is reminiscent of perhaps the greatest figure of humane, international socialism, the French national tribune, Jean Jaurès.

When the war that Reuter had foreseen was over, with the consequences for Europe and Germany that he had also foreseen, he had only one desire—to exchange his secure existence in Turkey with an arduous, uncertain, and hungry life in occupied Germany. In January 1947 he wrote, "it is my impression that we have a great chance and that people are much more open now than they were before."[27]

The disaster that Germany brought down on the world and that ended with its own collapse was a chance dearly purchased, but one for a new political beginning nonetheless. For Reuter it was a chance (given to few people) to translate his ideas into reality, a reality that present-day Berlin represents. In 1947 he formulated this idea himself. "Politics requires courage. It is our task to inspire trust and to convince by way of solid achievements. There are no textbooks for democracy, but we do have the powerful school of daily life that forms people. Mistrust is the worst poison in political life, and Europe's rebirth will begin with trust."[28]

We owe the new democratic order in West Germany and the

rebirth of Europe to the fact that after Germany's defeat there was no lack of democratic politicians of major stature. We need think only of Konrad Adenauer, Theodor Heuss, Reinhold Maier, Wilhelm Kaisen, Kurt Schumacher—and Reuter. Not that harmony or even trust existed among all these men, but all of them, learning from the past, wanted to build a new order. Despite their differences in goals and methods, they agreed that inner peace was essential for a free country. Much has been done in this respect; and much remains to be done, especially in what Reuter, in the 1920s, had called the field of political culture, that everyday sphere in which democratic attitudes have to be translated into practical behavior toward others who are not of one's own persuasion.

The second German republic was established under the shadow of the occupation but constructed by self-confident politicians. And among these politicians Ernst Reuter was one of the most prominent and represented not just for Berliners or Germans but for democrats everywhere the model of a democratic leader.* His life is proof of the practical effectiveness of democracy and of a free social order. Only in one respect did the postwar generation have things easier than we do today. The dangers then were great and immediate; ours are not so palpable, but they are ultimately every bit as grave. Reuter's legacy is his defense and enlargement of human, democratic, and liberal freedom—and that not only in the deeds of statesmen but in the conscience of German citizens.

In 1946, in one of his first policy speeches, Konrad Adenauer asked, "How was this fall of the German people into the abyss possible?"[29] This is the great question of German history, and it remains one that perhaps every thinking person is obliged to ask. There is no definitive and generally valid answer to this question, and as long as historical research is free, there will be none. But we can hope, in conclusion, that future historians will add a second question to this first and ask not only how National Socialism was possible; we can hope they will also ask how it was possible that

---

* And yet Reuter's son, himself an example of the engaged democratic citizen *and* the practical entrepreneur, recalled: "And it took long enough until Ernst Reuter was recognized as a German patriot even by his political enemies. . . . Bitter as it may sound, it is nevertheless true that it took the struggle for freedom during the Berlin blockade to make Ernst Reuter unassailable. Malicious exceptions, even in the party which calls itself Christian, occurred even then." Edzard Reuter, *Vom Geist der Wirtschaft, Europa zwischen Technokraten und Mythokraten* (Stuttgart, 1986), pp. 104–105.

after only one generation following Germany's collapse, this country often referred to as the "belated nation" has in fact assumed a leading role in the democratic world? And whatever the answer may be, the name of Ernst Reuter will be invoked as a foremost and shining example.

F O U R

THE BURDEN
OF SUCCESS:
REFLECTIONS ON
GERMAN JEWRY

This essay was written for a projected *Festschrift* for Lionel
Trilling; the book appeared in 1977, after his death.

I had wanted to acknowledge my abiding debt to a
teacher, colleague, and admired friend. Trilling's teaching
and writing exemplified the complementarity of literature
and history, and that complementarity has shaped my
own sense of the past.

These reflections on German Jewry were prompted by
Gold and Iron, but by explicitly relating the rise of Jewry
to the bourgeois ambitions of the last century generally, I
found illumination in the great novels and in the work of
Trilling himself. The essay, here reprinted without change,
was also intended to present a somewhat more balanced
assessment of German Jews and Germans than was then
current.

M EMORIES FADE—and the health of nations as of individuals
depends on some measure of release from the wounds
of the past. But memories not only fade; they are rearranged as
well, in accordance with some perceived need of the present.
Historians abet—and sometimes correct—this rearrangement of
the past so that a society can find a tolerable or livable past for

itself, for "try as we may, we cannot, as we write history, escape our purposiveness."[1]

Our recollection of the Holocaust is an example of this double process: for many, the memory has become a dim one and reminders are likely to stir embarrassment or resentment. The memory of the Holocaust has also become assimilated to our present needs and predicaments. For a shrinking number who witnessed the first moment of horror helplessly from afar, the extermination of a people will remain engraved in their minds. But even their immediate response was designed to salvage something of the collective self-respect of humanity, and many Westerners, face to face with the horror of the Holocaust, believed at first that somehow the perpetrators of this most calculated and perhaps most heinous of all crimes in Europe's history, the Germans, were uniquely evil—with the implicit belief that our civilization was largely exculpated and that such terror, foreign to our collective nature or experience, would not be visited upon the world again. This—here rendered most inadequately—was a not uncommon moral response of the late 1940s; it was also a professional response. Historians reinterpreted German history, often very fruitfully, in the light of the intervening disaster. The perspective of 1945 became a valuable hermeneutical instrument.

The judgment of the Holocaust as a uniquely German crime has begun to fade from our consciousness and our professional concerns. In the rearrangement of our collective memory, the gap between perpetrators, bystanders, and victims has been allowed to narrow. We have had to distance ourselves from the once comforting view that only Germans or National Socialists could have committed so terrible a crime in so meticulous a fashion; we have come to understand the many acts of compliance, collusion, or willful passivity on the part of so many others, inside Europe and even outside, that had made the "final solution" feasible. But there is more to our rearranging of the past than that, more too than the realization that Soviet terror had claimed even more lives than had the Nazis. In our present mood of willful self-denigration, we have come to assimilate the crimes of the past still further by linking them to our own; the gas chambers and the massacre of My Lai are somehow deemed comparable, and the very term *Holocaust* is often heedlessly invoked. All of this is morally problematical; to exaggerate guilt is no better than to repress or deny it. To understand the process of fashioning memories of the Holocaust is more than an historical exercise; it might well reveal that the historical fact of the extermination of six million Jews, however interpreted in the intervening thirty years, may have wrought more of an injury to our self-confidence, so often and in so many ways assaulted in the last century, than is realized.

In this rearranging of our collective memory, there has also been a reappraisal of German Jewry, of the earliest victims of National Socialist persecution. Gradually a negative judgment has sprung up, based on some ill-considered generalities and useful perhaps to present political or psychological interests, but neither reflective of the complexity of the issue nor without its own polemical design. I refer here to what an eminent scholar has recently called the " 'bad press' that German Jewry has had in recent literature."[2] It has become a common view to hold that German Jewry somehow represents the epitome of craven assimilation and submission; implicit in this view is that the fate of German Jewry and its character were somehow linked, and that character was therefore historically culpable.

Historians are only now beginning to study the German-Jewish community in depth and with some perspective.[3] I mean to limit myself to the setting out of what I consider to be the principal themes. If this essay suggests something of the complexity of the subject and thus cautions against facile generalities or dangerous analogies, it will serve some purpose. German Jewry has become a category of disapprobation; as such, it may neither do justice to the past nor serve as a correct guide to the future.

This essay is based on two assumptions. First, that the whole course of German history should no longer be seen principally from the perspective of 1945, that is to say, not from the disaster backward, with the inevitable consequence that the strands preparing the disaster are given particular attention and the others slighted, but from a particular past, with all its uncertainties, aspirations, and illusions, forward. The second assumption is that in such a new perspective on German history, the role of the Jewish community within Germany should be analyzed, freed from the many taboos that have always clung to the subject, because that role was a signal element in the history of modern Germany.

We must see the history of the German Jews as a special current, itself made up of many rivulets, within the broader German stream. It is a difficult subject for study because the formal integration of Jews into German life was something that German Jews desired; hence so much of what would be considered the essence of German-Jewish life remained unspoken, unacknowledged, and the study of it now is overladen with feelings of guilt and unease. And still one must try to recover something of the cast of mind and feelings of this community, for it illuminates the social history of modern consciousness.

For decades, most studies of German Jewry circled around the themes of "Jewish contributions" and of the unrequited love that Jews had for Germans. It was easy to fit the German experience into what has been called the lachrymose tradition in Jewish historiography, dwelling as it did on the sufferings of the Jews. (Sir Isaiah Berlin recalls an incident that epitomizes this tradition. He relates that "the late Sir Lewis Namier once reported that, upon being asked by a splendid British peer why he, a Jew, devoted himself to writing English history, and not Jewish history, he replied: 'Derby! There *is* no modern Jewish history, there is only Jewish martyrology, and that is not amusing enough for me.' ") But the history of German Jewry which ends in martyrology began in greatness. It is a momentous story in the history of Jewry and of Germany, and it exemplifies and illuminates the vast complexity of the transformation of Europe. It is a process to ponder and acknowledge, not so much because of its achievements or its sufferings, but because it may be one of the most dramatic instances of Europe's encounter with what we commonly call modernity, the uprooting of society in a spiritual, social, and economic sense. In that climate of nineteenth-century modernity, German Jews throve visibly—and suffered invisibly. As a group, they compressed the experience of European man becoming an individual; the process had begun earlier and has been defined by Lionel Trilling as leading a man to "have an awareness of what one historian, Georges Gusdorf, calls internal space. . . . It is when he becomes an individual that a man lives more and more in private rooms; whether the privacy makes the individuality or the individuality requires the privacy the historians do not say."[4] I would suppose that German Jewry—if we could ever recapture the welter of its innermost feelings—would be seen to have had a highly developed sense of individualism, with all the freedom and the loneliness and the self-doubt that the new condition entailed.

To understand what I have called the great leap forward it is necessary to recall the preemancipation condition of debasement and debarment, of legally defined and enforced marginality. Jews were tolerated because they were useful; they performed services that the society around them neither condoned nor could do without.

For centuries, the Germans had lived a divided existence, divided by confession, region, status, and divided also by their attachment to particularist rulers or separate communities. That ordered life has been sympathetically and brilliantly evoked in Mack Walker's recent *German Home Towns:* a world of established order, of community, a world limited in some ways by the nearest church steeple. It was a life of known obligations and expectations, with appropriate values and continued religious sanctions. Jews lived on the margin of that society; they lived on the whole an uncertain, debased existence, as befit a people that was still thought to be separate and inferior, to be in some essential ways depraved.* In German eyes, Jews were inferior because of their seeming aptitude for peddling and money changing and because of their religious customs, their strange, clannish orthodoxy, by their continued attachment to a primitive divine dispensation that had been fulfilled only in Christianity. It was a time when Jews and Christians were still divided by a common God, when to both the struggle over the religious patrimony assumed central importance. The separateness of Jews and Germans, then, was an acknowledged fact on both sides, and the ghetto nurtured a strong sense of Jewish identity and community.

Into this slowly changing world of the Germanies, where everything still had its ordered place and Jews were in a sense shielded from outside life and even violence by the walls and laws surrounding them, came the recognition, spurred on by precept and example from across the Rhine, that subjects should become

---

* The marginality of Jewish existence is illustrated by Mack Walker's definition of outsiders who "were excluded for some other reason denoting inferiority: the illegitimately born for example, or Jews, or indigent aunts, or menial servants, or immigrants from the country who settled in the suburbs. . . . Other laws on beggars, wandering tinkers and sharpeners, players, musicians, peddlers, Jews—the old dishonorable wanderers—reiterated the need to protect the community against such people." Mack Walker, *German Home Towns: Community, State, and General Estate, 1648–1871* (Ithaca, N.Y., and London, 1971), pp. 29, 271.

citizens, that rights granted would lead to a more ready acceptance of duties demanded, and into that period of the late eighteenth and early nineteenth centuries fell the concern with the emancipation of Jews. Some Jews had thirsted for that liberation while still cut off from the public and cultural life of the Germans; the desire for emancipation and the discussion of it arose during a momentous flowering of German thought, often called the great Idealist Age, and some Jews yearned to embrace the new faith of the Enlightenment and European romanticism. Within the various German states, the argument for emancipation was made: Jews were to be released from their special disabilities, gradually or all at once, and allowed to enjoy some of the attributes of recently promulgated citizenship. But emancipation, as recent studies have shown, was a gradual and grudging process; it was justified by the expectation that emancipation would lead to the moral improvement of the Jews, to their "civic betterment" (*"bürgerliche Verbesserung,"* in the classic words of Christian Wilhelm Dohm's essay of 1783), to their assimilation to Christian life, though the exact nature of that assimilation was rarely specified. The Jews in Germany were released from their disabilities gradually and on what might be called a moral installment plan: They were to remain indebted for the goods received for a long time, and until they had paid for them in full, the goods were not considered fully theirs. Some scholars have recently argued that from the beginning, emancipation included the presumption of the final measure of assimilation, i.e., conversion to Christianity. Not all the emancipators may have had this goal in mind, but the unanimous expectation of the moral improvement of Jews implied at the very least a blending into the German scene, an end to any kind of uniqueness or separateness in any realm. The debate over emancipation reflected the distinctive nature of German liberalism; neither the vision of a pluralist society nor a commitment to the natural rights of man inspired the emancipators.

"The march out of the ghetto" was painful and precarious, and it coincided—as none of the emancipators could have foreseen—with a general upheaval in German society, indeed, with one of the greatest upheavals of European history.[5] I refer, of course, to the upheaval which we invariably label as the emergence of a capitalistic-industrial society, gradually secularized and democratized. It was a world characterized by a sudden, ceaseless mobility across boundaries of thought, traditions, classes, received customs. Put much too simply, in that new society of the nineteenth century, the possibilities of the market replaced the constraints of birth, and wealth became the new criterion of success. It is a world that the great novelists of the last century depicted and that Karl Marx described in his own poetic-revolutionary manner in the *Communist Manifesto*. To a greater extent than ever before, if still much less than proclaimed in the mythologies of Samuel Smiles, and by the apostles of laissez-faire, the new economic order made possible an open society, a society based in part on Napoleon's revolutionary principle of careers open to talent. (Napoleon's call for such a society was a striking instance of a man raising his personal experience to the level of a universal principle. And Napoleon's entire career and most especially the dramatic act of his placing the crown on his own head were paradigmatic acts for the nineteenth century, with special relevance for Jews, a relevance duly felt by Jews. By the end of the century, it was widely thought that careers were open to wealth, not talent, and that the rich, often thought unworthy, were, in fact, throttling the very freedom that had created them.)

It is enough to recall that the economic upheaval coincided with a moral upheaval as well; just as the traditional social order was breached, so was the traditional moral-religious authority; the falling away from God, disguised, uncertain, and uneven though it was, was nevertheless a social fact, as was the emergence of the new faith in progress, rationality, and science, with its own prophets and practitioners. Secularization affected Jews as it did Christians; in some ways, it affected them more profoundly because their faith had ensured their survival as a distinct group; other groups had for a long time been able to define their identities in a religious and a national sense. For Jews, as the religious bonds were loosened and as the new secular faith of nationalism beckoned, the danger of ever greater alienation from their own traditional identity became considerable.

In this new world of the mid-nineteenth century, the symbols of success changed as well. The palaces and temples of the time were railroad stations and banks; the self-made men built themselves mansions of pomp, and the European plutocracy thought to dazzle the world by their visible presence, by the old manor houses they could buy or the new pomposities they could construct.

The new presumption was cast in stone and marble, and everywhere visible; the old prejudices against the new wealth, against money-grubbing, and against the new commercial dispensation were less visible, but nonetheless real and powerful. Historians—and political dogmatists—have often spoken of the triumph of capitalism as the chief characteristic of the last century. The triumph, in retrospect, may have been more apparent than real; at the very least, the prejudices against capitalism grew rather than diminished with time and received a new sanction from the various strands of socialism. Marx was one of the first to understand the dynamic and exploitative character of capitalism, but precisely because he denied or denigrated the autonomy of sentiments and misunderstood the force of nationalism, he did not envision the possibility of a strong nonsocialist anticapitalist movement arising; in Germany it played a decisive role.

In this uneasily capitalistic, secularizing age, German Jews did superbly well. Nimble and rootless, they seized every possible chance; economic opportunity beckoned for all, often at the price of moving to new and unknown quarters; Jews had little to lose and hence responded to the lure of the new city with untroubled eagerness. Once there, they excelled in certain traditional functions, quickly adapted to modern needs. The experience of Jewish success must yet be fully explored in all its ambiguous glory; I came upon it by reconstructing the life of Bismarck's banker, Gerson von Bleichröder. The Rothschilds, of course, were the visible pinnacle of power, and already in the 1820s they were referred to as the uncrowned kings of Europe. Perhaps it will suffice if I suggest some dimensions of that success: Jews attained a unique prominence in the new German society. Proportionately they were richer, better educated, and—at least in some areas—held better positions than their Christian colleagues and competitors. In some fields, such as banking and journalism, for example, Jews gained such prominence as to come close to dominance. They were disproportionately concentrated in a few large cities. These are the landmarks of their success, won in the face of barely suspended hostility. This success is attested by figures and by the reports of foreign observers.*

---

* One English observer, Shepherd Thomas Taylor, noted that in 1870, "whilst the Christians of Berlin have, as a rule, to bear the burden and heat of the day, a disproportionate share of

There was something asymmetrical in almost every aspect of the German-Jewish coexistence. The Jews were far more urbanized than the rest of the population; Jews had traditionally been banished from agriculture, and they were not about to return to the soil, where they would have met with considerable hostility from the existing population. (Wealthy Jews did buy themselves large, formerly noble estates and returned to the soil by becoming landowners and *Gutsherren* on a grand scale. The Junkers, obsessed with what they took to be their catastrophic economic decline, so injurious to themselves and to the traditional order of the state, always assumed that when penury would finally lead them to have to sell their ancestral home, a rich commoner, and usually the worst kind of commoner, a Jew, would replace them.) Jews shunned the industrial sector, where as either worker or entrepreneur they would have to deal with a large number of non-Jews. They flocked to occupations where they could operate alone or with one another—and this, too, fed the notion of the invisible Jewish power. Jews also made disproportionate strides in higher education and thus gave sustenance to the notion that Jews were somehow more cunning, more clever, more scheming, more—aridly—intelligent, and more given to "soulless" learning than others.

The story of German Jewry may well constitute one of the most spectacular social leaps in European history. Fifty years after emancipation, the Jews *had* bettered themselves, but in ways almost always antithetical to the wishes and expectations of the emancipators. They had bettered themselves in ways that the emancipators had hoped they would leave to Christians; it must have seemed as if they had transmuted their pauperish peddling into plutocratic grandeur.

Under the best of circumstances, this kind of sudden rise would have caused consternation; it is not surprising that many Germans

---

the material loaves and fishes falls to the lot of the more fortunate Jew. . . . [The Jews] inhabit the best houses in the best quarters of the town, drive about the parks in the most elegant equipages, figure constantly in the dress circle at the opera and theatres, and in this and other ways excite a good deal of envy in the minds of their less fortunate Christian fellow-citizens." Taylor continued that in England there would be far greater animus against Jews if they held a similar position; the whole problem, he thought, would disappear because "it would almost seem as if the end of Judaism were near at hand in Berlin." By this he meant that the traits of Jewishness were on the decline. Shepherd Thomas Taylor, *Reminiscences of Berlin During the Franco-German War of 1870–71* (London, 1885), pp. 236, 237, 241.

(and some Jews) viewed the new prosperity and prominence with misgivings and resentment. In the 1850s and 1860s, there was relative silence, in part perhaps because the society was far less aware of change than it was to become later; also among the literate groups there was a general presumption in favor of economic progress and laissez-faire, of which the Jews were at once exemplars and promoters. By the 1870s, a radical shift occurred: After a few years of frantic speculation, in part triggered by the German exultation over unification and the defeat of the French as well as by the sudden inflow of five billion francs as French indemnity, the Berlin stock market crashed, many of the newly and often fraudulently spawned corporations went bankrupt, and a serious and protracted depression ensued. Amidst this crisis, a storm against Jewish power and corruption erupted; pamphleteers began it, but by 1875 the most respectable papers of the old Protestant orthodoxy and of the embattled Catholic party were charging that Jews had suddenly come to dominate German life, and that they were using their new position to corrupt, exploit, and destroy the German people and its traditions. The variations on these charges were endless, but common to all of them was the fear that somehow the Jews had achieved a kind of secret domination—and as evidence was offered the position of Jews in the economy, in journalism, in banking. The more scurrilous the paper, the more lurid the picture of this spider which caught ever new victims in its web; in the more respectable papers, the charges were often made more in sorrow than in anger, and everywhere Bleichröder was held up as the principal exhibit of mysterious Jewish power, consisting of political connection, vast wealth, and boundless ambition. As I have pointed out elsewhere, Bleichröder was a Jew such as the most imaginative and enterprising anti-Semites could hardly have invented. He was the hostage of this first generation of new anti-Semites (the very term, "anti-Semitism," was coined in Germany in the 1870s). If he had not existed, they would not have been able to invent him. As Richard Hofstadter has pointed out, political cranks need this "quality of pedantry"; they need some basis in fact, some evidence to bolster their extravagant charges.* In the 1870s, this demonology was

* "One of the impressive things about paranoid literature is precisely the elaborate concern with demonstration it almost invariably shows. One should not be misled by the fantastic

broadened by the emergence of racial anti-Semitism, the "scientific" assertion that racial characteristics were hereditary and that the evil essence of Jews was thus ineradicable.

After the 1870s, the ideological attacks on the Jews were not born of economic distress or the products of vague economic forces. But they seemed plausible because of the economic and psychic dislocations of the day. The subsequent history of anti-Semitism had very little to do with social actuality or the real position of Jews, which in any case gradually weakened.

Nothing so enraged the anti-Semites as the notion of a secret Jewish conspiracy ruling the new Germany. Their warnings had resonance, in large part because in an economically minded century, Germans and others mistook wealth for power, but in fact the position of German Jewry demonstrated that while wealth begets the power to amass more wealth, while it commands special considerations and privileges, in the Germany of Bismarck (and subsequently) it did not command political power. Despite the suspicion, so carefully nurtured by many critics of the time, that wealth and power were synonymous and that hence Jews were to be thought as holding both, the structure and substance of German politics were remarkably sealed off from any possible Jewish penetration.

The role of Jewry was asymmetrical, as I suggested earlier. In Germany, Jews were tacitly banned from all positions of political power, indeed from all visible identification with *dignified* power. They could become *Kommerzienräthe* and, in rare instances and in some fields, university professors; a few of them, beginning with Bleichröder in 1872, were even ennobled. But the upper reaches of the state service and the sanctum sanctorum, the officer corps, were closed to them; in the Prussian army, they were unable to become regular officers and the prize that all bourgeois elements strove after—the coveted title of reserve officer—was beyond the reach of Jews after 1878 or so. Perhaps in no other country in which Jews enjoyed civic equality was the officer corps as important

conclusions that are so characteristic of this political style into imagining that it is not, so to speak, argued out along factual lines. The very fantastic character of its conclusions leads to heroic strivings for 'evidence' to prove that the unbelievable is the only thing that can be believed. . . . But respectable paranoid literature not only starts from certain moral commitments that can be justified to many nonparanoids but also carefully and all but obsessively accumulates 'evidence.'" Richard Hofstadter, *The Paranoid Style in American Politics and Other Essays* (New York, 1965), pp. 35–36.

as it was in Germany, and in none, I believe, were Jews so resolutely excluded. In Germany, there was no Dreyfus Affair because there was no Dreyfus. One has to remember what the army meant in the hierarchy of power and values; it embodied, certainly by consensus of the governing classes, the noblest traditions of valor, honor, service, manliness. The symbolic and psychological importance of that exclusion was incalculable, and Jewish acceptance of it—with only occasional protests—suggests not only that they had to some extent taken over the stereotypes of their excluders, but that they had it too good to cope psychologically or politically with remaining indignities, just as the German bourgeoisie was too prosperous and too fearful ever to mount the barricades.

Self-perception is never easy, and German Jews found it excruciatingly hard to assess their place in German society. Nor were their views uniform—far from it; the Jewish community was split into recognizable divisions, varying with economic and social status, and marked by different views on political and religious issues, and especially on the problems of Jewish destiny itself. The countercurrents were violent: The drive to ever greater assimilation seemed consonant with rational self-interest and sentimental identification with the German nation and its culture; but if assimilation was the goal, how far should it go, how much religious heritage was one to surrender, how many discriminations and indignities to accept in order not to call attention to the separateness of one's group? Should one accept the remaining barriers, perhaps expecting, as did the rest of the German bourgeoisie, that in time these lingering survivals of a feudal age would disappear? Should one not be grateful for the safety won—after all, was not the fate of Eastern European Jewry steadily deteriorating after Russia adopted a new repressive anti-Semitism after 1881, a constant reminder of how immeasurably far German Jewry had traveled?

Wealthy Jews, of course, tended to be the most conservative and hence were least likely to want to criticize existing German conditions. How were such Jews to adapt to the successes they had scored? Meekly, modestly, unobtrusively, as if Stendhal and Dickens had never portrayed the bourgeoisie's irrepressible drive to dazzling heights of opulence and vulgarity, to the reification of tastelessness? Were they to be better than the "bran-new" Veneerings, the Podsnaps, and the Merdles? The temptation to snobbery was irresistible, and the costs were great as well, for as Lionel

Trilling noted, "The dominant emotions of snobbery are uneasiness, self-consciousness, self-defensiveness, the sense that one is not quite real but can in some way acquire reality."[6] The record suggests that Jewish plutocrats in Germany were just as garish in their grasp for social prominence as any bourgeois anywhere; the life of Bleichröder showed how important this social ascent was to the most prominent of economic Jews of the German Empire. Their efforts earned them the disdain of the very group they most sought to emulate, the older classes. And in the process of ever reaching out and ever being rebuffed, some of the Jews earned the reputation of being especially pushy, vulgar, loud, brazen, and money-conscious.

In the 1880s, various leaders of German Jewry admonished their coreligionists to be more "modest," an injunction that a great many critics, Nietzsche and Burckhardt included, also preached. The German Jews, it has often been noted, were especially censorious of the so-called *Ostjuden*, with their less cultured ways and peculiar speech and garb—reminders perhaps of what once upon a time German Jews themselves looked like. But self-critical admonitions went out to German Jewry as well, and especially to the most affluent, who were also often less cultured and more visible than the rest of the community.

In the 1870s and 1880s, that is, in the beginning of the new anti-Semitism, the principal target was Jewish economic power. By the end of the century, Jews had also become remarkably prominent in the academic-scientific field. For whatever combination of reasons, German Jews achieved an unprecedented preeminence in the natural sciences, in the birth of what has come to be called the new physics, in chemistry, and in medicine. In these fields, Germans and Jews complemented each other and collaborated in what may well have been a singular crucible of genius. And yet even in that field, there must have been bred resentments and unease; for every Jewish discovery made, for every Nobel Prize won, there were ten Germans who felt aggrieved. Nor can it be forgotten that both Germans and Jews occasionally thought that there was a distinct Jewish component to Jewish success. In part, it was the spur to greater effort; the need to excel was instilled by tradition and nurtured by hostility. Not safety or security, though those too were present in the domesticity of German-Jewish life, but hidden wounds inspired visible achievement.

It was Freud who in 1926 suggested something of what might be called the Jewish source of his work. In his address to the B'nai B'rith, in which he averred that he was an unbeliever and even an opponent of all national, including Jewish, enthusiasms, he added, "But plenty of other things remained ever to make the attraction of Jewry and Jews irresistible—many obscure emotional forces, which were the more powerful the less they could be expressed in words, as well as a clear consciousness of inner identity, the safe privacy of a common mental construction. And beyond this there was a perception that it was to my Jewish nature alone that I owed two characteristics that had become indispensable to me in the difficult course of my life. Because I was a Jew I found myself free from many prejudices which restricted others in the use of their intellect; and as a Jew I was prepared to join the Opposition and to do without agreement with the 'compact majority.'"[7] It is a paradoxical fact that it was German Jews, so many of whom were thought to be in craven submission to the dominant group among whom they lived, who in the century between emancipation and extinction produced some of the most fiercely independent minds, willing not only to break with the majority but to expose the taboos that characterized German society. The Germans cherished a certain type of sentimental domesticity or, put differently, transmuted the aggressive strains of human nature to fairy tales; it was Heine who could in unmatched lyrics express these yearnings for love and beauty and with searing irony expose the taboos as well. The Germans were also always peculiarly reticent about matters of money and sex, both considered "dirty" and unmentionable; Marx and Freud dedicated their lives to analyzing the material and sexual origins of collective and individual behavior.*

The Jews had made an unprecedented leap, but their success, partial in any case, had brought them grave costs as well. So many

---

* Freud cited one splendid instance of Heine's satirical exposure of German sentimentality: "A great imaginative writer may permit himself to give expression—jokingly, at all events—to psychological truths that are severely proscribed. Thus Heine confesses: 'Mine is a most peaceable disposition. My wishes are: a humble cottage with a thatched roof, but a good bed, good food, the freshest milk and butter, flowers before my window, and a few fine trees before my door; and if God wants to make my happiness complete, he will grant me the joy of seeing some six or seven of my enemies hanging from those trees. Before their death I shall, moved in my heart, forgive them all the wrong they did me in their lifetime. One must, it is true, forgive one's enemies—but not before they have been hanged.'" Sigmund Freud, *Civilization and Its Discontents* (London, 1949), p. 84.

of them had willingly tossed most of their own traditions aside, content to merge with the dominant, secular, nationalist culture of the Germans. The varying degrees of hostility they encountered puzzled and divided them; the Jewish response to lingering resentment and burgeoning anti-Semitism, which by the end of the century included a new form of racism, was a composite of design and passivity. Different groups were predisposed toward different responses, and German Jewry embraced simultaneously a set of conflicting strategies.* Some counseled still greater efforts at assimilation, even conversion; others wished for a more assertive policy that would demand the implementation of civil rights which had been formally granted in the various emancipation decrees; others still embraced a new Jewish nationalism which in its own way echoed the charge of anti-Semites that Jews were an alien people that should be extruded from the German body politic. For all the conflict and unease within the Jewish community, there was a kind of unarticulated cohesion as well; religious and secular, conservative and radical Jews, however much they warred among themselves, understood that they shared certain traditions and certain talents, and they were at once proud and ashamed of these traditions. There remained a measure of cohesion that mingled pride with shame, that by being largely covert gave less psychic reassurance than it might have done. The spiritual stance of German Jewry can perhaps best be described by the word ambivalence: ambivalence about themselves, ambivalence about the Germans, ambivalence about their role in German life. The history

---

* It is worth recalling that Tocqueville, reflecting on the democratic inclination to elect mediocre leaders, observed that "when serious dangers threaten the state, the people frequently succeed in selecting the citizens who are the most able to save it. [But] extreme perils sometimes quench the energy of a people instead of stimulating it; they excite without directing its passions; and instead of clearing they confuse its powers of perception. The Jews fought and killed one another amid the smoking ruins of their temple." *Democracy in America*, vol. 1 (New York, 1945), p. 210. How could it be otherwise, given the myriad reactions of individuals at the time? Consider two statements from the early 1890s: the nineteen-year-old Chaim Weizmann, apprenticed in a German-Jewish school and in full rebellion against the assimilated principal who lectured Weizmann that the Germans would overcome their anti-Semitism as soon as they fully realized the magnitude of Jewish contributions, cried out: "Herr Doktor, when someone has something in his eye, he doesn't care whether it is a piece of gold or a piece of mud—he wants it out." In 1890 the great German novelist Theodor Fontane wrote: *"At least here in Berlin*, all freedom and higher culture has been mediated for us primarily by rich Jewry. It is a fact one has to accept finally, and as an artist or a literary person, one has to accept it with pleasure (because without it, we could not exist at all)." Weizmann, *Trial and Error* (New York, 1949), p. 32; Theodor Fontane, *Briefe*, vol. 2 (Berlin, 1909), p. 245.

of German Jewry in its century of seeming freedom described in a particularly intense and elusive manner what we commonly call the problem of identity.

In seeking to understand this buffeting, one must remember that Jews were nurtured in the political culture of modern Germany, and one must remember the degree to which the Germans themselves experienced the same fate, both internally and in their relations to the outside world, as did the Jews. Did the Germans of the new empire not astound the world by their material triumphs, by their great power, by what appeared to all as their disciplined genius? And yet their appearance aroused not only resentment but contempt, for they, too, were thought to appear simultaneously as craven and commanding. And the Germans faced this world in jackboots and with bombast, wishing to be loved and feared at the same time. They mixed arrogance and *angst*, and they too had deep misgivings about their identity and national destiny, and nostalgia for traditions lost. And did not Germans—at least those that were not titled or powerful—suffer the same kind of lingering nonage that the Jews experienced? For the Germans, in their erratic thrust for world power, their relationship to the great declining Imperium of Britain was the central political problem; the antagonism that developed between Britons and Germans was perhaps the single most important element in the later self-destruction of Europe. And the Anglo-German antagonism, while rooted no doubt in substantive conflicts and rivalries, was also nurtured by the multiple misunderstandings and misperceptions that the British formed of the Germans—misperceptions and suspicions that often paralleled the Germans' view of their Jews.

In their own great triumph, the German Jews anticipated and approximated the triumphs of their country. They contributed to that larger national triumph, and they too exulted in it. As we have seen, they were also the victims of their own success and that of the Germans, but their real tragedy began when the Germans suffered the defeat of 1918, embittered by the sense that the world had denied them their rightful place as Europe's imperial power, for which their military, industrial, and scientific might had predestined them. After 1918, the Germans experienced a succession of reverses, none of which they understood, all of which were made more galling by their feeling that they were being treated as the moral pariahs of the world. It was in those years of inflation and depression, of outraged nationalism and a sense of aggrievement at being treated as outcasts, that the accumulated anti-Semitism in Germany became concentrated into a frenzied political gospel and directed against a Jewish minority that had long since lost the strength or power it had once possessed..

But even then there was no single road that led to Auschwitz. What the National Socialists aimed at was the total repudiation of emancipation and the extrusion of Jews from German life. They proceeded slowly, by design and improvisation; what emboldened them was the passivity with which the German elites, long nurtured on a kind of presumption against Jewry, observed the elimination of Jewish colleagues and competitors from almost every sphere of activity. The outside world, which until the outbreak of the Second World War the Nazis watched with some concern, expressed but mild reproof and intermittent opposition. In the end, the Nazis, nurtured on a hatred of German Jews, unleashed their full wrath on European Jewry, made defenseless by Nazi conquest. For a generation, the memory of the Holocaust smothered the ancient prejudice against the victims; under the impact of new events and a new generation, the world may forget the fate of these millions, and their memory may be violated by polemical invocation on the one hand and increasing resentment or impatience on the other. The living wish to be freed from the incubus; the victims embarrass.

The term "German Jew," long since emptied of much specific historic meaning, has become synonymous with meek surrender, self-immolation, cravenness, with victims digging their own graves. This memory as the indictment of victims is a terrible simplification, unfaithful to the past and portentous for the future; for it could encourage truculence and moral defeatism. But the cultivation of this memory is nurtured by many sources; time was when the liberal mind essentially affirmed the rational, the secular, the democratic ethos. It is a terrible irony of our time that after having encountered and finally, at hideous cost, vanquished the embodiment of political irrationality, our culture is full of voices extolling the irrational. In the haunting, final words of *Sincerity and Authenticity*, Lionel Trilling evoked that new facile inclination toward irrationality, toward "an upward psychopathic mobility," that mocks the dead and threatens the living.

At such times, German Jewry will hardly be assessed with

sympathetic understanding. For the German-Jewish community epitomized too many of the things now held in disrepute: They lived by what were once regarded as the proper modern habits of rationality, discipline, repression, and with these came both self-denial and alienation. The record, moreover, bespeaks submission and servility; it also describes a great flowering of the human spirit and imagination. If, in the end, the hope for an untroubled German-Jewish partnership or collaboration is to be judged an illusion, it must be said that for a brief moment it was an enticing illusion, an illusion productive of greatness. For the rest it remains a subject that we must treat with a new candor and with the greatest degree of empathy as well as factuality. It is a subject that speaks to all those who are concerned with the questions of integration and pluralism. Would it be permissible to go even further—to say that such knowledge would illuminate the human experience in a modern, often hostile, society generally? It is a subject touched by the tragedy of our civilization and a wiser understanding may enlighten our present predicaments and diminish the danger that the pain of the past by twisted memory confounds the present.

II

The Lure of Power

I wrote the two following essays in the last three years for different occasions and without intending to republish them in consecutive order. They have a common premise: my belief that National Socialism was the great moral drama of our time and that the vulnerability of Germans, especially of the German elites with their claims to superior education, responsibility, self-awareness, and a sense of history, to Hitler's triumph was a fateful theme in that drama.

The first essay was originally delivered as the Leo Baeck Memorial Lecture in 1983—fifty years after Hitler's assumption of power. It tries to depict the style of National Socialist politics and to relate the movement's appeal to some older aspects of German life, to what I call "the silent secularization" of Protestant Germany and the manner in which Germans received their political education. It is here reprinted with some minor additions.

The second essay was originally delivered as a lecture at the University of Tübingen in 1984, on the occasion of my receiving the Leopold-Lucas Prize of the Evangelical Theological Faculty. I wrote and published the lecture in German, it was translated by Robert and Rita Kimber, and subsequently I revised and expanded it extensively. It argues that for many Germans, National Socialism in its deliberate pseudo-religious form appeared as a great temptation, as a promise of national salvation that harked back to earlier hopes and delusions. "Temptation" in the title suggests the irrational elements in submission; my chief concern is with the early period of Hitler's rule, when choice for or against him entailed little or no risk. I try to reconstruct the conduct of people under unprecedented, seemingly revolutionary circumstances, remembering that the German elites had little experience in collective civic action beyond voting.

In retrospect, I see that the two essays proceed from the most general statement to the most specific. I have tried to eliminate overlap as much as possible, but some themes necessarily recur.

The reader may sense a personal engagement and I realize that my own experiences may at times have intruded in these essays and also informed them. I plan to expand "National Socialism as Temptation" at some future time.

F I V E

GERMANY 1933: FIFTY YEARS LATER

Hitler's rule began on January 30, 1933, but the roots of his triumph reach deep into the history of our world. The day itself was marked by that murky mixture of delusion, drama, and intrigue that had brought Hitler to power and that continued to characterize his rule. In the next twelve years, the drama never ceased; for the first ten, it was a victorious scene and for the last two years it was a drama in total defeat. By terror and seduction, Hitler enthralled Germans and subdued an already enfeebled Europe. His regime dominated the lives of Germans and, ultimately, of non-Germans. It never achieved stability and boredom; it hardly provided any respite from passion and mass excitement. Much about that regime remains unclear or controversial, but few would now dispute that Hitler's German dictatorship was the most popular, the most murderous, the most seductive, and the most repressive regime of our century. After Hitler, nothing is quite the same—not in the world of the mind nor in the world of politics; not in Europe and not outside it. Hitler was the cataclysmic event of our time. We need seismographers of the spirit to understand the faults that made possible the earthquake, and in some way try to understand this worst of earthquakes in comparison to preceding, lesser ones.

January 30, 1933. The day had several faces. There was the

constitutional legality, the seeming guarantee of normality: The aged president, the eighty-five-year-old Field Marshal von Hindenburg, the very embodiment of tradition and authority, endowed the leader of Germany's largest party with the country's highest political office. But Hindenburg and his entourage insisted that Hitler had to have a cabinet in which non–National Socialists predominated numerically, because this would be an outward sign that the old elites, who for several years had tried to establish an authoritarian government without parliamentary or popular support, had finally succeeded in taking Hitler "captive"; *that* illusion was soon shattered. Representatives of the army, business, and the old civil service in Hitler's cabinet gave the new government respectability and the world at large the promise of moderation. At the moment of utter bankruptcy the old order turned to the leader they considered an Austrian outsider, a Bohemian corporal, a terrible vulgarian, with reluctance and restrictions, but turned to him nevertheless. Bereft of popular or parliamentary support, the old order embraced the morning-coated, stiffly bowing Hitler.

That same night, tens of thousands of his storm troopers staged a gigantic torchlight parade in front of the Chancellery, where Hitler and Hindenburg watched the uniformed, flag-carrying, chanting troops. That parade was at once a celebration of victory and a defiant demonstration of power—yet to be exercised. The ominous spectacle demonstrated once again the National Socialists' dazzling command of the pageantry of politics, of the orchestration of power. With torches illuminating the night, the eerie show of light and darkness was a signal of invincibility and a threat of intimidation. It was also a night that many thought signaled the beginning of a new, great era, a rebirth or regeneration of the German nation.

I remember the day of Hitler's assumption of power, his *Machtergreifung*, as the party instantly and dramatically dubbed it. I was not quite seven on that day, but a politically aware father and the fact that my native city, Breslau, was a stronghold of National Socialism (in July 1932, the NSDAP polled 46 percent of the vote there) had given me an early sense of outside danger. I remember as well the antecedent period of apprehension and uncertainty, symbolized by the daily marches of storm troopers with their rubber truncheons, their drums and flags, ever ready for clashes with rival groups, with communists in particular. I remember bringing the special one-page "extra" of the newspaper, with banner headlines that Hitler had been appointed chancellor, to my parents and knowing that it was terrible news. I can also remember on that day a long procession of communists, men, women, and children, marching behind red banners and chanting "hunger, hunger." I remember the subsequent days as well, the silence that fell over the family when the news came that a close friend and patient of my physician father, Ernst Eckstein, the leader of the SAP, a left-wing radical offshoot of the Socialist Party, whose house had been bombed earlier, had been tormented to death in a Nazi cell. I recall other political friends of the family fleeing or being dragged off to camps. It was the beginning of my political education.

The day itself, January 30, offers clues to the question that has haunted people for half a century: How was it possible? How could the National Socialists have risen from being a marginal group of right-radical misfits to being Germany's single largest party in 1932, with a higher percentage of votes than any other party in Weimar had ever won before? How could so many members of the German elite, so many guardians of the German spirit—pastors and army officers, civil servants and university professors—have found Hitler acceptable or patriotic or idealistic? The *Machtergreifung* marked the end of Weimar's agony and the immense appeal of the National Socialists. The two processes, the fall of Weimar and the rise of Hitler, were distinct if inseparable developments.

There was a diabolical complementarity between a twisted, tortured, partial genius who sought release in gaining power over men and a nation, humiliated and divided, that hoped for a return of national grandeur. Hitler needed power to exorcise his own fears and demons and, in turn, in his promise of absolute authority, his followers found solace, relief, and hope. As an outcast in the ideologically seething atmosphere of prewar Vienna, as a failed artist on the margins of society, as a demobilized soldier without purpose or place, he had experienced the injuries and resentments that Germans collectively suffered after the Great War. He found his own salvation in the manipulations of these resentments. If Germany had won the First World War, Hitler would have remained an obscure misfit; a victorious Germany would not have needed the delusions of salvation. Hitler proved the greatest magician-manipulator of the aggressive, violent instincts of an outraged, perplexed people that the modern world has seen. He knew how to attract and bind the anxious and the dispossessed. There is no reason to suppose that Hitler had ever read—or heard of—Dostoevsky's parable of the Grand Inquisitor, but instinctively he knew that people succumb to the promise of miracle, mystery, and authority.

Hitler's message was simple, at once revelation and prophecy, and he endlessly intoned it: Life is struggle, the basic struggle is racial, with a pitiless Jewish race pitted against a pure but trusting Aryan race. Jews and Marxists, the promoters and profiteers of the so-called November Revolution, were responsible for the defeat of 1918, for the shackles of Versailles, for the divisiveness and class antagonisms of the Weimar Republic. Hitler promised the redemption of the country, a *Volksgemeinschaft* at home that would transcend classes and, under the command of a Führer-genius, would restore greatness abroad. He would liberate his people from Versailles, from Jewish domination, from the Bolshevik threat; he would unify Germany and restore order and national power. A German imperium would be built in the east. There were sinister notes in the program: Germans needed *Lebensraum*, i.e., territorial conquest; Jews must be eliminated from German life, i.e., they must be hounded out; in the glorious unity of the Third Reich, there would be no parliamentary opposition from selfish interests or party profiteers, i.e., all opposition would be crushed, and all the corrupt elements that corroded Germany's greatness would be destroyed.

Hitler's way to power was through the orchestrated word, through the cunning, largely intuitive seduction by verbal and symbolic appeals to power and community. He and his ingenious satraps perfected the instruments of propaganda, borrowed in part from the blackshirts in Italy. Every speech and every rally was a celebration of passion and unreason. Providence had chosen Hitler as Führer and redeemer—the religious motifs were very strong. By 1930, the National Socialists had mastered this theatre of politics, but behind the public show was the painstaking organization of the party. The elements are familiar: orgiastic meetings, disciplined celebrations that recalled the exuberance of earlier youth movements and the trappings of an army. The National Socialists learned to play on the dreams of the young and the grievances of the old. At the meetings and marches there was always the promise of community, the frenzy of collective response, the certainty that came from glorifying a single leader, the salute to him, the common insignia. It was all so simple—and so meretricious—but his followers were transported. They were caught up in the movement in a way that mere voters for other parties were not, though perhaps the communists had a comparable fervent faith, albeit not the same fanatic will to be enslaved in exaltation.

It would be wrong to make light of Hitler's triumph; half a century later it can seem an easy feat, given the congruence between Germany's public, political debility and Hitler's style. The Germans had been buffeted since 1914, humiliated since 1918, economically entrapped in 1923, and tried again by the Great Depression. In many ways, Weimar continued the agony that began in 1914. Its successes, substantial in domestic and foreign policy, were undramatic, as was Weimar's political leadership. Hitler's political opponents were divided.

And still it would be wrong to trivialize Hitler's triumph: It could blind us to the contingencies in his rise. It could blind us to the unpalatable truth that Gordon Craig put starkly: "Among all of the prominent figures of the Weimar period, [Hitler] is the only one of whom it can be said unequivocally that he possessed political genius."[1] The success depended upon lucky breaks and on the misfortunes of his opponents. It was not inevitable; indeed the party itself was in gloom and disarray in the two months before January 1933. There were historic conditions and deeply rooted traditions in German life that favored his rise, but all of German history was not a prelude to 1933. Hitler's triumph was—and remains—astonishing.

Historians have attributed Hitler's success and the enthusiasm or acquiescence of a majority of Germans to many factors, among them certainly economic misery and the state's seeming inability to deal with heightened anxiety and the disillusionment of millions. We know of the fragility of Weimar and the suppressed fury of the old governing classes that saw their power decline with Germany's after Versailles; they confounded injury to class and injury to nation and did not see that their own chauvinism and class egoism, their own violent opposition to democracy, had brought Germany most of its grief. We remember the weaknesses of the constitution and the predominance of an old conservative elite in the judiciary and the civil service generally. The army behaved like a state within a state, and the political parties—by 1930, six major ones and eleven minor ones—were doggedly fighting narrow battles and seemed incapable of working efficiently within the parliamentary, multi-party system. There was also increasing civil disorder and street violence and a Moscow-led Communist offensive against the Republic in general and the Social Democrats in particular. Historians also emphasize the resentment caused by Versailles and the social burdens of an unprecedented inflation by which the state in effect expropriated its own middle class. Some of us have stressed the illiberal structure of Germany's political culture, its tradition of anti-Semitism, its resentment against "the West," against capitalism, democracy, modernity. Anxiety was rampant in German society, and the onset of the Great Depression—which in Germany as elsewhere deprived millions of livelihood and hope—added existential fear to latent anxiety. As Franz Neumann pointed out long ago, that anxiety predisposed a people to fasten on notions of conspiracy and thus to give further credence to Hitler's diatribes against Jews and Marxists.[2]

In order to attain power, Hitler needed the legitimation of electoral support; in the election of 1930, at the beginning of the Great Depression, which the Brüning government sought to fight with orthodox deflationary measures, the NSDAP gained 18 percent of the vote. In July 1932, it won 37 percent of the vote. A recent study calls into question the traditional view that the lower middle class was the group most vulnerable to NSDAP blandishments. The Protestants and the young, especially students, flocked to Hitler early and in disproportionate numbers. The upper classes, the well-to-do marked by *Bildung und Besitz*, voted for Hitler—also disproportionately; the same was true for Protestants in rural areas.[3] But Hitler needed the support or acquiescence of the old elites as well; only they could confer respectability on him and the party and could reassure voters and rulers that the NSDAP was neither as radical as it sounded nor as violent as it often acted. As early as 1929, in their vile attacks on Stresemann and the Young Plan, the conservative parties included Hitler in their ranks, and the experiment was repeated in the so-called Harzburg Front of 1931. Kurt von Schleicher, intimate of Hindenburg and political general par excellence, exclaimed that if the National Socialists did not exist one would have to invent them.[4] But there was reluctance as well, characterized by Hindenburg's remark in 1932 that he had no intention of handing Germany over to Hitler "like a laboratory rabbit."[5] In the end, of course, Hindenburg did just that, and Hitler, suspecting Schleicher of wishing to "uninvent" the National Socialists, had him murdered.

It is puzzling that amidst the plethora of studies on virtually all aspects of National Socialism there is no single, comprehensive work on the responses of the old elites and the self-acclaimed guardians of morality to the National Socialists. To judge the range of responses one must ask: What could they have known about Hitler before the actual seizure of power? Why the passivity and acquiescence on the part of so many? Given what was then known or knowable about Hitler's movement, could they have understood the radical evil that Hitler represented? Of course, it was difficult to read the signs correctly. By 1932 the economy was in collapse and the state enfeebled. For many, National Socialism seemed to offer the one solution that would satisfy both material interest and nationalist sentiment; if the National Socialists were guilty of excesses in rhetoric and in street action, this was not the time for niceties. In 1932–33, the great Rhenish coal magnate Paul Silverberg, a Jew baptized at birth, favored the inclusion of National Socialist leadership in the government as the only means of returning to economic and political stability.[6]

Hitler's victory was made possible by the millions who voted for him. But it was also essential to have tens of thousands of the elite believing that he was perhaps the legitimate if uncouth heir and true redeemer of ancient tradition rather than its traducer. There were many Germans who hesitated, who wondered, like the blind Isaac: "The hands are the hands of Esau but the voice is the voice of Jacob."

It has often been said that the underestimation of Hitler was one of the principal reasons for his success. But Germans not only underestimated him, they misperceived him. They saw in him an exaggeration, a caricature of something old and known; they adjusted him to their own limited imagination. They were prisoners of their past, and they failed to see the radical difference, the true evil, that Hitler represented.

Hitler was a genius at dissembling—yet reckless at revealing his true nature. After the failed Putsch of 1923, he had mouthed constitutional pieties, but *Mein Kampf* was a battle cry for war, and the hatred that he spewed out on the platform his thugs carried to the streets. In August 1932 in Potempa, in Upper Silesia, five of his storm troopers beat a Communist worker to death in front of the man's mother. When the five men were sentenced to death, Hitler sent a telegram pledging the murderers his "unconditional fidelity."

Hitler's political opponents—those who had a professional interest in defeating him—also underestimated or misperceived him. Communists and conservatives both thought they could use him. The Communists, prisoners of Stalin's policies, hoped he would be a tacit ally in wrecking Weimar; they concentrated their attacks instead on the all-too-meek Social Democrats, whom they branded as "social fascists." The Socialists in turn thought the National Socialists the instrument of capitalism, the tool of reactionary forces, the recipient of bribes—as if people had to be bribed to be transported into a state of permanent exaltation. Few on the Left understood the psychological appeal of National Socialism, and Marxist orthodoxy ill-prepared them to grapple with the power of unreason. They believed that at worst they would have to suffer a period of repression such as they had suffered under Bismarck, a period of martyrdom that might perhaps bring about an heroic renewal. For all the candor of Hitler's threats, and despite the lessons of Italian fascism, with Matteoti murdered and Gramsci imprisoned, the Left did not anticipate the terror with which the National Socialists, if ever in power, would destroy all opposition, actual or imagined.

On the Right there was much murmuring about the vulgarity of the upstart, but the Right also sensed a congruence between itself and the NSDAP, at least on major issues such as anti-Marxism, the enslavement of Versailles, the un-Germanic character of much of Weimar, the dominance of Jews. Even some of those who disliked Hitler had a reluctant admiration for his avowed ends and for the superb organization of his party. The traditional Right and Right-Center gave Hitler what he needed—not so much money, on which so much historical interest has fastened in recent years, but respectability.

Among the most aggrieved groups in Weimar were the East Elbian agrarians, impoverished and politically disinherited. They had been an economically declining class for at least half a century; after the collapse of the Empire and the defeat of what they considered *their* army, they had lost their privileged position in state and society, a loss they identified with the humiliation and betrayal of the nation as a whole. The national organization of the German nobility, the Deutsche Adelsgenossenschaft, founded in 1874 by East Elbian estate owners *(Rittergutsbesitzer)*, adopted a virulently anti-Weimar policy by sentiment and material interest. The honorary head was Hindenburg, whose own attitude toward National Socialism was by no means unambiguous. And the organization, though self-consciously Christian and full of laments about the "godlessness" of the people, moved ever closer to the NSDAP. Always anti-Semitic (having already excluded Jewish nobles from belonging), always hypernationalistic, the head of the organization sought to rouse his fellow members in 1932: "We are at a fateful moment. With elemental power, the Nordic soul in our people wrestles with the unnatural powers that a westernizing un-Germanic democracy has bestowed on us . . . noblemen do not belong in the ranks of whining pacifists but there where blood flows." Whatever one's personal view of the National Socialist movement, "there are such enormous forces in it: it is a matter of engaging it, in the sense of [achieving] a political leadership of the state governed by our spirit."[7] Translated freely, to catch the military overtones of the original, the sentiment reads: "Throw in the most powerful battalion; it will fight and win our battle." How prevalent a sentiment that was! How often groups deluded themselves into thinking that they were protecting German ideals and not narrow, selfish interests! How common was the notion that the National Socialists were an undirected army whose views, by and large, coincided with one's own!

Still, Hitler could be understood and was understood—the more prominent he became, the clearer the evidence. Even as early as 1922, Thomas Mann understood the subterranean mood of contempt and disdain for Weimar that joined together young assassins of the Right and patriotic or nationalistic members of the declining elites. In a major address in 1922, he sought to persuade hostile students that the Republic was respectable, consonant in fact with Germany's past and with her poets (Novalis in particular) as well. He warned against the constant romanticizing of war and avowed that "obscurantism, its political name is reaction, is brutality. . . . War is deception." The students noisily objected to his assertion that "in all the world there is no reason to think of the Republic as (merely) the property of cunning Jew-boys."[8] Mann knew of the temptations of a certain kind of Germanic idealism, devoid of all sense of reality, full of longing for some national redemption and full of contempt for humdrum democracy. Thomas Mann, so bourgeois, so remote, had an uncanny sense of that voluptuous underworld of false promise and real decay, and he sensed the dangers of this murky movement of young nationalists. In 1930, in "Mario and the Magician," he portrayed a malevolent magician who in an atmosphere of exaltation and uncertain distress knows how to seduce his audience, knows how to play on the intuited wounds of the servant, Mario, how to coax Mario into submission. In the same year, Mann delivered a passionate defense of the Weimar Republic and proclaimed his support of the Social Democrats.

But even without Mann's intuitive gifts and familiarity with political irrationality, one could have understood the power and the nature of Hitler's movement. In 1932 Ingbert Naab, a Capucin priest and well-known publicist, published a tract entitled *Is Hitler a Christian?* He acknowledged that Hitler's followers thought of him as a bulwark of Christianity, whereas in reality "he violates the foundations of Christian morality and he rapes freedom. . . . With its clear firmness, the Catholic Church will overcome the waves of this movement too. The costs will have to be borne by German Protestantism, which sees only the grave national misery and because of it permits the fundament of a Christian view of the world to be destroyed in many of its followers." Naab appeals to the educated followers of Hitler: "Where is their education? their knowledge? their logic? Why don't they see the great internal contradictions? Don't they also lack character? . . . We don't know what will happen to our poor fatherland. But we do know that if we must live through a truly hard catastrophe then a high percentage of our educated world will bear a good part of the guilt. And the balance sheet of guilt comprises inadequate knowledge, missing logic, weak character, hypocritical Christianity."[9] And in a Reichstag speech in 1932 a rising star of German social democracy, the young Kurt Schumacher, defied the Nationalist Socialists: "National Socialism is nothing but the appeal to the *Schweinehund* in man."

Of course people knew. Most recently we have the testimony of Raymond Aron, who from 1931 to 1933 was in Germany as a young university lecturer and who testifies that it was then and there that he received his "political education," then and there that he recognized the force of the irrational in politics, and then and there, instantly, that he understood "the Satanic" in Hitler.[10]

No, the real question is why so relatively few uncommitted intellectuals acquired the same political education that Raymond Aron acknowledged. He himself ruefully noted that his friend and later political opponent Jean-Paul Sartre drew no such benefit from his German sojourn. Neither intellect nor Jewishness could shield one from political misjudgment. Thus Ernst Cassirer, a great German philosopher, is supposed to have said, "This Hitler is an error of history. He does not belong in German history at all. And therefore he will perish."[11] After the first great victory of the National Socialists in 1930, Einstein wrote that he saw in the movement "only a child's sickness of the Republic. I am always for solidarity among Jews, but no reason for a special reaction to the electoral results."[12]

Before January 30, 1933, there was sufficient evidence of Hitler's malevolence, and enough warning voices from different quarters, so that passivity or conniving uncertainty suggests willful ignorance, suggests that primacy of material or ideological interest was asserted, put ahead of civic rationality or basic morality. Perhaps the people who hesitated were confounded by the nationalist fervor of the movement, by their own despair over existing conditions, and perhaps they saw in "the promise of national ascendancy . . . an opiate against the fear of social descent."[13] The process of Nazification was even more complex and difficult to understand than the process of de-Nazification. Who were the truly culpable ones—those who joined the party, those who were its fellow-travelers *(Mitläufer)*, or those who kept their benign distance from the melee but saw the good in National Socialism, condoned its excesses, supported its ends?

Consider Franz von Papen, a frivolous reactionary and intriguer, who at the height of the economic crisis headed a government risibly bereft of support and who hoped to use Weimar's end in order to restore the monarchy. In October 1932 Papen declared that he and his government represented a new "politics of faith. What is essential about every conservative worldview is its being anchored in the divine order of things. This, however, is also its radical difference compared with the doctrine embraced by the

NSDAP. What gives the latter the nature of political religion is its axiom of the 'exclusiveness' of the political 'all-or-nothing' [and] its mystical Messiah-faith in the 'word-mighty' Führer as the only one summoned to control destiny. And it is here where I see the irreconcilable difference between Conservative politics rooted in faith and a National Socialist faith rooted in politics. . . ."[14] Three months later, Papen reconciled the irreconcilable—and thus became the ultimate gravedigger of Weimar.

The men who persuaded Hindenburg to appoint Hitler chancellor thought they could control him, thought that though he had delivered the support of the masses, power, of course, would remain in traditional hands—of the army, of the landed and indebted Junker, of business. They could not believe that the inexperienced upstart would know how to move the levers of government. But these clever conservatives did not reckon with Hitler's will to power, the cunning with which he would consolidate his rule. Even today the rapidity and totality with which he established his dictatorship astounds us.

Within weeks of January 30, 1933, Hitler had intimidated and ultimately eliminated most organized opposition to him. The twin instruments of propaganda and terror coerced and cajoled a people to give up what for so long they had taken for granted: the formal rule of law, a free press, freedom of expression, and the elementary protection of habeas corpus. Bogus legality covered his action. Less than a month after the *Machtergreifung* and within hours of the Reichstag fire, Hitler persuaded Hindenburg to issue emergency decrees that suspended civil rights and established a constitutional basis for the German dictatorship. A few days later, general elections gave Hitler and his ally, the German Nationalist Party, a slim majority. And by the end of March a great pageant at Potsdam symbolized the reconciliation of the old Prussia with the new National Socialist Reich, and the Reichstag voted Hitler four years of dictatorial power—with only the Social Democrats in opposition, the Communists already having been imprisoned or debarred. German civil servants and their charges, i.e., the right-thinking citizenry at large, had the comfort or threat of knowing that the National Socialist arbitrariness was fully clothed in the mantle of legality. In April 1933, most Jews (front-line soldiers from the Great War were temporarily exempted) were deprived of their civil service jobs—their university, clinical, or judicial appointments—simply on the basis of their race. That act, ceremoniously called an act for the restoration of the professional civil service, also had all the trappings of legality.

But the National Socialists never acted on one track alone. Themselves protected by the powers of the state and the judiciary, they also resorted to the physical means of power. By March, the first concentration camps were established and well publicized; their existence, after all, was part of the politics of intimidation, and the KZ *(Konzentrationslager)* became an ominous household word, connoting illegal arrest and torture.* On April 1, the NSDAP called for a boycott of all Jewish establishments, but there was little popular sympathy for this at home and hostility abroad. In May, the National Socialists staged a great book-burning ceremony in which "decadent" works written by Jews and non-Jews, including those by Freud and Einstein, were consigned to the flames. In May labor unions and in July political parties were officially banned. By mid-1933 the National Socialist dictatorship was in place. Hitler had achieved in months what Mussolini never and Stalin only after many years achieved: the supreme role of the party in the state and the unchallengeable power of the leader. The National Socialists called it *Gleichschaltung,* "coordination"; there was no opposition left, no expression of contrary views. The elements of totalitarian rule were successfully superimposed on what remained a remarkably normal civil society. The very normality of German life—the continued presence of Hindenburg, the restored order, the economy recovering by its own rhythm and by the steady increase of public spending—reassured Germans and non-Germans.

Hitler's swift triumph must have appeared as a kind of foreordained continuation of his march to power; in fact, he and his lieutenants were ever anxious about the reaction to him at home and abroad. But in the first few months of Hitler's rule there was very little active opposition. And at every point he was emboldened by silence, acquiescence, or support. There were exceptions, of course: early on, a small group of Protestant pastors objected to the establishment of what was called the German Christian move-

---

* In July 1933, the German writer Erich Ebermayer wrote in his diary: *"Whoever disappears in a KZ is placed outside the law and expelled from humanity."* (Italics in original) Erich Ebermayer, *Denn heute gehört uns Deutschland . . . Persönliches und politisches Tagebuch* (Hamburg and Vienna, 1959), p. 145.

ment—a travesty of Christianity—and the Aryan paragraph in the law restoring the professional civil service, which forbade converted Jews from being Christian pastors. Martin Niemöller and Dietrich Bonhoeffer saw in that paragraph the irreconcilable antagonism between racism and Christianity, and gradually parts of the Protestant and Catholic clergies began to struggle with National Socialism, but by the time the churches acted, the regime fought back, eventually sending thousands of priests to prison and concentration camps. In any case, the more the churches caused trouble, the stronger became Hitler's resolve that after a successful war he would put an end to Christianity.

In 1946, Konrad Adenauer, hardly an indulger in national self-recrimination, wrote to a priest: "I think the German people and the bishops and the clergy bear a heavy guilt for what happened in the concentration camps. It is true that perhaps later [after 1941?] there was not much that could be done. The guilt was incurred earlier. The German people, to a large extent bishops and clergy as well, accepted the National Socialist agitation. It allowed itself to be regimented (gleichschalten lassen) almost without resistance, even in part with enthusiasm. I think that if all the bishops had, on an agreed-upon day, spoken publicly from the pulpit against National Socialism, they could have prevented much from happening. If the bishops had gone to jail or to concentration camps because of such an action, that would have done no harm, on the contrary. But none of this happened, and therefore it is best to remain silent."[15] Adenauer's was a summary indictment, but resistance became increasingly hard—and necessary—as the terror became ever greater. Yet the nagging question remains: Why was there so little resistance at the very beginning? After all, in early 1933, members of the elite—clergy and professors, officers and famous artists—could have protested the actions of the regime without jeopardizing their lives and probably without jeopardizing their careers. I single out the elite because it claimed and possessed special privileges, special knowledge, and its members could have acted with some kind of corporate impunity unavailable to less fortunate people; in the beginning, the regime would have hesitated to deal harshly with opponents of impeccable conservative distinction. In those early months, protests would not have entailed martyrdom—and would have changed the course of history; in 1944, hundreds of the same elite did risk and suffer martyrdom—

without effecting change. Yet in virtual silence, the elites witnessed the extrusion of Jewish scientists, the imprisonment of political opponents, the reintroduction of torture, the throttling of freedom; in silence, they witnessed the burning of books and the elimination of "Jewish" art and artists.

The reasons for this silence were many and complex, no doubt. German elites had little training in moral protest or political opposition; they were peculiarly tied to the authority of the state. And rationalizations must have come readily to mind: The regime is going through its infant stage; in time it will become domesticated. On the whole, their objective interests were not yet threatened by the new regime; the ouster of Bruno Walter or Albert Einstein was perhaps an unfortunate excess, but one could live with it. The reasons for passivity included opportunism, careerism (the removal of Jews and socialists, after all, opened vacancies), and confusion. Also, Germans cherished "bourgeois freedoms" that had long existed in Germany less than they cherished the dream of a strong and united nation. So as the German elites reacted to Hitler with silence, acquiescence, fear, complicity, and enthusiasm, they were encouraged by memories of how bad Weimar had been, or how pervasive the "corrosive" Jewish influence had been; and they were reassured by colleagues in the army and the universities, by the example of generals who favored the regime and famous philosophers such as Martin Heidegger, who as rector of Freiburg in 1933 fervently embraced the new regime.

To some, no doubt, silence was an act of decency, already the first step toward an "inner emigration." But it has to be emphasized that most members of these elites had a special vulnerability to National Socialist rhetoric and ideals. Hitler's promises had an immediate resonance in groups that had been brought up on older dreams of national rebirth, on deeply rooted anti-Western sentiments, on all manner of cultural despair.[16]

At the other end of the scale—among the objects of Hitler's relentless hatred—did German Jews grasp the enormity of the sudden danger? Their survival depended on it. At a later time, whether Polish or Russian Jews understood the National Socialists correctly mattered little; they were victims without hope. But for some five years most German Jews were more fortunate. The Hitler regime, for reasons of prudence and because even the brutality of National Socialism needed time to ripen, gave most "non-political" Jews time to leave, a possibility of escape, even though under increasingly difficult circumstances. In fact, the regime at first wanted nothing more than to extrude the Jews, to make the new Germany *"judenrein."*

Yet Jews were slow to emigrate even when opportunities existed; as demand rose, so did the inhospitality of other nations. Out of 525,000 Jews who lived in Germany in 1933, about 270,000 to 300,000 emigrated; the largest number of emigrants left in 1938. Of course there were distinctions among those who left. The young or the most immediately persecuted left early; the aged stayed on altogether.[17] Some Jews abandoned hope very quickly; others were torn between hope and resignation; they had their own reasons for a willed blindness in regard to Hitler.[18]* They too misperceived him and some paid the ultimate price for a delusion tinged with patriotism. The reluctance to emigrate sprang from as many motives as the silence of the elites: the hope for amelioration, the fear of the unknown, considerations of age, family, health, spirit. Reluctance to leave one's home, to acknowledge that one is no longer wanted in a society in which one feels at home, to abandon one's mother tongue—all this is perfectly human and can be scorned only by those who cannot muster sufficient sympathy for the trials of uprooting.

Jews were also torn between believing atrocity stories about the National Socialists, stories that often tended to paralyze action, and hoping that things would improve. Some Jews thought that in time the National Socialists would moderate, that anti-Semitism had had a long history in Germany, that these new manifestations were but the old anti-Semitism revisited. Some upper-class Jews—thinking of their "inferiors," of modern analogues to Jewish peddlers or sharpies of various sorts—could even sympathize with

* George Clare, an Austrian Jew, recalled that his father, "himself a veteran of the Great War, could not help admiring in some ways this former Lance-Corporal, who had risen so high, and I, the boy nurtured on the *Gute Kamerad,* on so many stories of German valour, on the stab-in-the-back legend, on endless talk about the inequities of the treaties of Versailles and St. Germain, read with fascination the speeches of this man, who promised to make Germany great again.

"We knew about his anti-Semitic tirades, of course; we knew about the 1933 anti-Jewish boycott, but, strange as it may seem—it was really a form of self-protection, foolish certainly, but very human—we looked for, and found, excuses for these excesses, having used anti-Semitism to help him achieve power, like so many demagogues before him, did Hitler have any choice but to allow his stormtroopers their field day?" *Last Waltz in Vienna* (New York, 1983), p. 121.

elements of anti-Semitism. There were Jews who well before Hitler cringed at what they took to be unpleasant Jewish characteristics and nevertheless inveighed publicly against anti-Semitism. So it was not difficult to delude oneself and hope to be spared; Jews could take comfort from the fact that there was so little spontaneous anti-Semitism in early 1933, that official boycott actions had indifferent results, that Germans continued to flock to Jewish physicians and Jewish lawyers; even a measure of sociability was maintained in the first few years. Just as every German had "his decent Jew," or so Himmler complained, so most Jews had their decent "Aryan" who continued to have contact with them. Jews, too, could be deceived by the specious normality that the regime allowed to continue.

Two historic developments seem to me to have had a special bearing on the vulnerability of Germans to National Socialism. In singling out these distant and complex processes I do not mean to underestimate the immediate, material, and documentable reasons why people embraced National Socialism or acquiesced in it; I simply mean to recall some cultural contexts that shaped people's sentiments and habits, that fashioned the manner in which they responded to politics. For in confronting National Socialism, Germans responded to something far deeper than a political choice. For many of its adherents or sympathizers, National Socialism was a promise at once of immediate melioration and of satisfaction of a deeper yearning, a longing that had expressed itself before in sudden eruptions of the spirit. German politics was certainly dominated by what Lenin once called "who—whom," by the defense of the material interests of the upper classes, but it was also the scene where from time to time the stirrings of the German soul found turbulent expression.

It is a commonplace to see in the nineteenth century the century of secularization. In some countries, there were battles over secularization, as there was in Germany at the time of the *Kulturkampf* in the 1870s. After the *Kulturkampf*, Protestant Germany, where in the 1920s and 1930s National Socialism won its decisive triumphs, experienced what I would call "silent secularization," a term adapted from the medical vocabulary which describes an unnoticed heart attack as a "silent" one. Protestant secularization was largely "silent," a protracted transformation characterized more by concealment than by confrontation, more by pretense of

continuity than by an acknowledgment of a profound break. Here
I would recall Nietzsche's all-too-familiar outcry that: "God is dead.
God remains dead. And we have killed him! . . . The holy and
most powerful the world has yet owned, it has bled to death under
our knives—who will wipe this blood off us? The tremendous event
is still on its way . . . it has not yet reached the ears of man. . . .
This deed is still farther from them than the farthest star—and
yet they have done it themselves."[19] In Protestant Germany, the
death of God remained an unacknowledged secret, disguised,
transmuted, denied—denied at times by the very voices that warned
against the secular wave, the godless world.

In the West generally, secularization described the attenuation
of religious commitment, faith, and conduct. It meant the withdrawal of belief from the centrality of a Christian order; at the
same time secular institutions and secular life assumed an aura
and an awe previously reserved for the religious life. In Germany,
the great achievements in higher criticism applied historical standards to revealed religion; scientific-rational thought undermined
the authority of theology and revelation. By the early nineteenth
century, Neo-humanism had already created a new faith: a faith
in education and self-realization, and it was this faith that provided
justification for life. The new faith did not deny Christianity; it
supplanted it, particularly among the educated classes.* The secret
ideal was the classical world, a glorified Greece. About fifty years
ago, a book called *The Tyranny of Greece over Germany* appeared,
and the title evokes a state of mind. But even that process was
disguised, and it was perhaps symptomatic that one of Nietzsche's
greatest and earliest diatribes was directed against David Friedrich
Strauss's work *The Old and the New Faith*, a hapless effort to reconcile
the two modes, to offer some kind of synthesis of science and
watered-down theology.

There were gradual changes in the religious lives of people as
well. Church attendance declined; the prosperous classes began to

---

* In a new edition of Friedrich Schleiermacher's speeches, *Über die Religion*, Rudolf Otto
describes the religious situation in the period around 1800: "But confronted with this aesthetic
sensibility on the one hand and these moralistic tendencies on the other, religion had been
backed into a corner. It was superfluous; it was not in keeping with the times anymore. No
one hated religion, but it was looked down upon as something that was no longer needed.
You could be educated and full of ideals; you could be an aesthete; you could be a moralist;
but you could not be pious." Friedrich Schleiermacher, *Über die Religion: Reden an die Gebildeten
unter ihren Verächtern*, 5th ed., ed. Rudolf Otto (Göttingen, 1926), p. iv.

have the sacraments of baptism and marriage performed at home rather than at the altar, a practice that could be seen as a further sanctification of the home. But there was a more serious estrangement between Protestant Church and people: in the course of the nineteenth century and at a time of liberal thought and socialist organization, the Church remained unswervingly conservative, unquestionably supportive of the established order. It had its philanthropic spokesmen for the poor, but not moral defenders of the rights of the dispossessed and endangered. Despite intermittent efforts by men like J. H. Wichern and Friedrich Naumann, the church practiced social indifference, with the result that the urban and recently uprooted poor remained outside the flock.

The Protestant ministry became the king's spiritual guard; it exalted king, nation, *Volk*. Indeed the *Volk* was the embodiment of the divine on earth. Enemies of the nation or the state, domestic and foreign, were traducers of God's dispensation; good Christians had to be faithful servants of the nation. The identification of the divine with the fate of the nation and its existing order—true for much of Europe in that age of nationalism—seemed to vindicate the sentimental smugness with which upper-class Germans viewed German politics before Weimar. God was the guarantor of the nation's ever-growing power and importance. God had given Germany its victory in 1871 and Church and Monarch routinely implored and expected divine blessings on a Germanic Christian State.

Throughout the century, the awe once reserved for the worship of the divine came to be associated with this world's institutions and practices as well. Both German Idealism and liberal Protestantism endowed the state with its own nimbus. The state in turn demanded veneration, sacrifice, and service, celebrated in shrines, holidays, hymns. Other public institutions acquired a new sanctity: the German universities, transformed by Humboldt's ideals and reforms, came to be hailed as temples of culture and wisdom, certainly by their professors, many of whom were sons of Protestant ministers. Pedagogues were the high priests of learning, artists came to be regarded as prophets; the German cult of genius acknowledged the artist as a mysterious, divinely inspired creator of a higher truth. (The German historian who in all seriousness suggested that Goethe's works be added to the Book of Revelation merely provided a caricature of reality.) Richard Wagner became a kind of demonic deity, with Cosima his grasping priestess. Germans accorded a special veneration to family and friendship, to art and cultivation, to scholarship, and these were specially celebrated. The very neologisms of the end of the nineteenth century—*Kunstreligion* and *Kulturreligion*—suggest a phase of secularization.

The prominence of German Idealism and German metaphysics facilitated the disguise of secularization. In Protestant Germany there were no battle lines drawn between believers and non-believers, between clerics and anticlericals. "The retreat from Christianity," as Langmead Casserley called the process, or "the unchristening of Europe," as C. S. Lewis called it, occurred discreetly—and the very silence or concealment added to the sense of guilt and to the hypocrisy of Wilhelmine society.[20] Decorum was all important.

Max Weber pointed to disenchantment, *Entzauberung*, as a characteristic of the modern world. For much of the bourgeois world, the transmutation I have depicted disguised *Entzauberung*, but the sense of void, of infinite boredom and pervasive falsehood, oppressed some of the young and many of the artists—and they proclaimed their yearning for a life more natural, more honest, less humdrum, less materialistic. "In the 1880s passed over western Europe one of those movement of mind that history perceives but cannot easily analyze or define. It was something to do with a reviving sense that the world holds mystery and that the prosaic explanations of the age after the romantics will not satisfy."[21] The German Youth Movement, begun in the 1890s and alive till the beginnings of the National Socialist regime, embodied this fervor and impatience. The young felt dispossessed, disinherited, misunderstood, and they clamored for a new faith and a new community. They craved "a moral equivalent of war," and if it could not be moral, then a cry for blood was acceptable as well. The mood was European and in many ways it resembled a kind of yearning for something that later would be called fascism. It sought a new order, a new authority, but it described an aesthetic hunger and a moral command as well. Some of the best minds were tempted by this mood—and the worst rabblerousers spread it.

Before 1914, German Protestantism had become the *Staatskirche* par excellence; the upper classes, embracing a theologically diluted faith that mixed Christian rhetoric, Luther's ethos of work and obedience, and the teachings of German Idealism, believed that the union of throne and altar was sacrosanct and infinitely reassuring. This union constituted what Walter Bagehot called the dignified parts of government; it guaranteed the stability of their world. They probably gave little credence to the traditional faith, but they believed that religion was necessary for the lower classes— for the very classes they had neglected and feared had become "godless." Ironically, they would have agreed with Karl Marx's definition in 1843 that "religion is the sign of the oppressed creature, the heart of a heartless world, the soul of a soulless environment. It is the opium of the people."[22]

Silent secularization diminished spiritual sustenance without acknowledging the change. So much of reality was denied in German society: Mammon was privately worshipped and publicly denounced; physical passion was to conform to respectability. Concealment was an important element in what I would call the sentimental and inadequate self-awareness of the Germans. Until the novels of Theodor Fontane and Thomas Mann, there were few, if any, great realistic novels in Germany; there were no analogues to Dickens and Trollope, to Balzac and Flaubert—and in the nineteenth century, the great novelists were also the moral teachers of the Europeans.

During the Great War, the identity of Protestantism with the German nation became the clearest tenet of Protestant faith, exalted in sermons by which the priesthood blessed the slaughter as a holy sacrifice and invoked God as the guarantor of German righteousness and ultimate victory.* In its moment of supreme need (and unacknowledged greed) the nation, long celebrated as the embodiment of the divine on earth, received the unconditional sanction of the church. For its sake, all sacrifices were justified. The Christian God had always been conscripted in European conflicts, and

---

* There was Protestant distress as well. The 28-year-old Karl Barth was appalled by Protestant enthusiasm for the war and in August 1914 wrote his revered teacher and restrained supporter of the war: "But why don't you leave God out of this whole sinful worldly necessity?" Much later Barth remembered his dismay at the "Manifesto of the Ninety-three," by which German notables, including leading theologians, expressed their unconditional support of Germany's war effort: "Because of that and because of everything else one read of German theologians then . . . a whole world of theological exegesis, ethics, dogmatics, preachings which till then I had believed in as fundamentally credible, was shaken to its foundations." This revulsion from clerical subservience to the state proved decisive in the formulation of his radical theological thought. *Karl Barth–Martin Rade: Ein Briefwechsel* (Gütersloh, 1981), pp. 28–29.

certainly the Prussian kings had always so used Him. But as the
Great War became the most demonic of European conflicts, so the
invocation of God was at once the most intense and ultimately
the most destructive.

The defeat of 1918 was a devastating blow to German Protestantism: It severed the alliance of throne and altar and the altar
was left unprotected in a hostile world. German Protestants—
particularly strong in the economically declining provinces of
northern and eastern Germany—identified with the humiliation
and degradation of the nation. Defeat and revolution brought
Protestants and Catholics closer together, but the latter had the
external support of the Vatican and the internal instrument of a
major political party. The Protestants felt endangered and belea-
guered. Both confessions often lamented "the state without God,"
thus saddling the young Republic with yet another sin.[23]

In Weimar, German Protestantism had to confront its failures:
its enfeebled faith, its failure to establish a link to the urban lower
classes. The workers had their party and their faith, the Catholics
had a strong party that had a decisive voice in Weimar life. But a
religion that had been tied to a deposed monarchy and to a
privileged order that was itself on the desperate defensive in
Weimar had none of its traditional support—and hence found
Weimar an uncongenial, threatening culture. Gone was the old
Lutheran pathos of obedience; at best there was a kind of sullen
aloofness, but aloofness and resentments are never apolitical.[24]

How could one preserve a *Kulturreligion* when the great revolutionary artists and writers of the 1920s unmasked the old
sentimentalities and mocked what to others was sacrosanct? The
institutions that a secularized Protestantism had endowed with
sanctity—the state, the nation, the universities—they too had
suddenly become devalued. Protestantism was no longer the spiritual arm of the secular power, the favorite of a much-revered
state; in the Weimar Republic, church and state were separated,
partly by law, largely by material and spiritual interest.

The second historic process that made Germans particularly
vulnerable to National Socialism was the manner by which they
acquired their political education. The Great War politicized them,
taught them the inescapability of politics, but did so at a time of
passion and pervasive angst. The war inculcated not civic rationality, but ideological simplicity and vast distrust. The Germans did

not have a protracted or unifying course in politics or self-government.* The emotional vocabulary continued under Weimar; in many ways National Socialism was a continuation of wartime politics and psychosis by other means and under different circumstances.

It has often been said that Germans were even more remote from reality, more *wirklichkeitsfremd,* than other people. In the nineteenth century, they made a virtue out of the private realm. The Idealist injunction of self-cultivation, the veneration of art and culture, the special place of the family and of friendships, the often sentimentalized domesticity of German life—all these virtues were remote from concern with public affairs. "To a German who had imbued himself with the spirit of Dürer, Bach, and Goethe, *vita contemplativa* was the highest form of life."[25] Great men or events would stir Germans from their domestic slumber: Napoleon, the revolutions of 1848, Bismarck, unification. But these were particular moments of collective drama, often identified with Great Men in History, with the demonic elements celebrated by Goethe and Hegel. Ordinary politics rarely engaged the Germans. Their life was work or business, though for many of them music, art, and literature *were* nurturers of life. The drama was private, and indeed the cultivated elite maintained its anti-democratic prejudices by insisting that democratic politics or parliamentary rule would jeopardize the older, nobler ideals of self-cultivation. Thomas Mann celebrated the apolitical and Robert Musil and Stefan Zweig described the world of the apolitical elite.

The Great War shattered that world; public drama suddenly engulfed the private world. At first, Germans responded with an orgy of nationalism, with an unprecedented exaltation. So did the rest of war-starved Europe. The famed spirit of August 1914 expressed a great yearning for a different world, a world of action, sacrifice, unity, a release from bourgeois boredom.† War as the

---

* Even after 1945, Karl Jaspers warned ambitious American reformers: "You should not give such big tasks right away to people who are political children or who are politically corrupted. Self-education in politics must proceed step by step." Quoted in Karl Otmar von Aretin, "Der deutsche Widerstand gegen Hitler," in Ulrich Cartarius, ed., *Opposition gegen Hitler* (Berlin, 1984), p. 20.

† In 1915, Thomas Mann recalled that earlier euphoria: "Let us remember the beginning—those never-to-be-forgotten first days, when what we no longer thought possible, happened. We had not believed in the war, our political insight had not sufficed to recognize the necessity of the European catastrophe. But as moral beings—yes, as such we had seen the trial coming—

redeemer, unifier, cleanser—that was one of the great delusions of our century.

Germans learned about the dominance of politics at a time of maximum mobilization and maximum impotence. For the first time, an entire society was mobilized and regimented, and official-dom sought to maintain by propaganda the fever pitch of exaltation that had sprung up spontaneously. But four years of war—with millions killed and maimed, with children undernourished, with a mounting suspicion that the war was senseless or made sense only because of the greed and fear of the upper classes—extinguished that first enthusiasm. People had never been so powerless to shape their own lives, to protect their private realm. Everything was at the mercy of the Moloch; one lived in the shadow of death and in grief or anticipatory grief.* At most, one could cheat at the margins: buy on the black market, bargain for some brief dispensation. The old expectation of achievement and reward broke down; when sacrifices were demanded, they were unequally divided, and the children of the poor suffered while the well-to-do managed. And still the official litany continued: The fatherland is in danger; the death of a soldier is a hero's death, a sacrifice like Christ's. Envious England was determined to throttle its innocent rival. Politically uneducated Germans lived through four years of war, during which they were promised that their sacrifices brought glory to the nation and in the end would bring victory as well. The harsher the regimentation, the cruder the propaganda, the longer the war, the more the Germans became suspicious of each other.†

---

and still more, in some way we longed for it, felt in the depths of our hearts that the world, our world, could not go on like this any more. We knew that the world of peace, that *can-can* culture . . . horrible world, which now no longer is, or no longer will be, after the great storm passed by. Did it not crawl with spiritual vermin as with worms? Did it not ferment and stink of the decaying matter of civilization?" *Friedrich und die grosse Koalition* (Berlin, 1915), pp. 12–13.

* Consider one example: Dietrich Bonhoeffer's twin sister wrote about their war experience when they were about ten years old: "We heard of the death of our grown up cousins, and the fathers of our schoolfellows. So after the evening prayers and singing . . . we lay awake a long time and tried to imagine what eternal life and being dead were like. We endeavored every evening to get a little nearer to eternity by concentrating on the word 'eternity' and excluding any other thoughts. . . . I believe this ritual saved Dietrich from being 'devoured' by Satan." Eberhard Bethge, *Dietrich Bonhoeffer* (New York, 1970), p. 23.

† The moral effects of the Great War on Germans have been caught in a neglected work, Albrecht Mendelssohn Bartholdy, *The War and German Society: The Testament of a Liberal* (New Haven, Conn., 1937). He noted for example that "the men in the trenches had comradeship to comfort them, while the people at home, as soon as the blockade made itself felt, had to

Political education and the urgent need for civic rationality came at a time of organized mendacity and pervasive hatreds. Systematically the government lied to its own people, lied about war aims and the chances of victory. The Germans were taught to hate their enemies and they learned—by bitter experience—to distrust each other, class by class, interest against interest. That is why the defeat of 1918 stunned the Germans—and could so quickly be translated into charges of betrayal and subversion.

Thus while the Germans learned about the centrality of politics in the Great War, they learned about it in a distorted and divisive manner. And they could never discard the categories they had come to use during it, especially the category friend or foe, first applied to foreigners and then gradually to fellow Germans as well. Wartime rhetoric is always specially charged and in Germany the confusion between sacred and secular reached new heights: salvation, rebirth, resurrection, revelation, martyrdom—these terms were constantly invoked to rally the people. The November Revolution made visible and rendered permanent the discord in German society.[26] Peace came in an admittedly harsh form, with unanticipated losses and as a stunning reversal; but even without Versailles, the Germans would have been sullen and divided; the nation felt itself betrayed.

Nor was there a period of healing, a return to reasonable privatism. The collapse of the old order and the establishment of an unpopular republic led to conditions of intermittent civil war, insurrections alternating with individual assassinations, and in 1923, in a rare exercise of despair, a bourgeois government allowed uncontrolled inflation to expropriate its own middle class, while foreign troops seized the Ruhr, the heartland of German industry. After a short respite, largely financed by American loans, an unprecedented depression engulfed the country, and people in all

face competition and the struggle for life in its ugliest form, and likewise had before them, day after day, the spectacle of the prosperous and influential profiteer." Speaking of representative memoirs of Germans in public life, he wrote: "The great mass of those who emerged from the War resigned and discouraged, of course, are silent. The bulk of such memoirs, therefore, favor the belief that war is one of the great forces of life. Men have to do battle, show themselves the master, in order to make plain their true measure of strength. Between the lines of these life stories, however, the tale of the scourge of war and its punishment of the good and great, and rewards for the coward and the braggart, is told in unmistakable signs." The dream of achieving "uniformity of mental attitude, attained through uniform education and a prescribed common stock of knowledge in a community of one single racial denomination, is the gift of the War to the German nation." (Pp. 286, 292, 285.)

camps came to doubt that the existing and enfeebled political system could deal with its several crises. Most Germans cherished delusions of national grandeur, hoped that Versailles marked a temporary reversal in the march to power; instead the country staggered from disaster to disaster. The contrast between expectation and reality was cruel and in a society rife with class antagonisms the temptation to blame disaster on enemies proved irresistible. In short, the Germans continued their political education in bitterness and doubt, in the absence of clear persuasive leadership, in the absence of any kind of consensus in public opinion. Their fears and passions were mobilized when their powers and their understanding were weakest.

A succession of disasters, a growing sense of civic and economic disorder, a feeling of national humiliation and of collective danger in divisiveness—all of these were factors in Hitler's triumph. So were the very special material interests that sought to destroy Weimar and that hoped to use Hitler for their own ends. But among the deeper causes for the special vulnerability of Germans to Hitler were what I have called silent secularization and a distorted political education.*

Instinctively Hitler played on public grievances and unacknowledged wounds, on German humiliation and distress, but did so in a style that reached even deeper and touched Germans where a great unacknowledged void existed. He did so cynically and deliberately, convinced of the gullibility of the masses. He may also have done it half-consciously for, as a son of the Dual Monarchy, he grew up in a society far less secular than postwar Germany had become. A rather unconventional and strongly anti-hierarchical Catholic historian, Friedrich Heer, wrote that "the Austrian Catholic Adolf Hitler found in the Catholic Church which he hated, despised, admired, and imitated, not a single opponent who was his equal." Hitler's rhetoric was religious; he dissolved politics in a religious aura, and all the theological terms which had

---

* As a mere example of an early similar diagnosis, consider this excerpt from a draft article by an American officer in Germany, written in June 1924: "The Racial Party [NSDAP] is today a factor in German politics. Its virulence and illogic count against it less than in other European states, so poisoned has become the political atmosphere in Germany. Not even mediocre leadership and total lack of understanding of foreign policies have checked its rise. . . . And the childlike political simplicity of the German people prevents the belief that they will soon see the sterility of its political formulas." *Berlin Alert: The Memoirs and Reports of Truman Smith*, ed. by Robert Hessen (Stanford, Cal., 1984), p. 74.

been previously secularized were now the great standard themes of his appeals: He promised deliverance and redemption, rebirth and salvation, even as he reviled the Reich's enemies as godless and satanic; he did all that in the name of Providence, for he believed that Providence had selected him to deliver the German people. In the beginning of his chancellorship, when he was still seeking to beguile his conservative allies, he appeared at his most devout. In the first government declaration to the German people, which Hitler broadcast on February 1, he spoke "of the terrible legacy which we take over," of how after the November Revolution, when "the German people forgot the highest treasures of its past, of the Reich, its honor and its freedom . . . the Almighty withdrew His blessings from our people." After promising a national rebirth, he concluded: "May the Almighty God accept our work in His grace, justly guide our wills, bless our intent, and endow us with the confidence of our people."[27] Certainly his closest followers thought him great and providential; in 1937, Goering confided to an American that there had been only three great men in history: "Buddha, Jesus Christ, and Adolf Hitler."[28] In his wartime diary Goebbels recorded that Hitler was deeply religious, if very anti-Christian.

Hitler's "sermons of a pseudo-religion" appealed to an uneasily secular people; "Non-recognition of reality is the principle of salvation."[29] There were many reasons why Protestants in particular were disproportionately drawn to Hitler, but we know from individual witnesses that his pseudo-religious, chiliastic promises attracted them far more than any other part of his rhetoric or program.* A theologian from the University of Erlangen welcomed "the German transformation as a gift and miracle of God."[30] Here was the echo of a century of nationalist-religious rhetoric. The lapsed Catholic capitalized on enfeebled Protestantism.

In 1933 the Germans, deluded and self-deluded, surrendered to a false prophet and partial genius and in time his boundless

---

* This is how an enemy of the regime described the mass meeting at which Hitler opened the election campaign on February 11, 1933: "Hitler is greeted with an incomparable storm of applause. Then he gives a far-ranging speech which rouses all to a momentous pitch. The man obviously grows with the task that has become his. At the end he begins to pray, as it were, and concludes with the word 'amen.' Exactly the right mixture for his audience: Brutality, threats, great bragging about power (*Kraftprotzentum*) and then again humility before the oft cited 'Almighty.'" Erich Ebermayer, *Denn heute gehört uns Deutschland* . . . (Hamburg and Vienna, 1959), p. 21.

hatred consumed his enemies and inflicted suffering on the very people who in supporting him had sought to escape suffering. Still, at first, some of the promises were redeemed: German power was restored, Versailles was repudiated, a great army was rebuilt, and the economy recovered. Every success from Autobahn to prospective Volkswagen, from the reoccupation of the Rhineland to the annexation of the Sudetenland, was magnificently dramatized. So was the putative union of the country—putative because Hitler's enemies had been murdered, hounded to concentration camps, or cowed into silence. Jews were extruded from German life and pushed into exile or subjected to ever greater persecution.

Most Germans remained loyal to the regime, certainly through the bloodless victories of 1938; most, indeed, remained faithful to the end. The regime was popular, the Third Reich did satisfy national yearnings and gave many people material and spiritual rewards which made them oblivious of costs, sometimes even their own included. There were those with misgivings and apprehensions. Some who had hoped for deliverance in 1933 came to realize the dangers and went into "inner emigration," retreated once more to the private realm, comforted by the pathos of obedience, intimidated by the presence of terror—and only a few, most prominently in 1944, became martyrs of resistance.

National Socialism needs to be remembered—and not only in scholarly monographs or trashy films, but in the moral consciousness of all of us. There is an appropriate epitaph for it, as for the Stalinism which evoked Nadezhda Mandelstam's outcry: "Silence is the real crime against humanity."[31]

S I X

NATIONAL
SOCIALISM AS
TEMPTATION

*"No passion so effectually robs the mind of all its powers of
acting and reasoning as fear. For fear being an apprehension
of pain or death, it operates in a manner that resembles
actual pain. Whatever therefore is terrible, with regard to
sight, is sublime too, whether this cause of terror be endued
with greatness of dimensions or not; for it is impossible to
look on any thing as trifling, or contemptible, that may be
dangerous. . . . And to things of great dimensions, if we
annex an adventitious idea of terror, they become without
comparison greater. . . . To make any thing very terrible,
obscurity seems in general to be necessary."*

EDMUND BURKE, "A Philosophical
Inquiry into the Origin of our
Ideas of the Sublime and Beautiful"

[I]

IN THE BEGINNING was the question: "Is National Socialism
Germany's Salvation?" That was the title of a lecture that Theodor
Heuss gave in Tübingen in 1931; and, while making all due
allowance for National Socialist goals and desires, he answered his
own question with a sober, ironic no.[1] The very asking of this
question called attention to the promise the National Socialists
were holding out: Germany, they suggested, needed salvation. The
Führer, Adolf Hitler, would be her savior.

That was the claim of National Socialism. It would free a
divided and humiliated nation from all its ills, most of which could
be attributed to the so-called November criminals, the Marxists

and the Jews. These enemies of the nation, working from within, had stabbed Germany in the back and robbed her of power and honor. National Socialism promised a radical new beginning, a national rebirth, a national community of the Aryan race, a strong country that would shake off the chains of Versailles and again become a great military power, that in the end would conquer the *Lebensraum* it needed. The class struggle would be overcome; the people would be united again; a powerful Führer would rule the Third Reich; enemies of the state would be driven from the land; and the Jews, who were responsible for Germany's woes, would be excluded from the national community; there would be no more parties; the Führer, as a forceful dictator, would embody the will of the people.

That is a rough summary, in words, of the program. But the National Socialists turned politics into national drama. Hitler and his lieutenants were stage directors of national emotion, magicians who manipulated the Marios among the people. They were, on the political stage of the Weimar Republic, what Max Reinhardt or Leopold Jessner was in the actual theater. Joachim Fest has rightly stressed the "liturgical magic" of National Socialist demonstrations, a magic that gave back to the people their "lost sense of belonging together and their feeling of collective camaraderie."[2] In a "sharp attack on the National Socialists" in his last speech in the Reichstag in 1932, Theodor Heuss spoke of the National Socialists' "fantastic propagandistic achievement, that practiced interplay that embraces both the hero and the saint at once, alternating between the great, victorious man at one moment, the martyr and his persecuted innocence in the next."[3]

The National Socialists transformed politics into permanent delirium. The great appeal of National Socialism lay in the Führer's unique form of demagogy and in the dramaturgy of National Socialist spectacle, that symbolism which had borrowed a great deal from the church, the youth movement, the army, and Italian fascism, yet which, for all its borrowings, National Socialism molded into a new style. Before 1933, the threat of terror and violence was part of this style; after 1933, the threat became brutal reality. But violence—particularly in a country that was feeling defenseless and victimized—impressed people, intimidated them, and disgusted them. Some may have registered all three reactions at once.

But despite all the delirium National Socialism induced, we

must not forget that Hitler never entirely hid his brutality. On the contrary, *Mein Kampf*—the title, *My Struggle,* alone is revealing enough—was a thinly disguised call for another war. And what else but a prelude to violence were the uniforms and clubs, the flags and the daggers, the war songs and the mass demonstrations? And did not Italy's milder fascism rule by murder and terror, too? Hitler had an insatiable will to power; he needed power to subdue his own demons. The SA (storm troopers) fought ferocious battles in the streets and glorified the victims from their own ranks. There were enough signs that any observer with his eyes half-open could not miss and that must have made clear that the Third Reich, if it were to come about, would impose a reign of terror on Germany.

The temptation before 1933 was to believe in Hitler as a savior, to believe in a national rebirth. The path to National Socialism led through a wasteland of personal fears, collective anxiety, and resentments. The temptation was to surrender oneself to a dictator, to believe in a miracle. Hitler evoked human will and divine providence. The religious-mystical element in National Socialism was uncannily appealing to unpolitical people, to unrealistic people at odds with their world and accustomed perhaps to the dream of heroic irrationalism. The temptation was to abandon oneself to this national delirium—despite (or even because of) the threat of violence. National Socialism's certainty of victory and its promise of national unity dazzled disillusioned Germans. Here at last was a call to the national spirit. Many people found it easy to overlook and excuse what was ominous and radically evil in National Socialism. They clutched at the pseudo-religious aspect of it, the promise of salvation held out so cleverly and on so many levels. One had to disregard a great deal and ignore many warnings to adopt this faith. Most of its followers probably had their own ideas of what National Socialism really was. Some things they refused to believe. They clung to what had particularly impressed them or what seemed needed, and they took the general message, the pledge of a strong national community, as the heart, the universally valid essence of the National Socialist promise. The zeal of the millions who joined the movement even before 1933 calls to mind Nietzsche's dictum: "Weariness that wants to reach the ultimate with *one* leap, with one fatal leap, a poor, ignorant weariness that does not want to want anymore: This created all gods and other worlds."[4]

The elites succumbed to this weakness as well; they too fell for the temptation. Their failure was decisive—and remains portentous. Once Hitler had decided that he had to gain power through "legal means," i.e., through the processes that a free society allowed and not through a coup d'état, which he had attempted in 1923, he needed a mass following. Under the conditions of the Great Depression he was able to recruit such support. But such was the character of Germany's political culture that Hitler also needed the support or at least the acquiescence of the old German elites as well, the guardians of morality: pastors, professors, officers, civil servants, industrial magnates, landed nobility. It was of course a complementary progress. The mass support impressed the elites, the support of isolated churchmen or other dignitaries helped to win voters and marginally helped to fill the coffers of an impecunious party. As we shall see, members of these elites rallied to Hitler and his movement. Some did so before 1933, many thereafter. It is their conduct, more visible, somewhat more documentable, than that of the anonymous voters that especially concerns me. Much attention has been focused on who voted for Hitler and who paid him. The so-called masses and the magnates have been held responsible, and their culpability, real or putative, has shielded the conduct of elites.

In analyzing such behavior, especially that after 1933, we have to use tact and caution and recall Ralf Dahrendorf's warning: "No one who has not himself been led into temptation has the right to pass moral judgment on others."[5]* And here I want to make a personal remark: I was spared this temptation, not through any special virtue on my part but because I am a full-blooded non-Aryan for whom temptation was forbidden. I recall very vividly how enthralled my schoolmates were by the Hitler Youth, how appealing and binding that communal experience had been, and

* In February 1946, Ernst Reuter, still in Ankara, wrote to the BBC, which had just broadcast a harsh program on Furtwängler during the Nazi era: "In the long years in which I had to live in involuntary banishment I have resisted with all my strength this cheap passion for throwing stones [Steinigungssucht]. Only one who went through the torment of the concentration camp, only one who looked his tormentors in the face and still could remain faithful to his convictions, ready to stand by them at the risk of his life, has, it seems to me—the right—if anyone has it at all—to pronounce such a sentence of stoning, and precisely he—grown wise in suffering—will be ready to render such a judgment only after the most careful examination." Ernst Reuter: Schriften Reden, ed. Hans E. Hirschfeldt and Hans J. Reichhardt, vol. 3 (Berlin, 1974), p. 618.

how painful exclusion could be. For me there were other temptations, particularly after I had left Germany as a twelve-year-old boy. I do not mean to pass any facile judgments here; rather, I want to take the German elite and National Socialism seriously and bear in mind the remark of the poet Gottfried Benn: "We were not all opportunists."[6] We have to understand the people of that time and realize that, to a certain extent, they may have been innocent, unknowing. But for all that we cannot avoid measuring the followers and advocates of National Socialism by the standards of their own contemporaries. We must bear in mind the actions and attitudes of those who resisted temptation, of those who did not rally to the great national revival; one must remember the whole range of non- or anti-Nazi responses. There were those who warned or protested while this was still possible without great risk. There were others who had believed in National Socialism and who at some later time recanted—not just in silence but in deeds that led to death. They bear witness to my contention that National Socialism could be a great temptation, that a certain kind of idealist could succumb to the movement as a means of identifying with the nation, of restoring a sense of belonging that had ceased to exist under Weimar, of finding a cause that would demand sacrifice—and not for reasons of petty careerism. The prudent succumbed with reservations; the virtuous, if they succumbed at all, often fell under the spell with all their fervor.

We cannot expect anyone to become a martyr. The time of the Third Reich was a shameful period in which sordidness and brutality, lies, opportunism, and cowardice celebrated their triumph. The historian and citizen should be all the more grateful that even in that time—or perhaps because of that time—there were men and women whose moral stature, decency, and self-sacrifice should remain unforgettable.

National Socialism was a new phenomenon in German life, and most Germans reacted to it in much more complicated, vacillating, unclear, and inconsistent ways than we ordinarily assume they did. There were, of course, zealous disciples and determined opponents; but then there were disciples who evolved into opponents, and the opponents were not without their doubts either. Before Hitler's assumption of power there was choice; clear decisions had to be reached, often in public view. In some elections of 1932, Hitler received 37 percent of all votes: an unprecedented triumph, confirming, in a way, his self-proclaimed role as savior of the nation.

But quantitative data do not give us qualitative answers: Why did every third German vote for Hitler? The importance of his appeal seems clear, the appeal of a carefully constructed cult of one man, who could spew out maledictions and promises with the same passion.[7] For many people, especially for Protestants and for the young, there seemed no alternative to Hitler. The bourgeois parties seemed condemned to mindless marginality. Not all of his supporters were unconditional believers in Hitler; not all those who voted against him were immune to his appeal.

Questions about human behavior and motivation are always difficult for the historian, and they are particularly recalcitrant for the National Socialist period. The great appeal of National Socialism—and perhaps of every totalitarian dictatorship in this century—was the promise of absolute authority. Here was clarity, simplicity. Yet for many Germans, National Socialism was not so clear and simple at all. They were impressed by its successes but at the same time troubled by the use of terror and worried about the future. National Socialism left many people "trembling with joy," *freudeschlotternd*, to use a term spawned by Karl Kraus. Doubts could still linger behind a "Heil Hitler." Those who took the route of "inner emigration" might still harbor secret admiration of the Führer, and this was true even for some Jews. Many people may have joined the party and publicly declared their allegiance to it. Yet in private, among trusted confidants, these same citizens would express their reservations, buying, as it were, a kind of moral reinsurance.

Where can the historian find the sources he needs? Given the nature of the regime, one's private, innermost thoughts would most likely have to be kept in silence. Censors prohibited any kind of open expression of opinion; they also intercepted mail. House searches made the keeping of diaries precarious; the fear of denunciation—by servants or even one's own children—inhibited conversation. For many Germans there was ambivalence; public silence may have covered a measure of private silence. How clear were individuals about their own motives? How vacillating, how cautious were they, even in their own minds? How strongly were they influenced by the behavior of others? How aware were they of their irrational and unconscious drives and desires?[8] There were surely many Germans who were neither for nor against National Socialism, who let themselves be influenced by events, and who, with outward gestures of conformity, bought themselves inner sanctuaries within which they remained undecided and indecisive.

[II]

To understand the appeal of National Socialism and the susceptibility of Germans to it, particularly the susceptibility of the German elite, one must remember immediate social reality and deeper emotional-intellectual stirrings that prepared Germans for belief in an authoritarian savior. I shall mention below the immediate reality—the buffeting of Germans after 1914, especially after 1918; in the previous essay I have talked at length about "the silent secularization" in Protestant Germany, that is to say, in that part of Germany which so overwhelmingly supported Hitler.[9]

Especially in Protestant Germany, Hitler's claim to be the providential savior had a strong resonance. His religious invocations suited a society which for generations had seen the intertwining of the divine and the secular. As religious faith waned, the secular (the nation or the *Volk*) was sanctified. Above all, one was taught to sacrifice for the state, as one once had sacrificed for God, and to yearn for the community of the *Volk*, as one had once been given strength by a congregation of the faithful.[10] National Socialism heightened this identification of nation or racial *Volk* with the divine to still greater dramatic exaltation. National Socialism as "disguised religion" is an old story, both complicated and obfuscating, but one that still alerts us to a reality we cannot ignore. We know that it originated in Catholic Bavaria but found its mass support in the Protestant north and east.

The German elites had a *Lebensgefühl* that made them especially vulnerable to National Socialism, a sense of life that corresponded to psychic needs, material interests, and idealistic intellectual attitudes. This sense of life had long been in the making and took many forms, but it provided the vocabulary with which to explain one's affinity for or at least one's understanding of National Socialism. One powerful strain in this *Lebensgefühl* was an intellectual movement in Europe that has often been called the "conservative revolution" and that had its roots deep in European culture. We can regard it as a kind of yearning for a "healthy" fascism. Nietzsche and Dostoevski were the intellectual ancestors of this revolution, and Lagarde, Langbehn, and Moeller van den Bruck representative examples of it in German life.[11] The rebellion of the German mind against the West, the hatred for Modernism— in economics, politics, art—and for anything that could be described as liberal. All those things had taken hold not only of these three prophets from three different generations but also of many intellectuals, particularly in postwar Germany, where the Treaty of Versailles had only intensified hatred of the West.

But as early as a hundred years ago the new yearnings and the new understanding of man were translated into political terms in France. The key names that come to mind here are LeBon, Sorel, Bergson, and Durkheim, but more important still, Barrès, Maurras, and Édouard Drumont. After 1880, a longing for a radically new society, for a new social commitment and authority, emerged in most of Europe; and with it came a passionate rejection of the existing system, a battle against the modern world per se: its materialism and corruption, its democracy and parliamentary system, its overly tolerant liberalism, its exploitative and purely materialistic capitalism. All that should be cast aside as a betrayal of the true nation. And everything modern was often seen as the work of the Jews. Drumont's *La France juive,* that singular attack on the dominance of the Jews, was one of the most successful books of the late nineteenth century. Maurice Barrès wrote a novel about the uprooted, and the main yearning of those generations was to free themselves from a rootless freedom. They wanted a new religious commitment, a new national order, strong human beings in a united nation. The Germans of that time were already dreaming of a new Caesar, a Führer. These attitudes were widespread among French intellectuals, but political life continued to be dominated by the republican reality, which, for millions of Frenchmen, still retained its own mythology, namely, the ideas of 1789. It would take the defeat of 1940 to bring French fascism closer to achieving power. The earlier, passionate criticism of the republic had not been able to foment a revolution from the Right.[12]

In 1927, Hugo von Hofmannsthal described the essence of the conservative revolution: "It is not freedom they are out to find but communal bonds [*Bindung*]. . . . Never was a German struggle for freedom more passionate and yet more tenacious than this struggle in thousands of souls in the nation for true coercion [*Zwang*], this refusal to surrender to a coercion that was not coercive enough."[13] We must not forget how strong and widespread this longing for new communal bonds and order was. It, too, is a fact we have to take into account; and it, too, was partially responsible for the great echo that fascism found, particularly among intellectuals, when it finally did appear. Fascism had its intellectual disciples just as communism did. Fascism without terror and National Socialism without war and without the persecution of the Jews would perhaps have been even more popular, but war and terror were indispensable ingredients of the new "idealism." To quote Nietzsche again: "The whole great tendency of the Germans went against the Enlightenment,"[14] against rationalism. The belief in a special path for Germany—neither Western civilization nor Eastern barbarism, neither capitalism nor Marxism—was incredibly strong and persistent.

In the final years of the Weimar Republic, right-wing intellectuals achieved considerable prominence with books and pamphlets that often bore the mark of Spengler's and Moeller van den Bruck's thoughts. Spengler's idea of a "Prussian socialism," a rigorous, authoritarian socialism that was based on national community and not on the Marxist class struggle, was often confused with National Socialism. Hans Zehrer's circle at *Die Tat* and Edgar Jung's *Herrschaft der Minderwertigkeiten* (Rule by Mediocrity), a single-minded attack on the parliamentary system, fall into this line as well. After the presidential election of 1932, Jung wrote that what was at stake in it was "the liquidation of Weimar liberalism along with its defeatism in both domestic and foreign policy. This moribund liberalism was in dreadful condition. . . . We are pleased not only . . . over the National Socialists' growing constituency but we have done our best to contribute to that growth. Working patiently with small groups and one-on-one, particularly among the educated classes, we helped prepare for that day when the German people gave their votes to National Socialist candidates. . . ."[15] Just two years later, after he had written a speech for Franz von Papen denouncing the "unnatural totalitarian claims" of National Socialism, the National Socialists murdered Edgar Jung on July 1, 1934. Despite his rejection of the Weimar "system" and despite his avowals of 1932, Jung became an early and determined opponent of the National Socialists, and he was one of their first victims from the ranks of the conservative revolution.

In 1931 Hans Freyer, the well-known German sociologist, published *Revolution von Rechts.* Freyer's career has an almost paradigmatic quality. The son of a Protestant minister, he began studying theology but then switched over to the humanities and sociology. All his life he wanted to be a kind of minister to the national soul and tried, with his activist scholarship, to lead Germans toward a new national community. The youth movement had formed his speech and manner, which is to say that he passionately opposed liberal, bourgeois, materialistic society, both from intellectual conviction and from his own existential experience. In *Revolution von Rechts,* he invoked the historic necessity for a conservative revolutionary solution—this at the very moment when Lucifer was at the gates. Freyer, who was a professor at the University of Leipzig, did not officially embrace National Socialism before 1933; but, without mentioning the party or the Führer in his tract, he argued for *his* idea of National Socialism. At that time it was prohibited for civil servants or soldiers to join either the NSDAP or the Communists. But Freyer's antidemocratic arguments, his call for an authoritarian state that would do away with class struggle, his nationalistic passion, and his activist's style all suggested leanings toward Hitler's NSDAP. After Hitler assumed power, Freyer praised National Socialism both as the crowning achievement of the anti-modernist cultural aspirations and of the youth movement of the nineteenth century and as a recognition of the unique meaning of political leadership. The National Socialists eventually came to mistrust him and considered him an opportunist. After a few years of zeal, Freyer's enthusiasm waned. For many who came from the ranks of the conservative revolution, the fulfillment that National Socialism brought them at first turned to disappointment in the end.[16]

The so-called conservative revolution and National Socialism had much in common: their critique of the existing system, their call for a national community, their striving for a new faith. But the conservative revolution remained only theory and dream; it fought solely with ideas. Nevertheless, its advocates did National Socialism a great service. It was they who led the upper classes into the Third Reich. Thomas Mann called them the "bellwethers of misery" and felt no sympathy for their fate.[17] The disciples of the conservative revolution were disappointed by the reality of National Socialism. In history as in life, to achieve a long-sought goal can bring about great disappointment: reality is less perfect than the long-cherished dream.

The temptation of Christ in the Bible came after forty days and forty nights in the wilderness. In the last years of the Weimar Republic, many Germans felt as if they were in a wilderness—lost, desiccated, in mortal peril. They had suffered a defeat which had left them enraged and humiliated, an inflation which had expropriated the middle classes and which could be blamed on the vengeful victors of Versailles and from which, it was alleged, a few Jews and other greedy entrepreneurs profited. Finally they were overwhelmed by the Great Depression, which, by 1932, had put six million people out of work. A divided and uncomprehending people felt lost and anxious; intellectuals of all stripes felt that the "bourgeois epoch" was finished; in 1932 Karl Jaspers wrote that what was real was "the consciousness of danger and of loss."[18] By the early 1930s, the intellectuals' feeling, long nurtured, that bourgeois society was, and deserved to be, doomed, coincided with a people's realization that a political and economic system had broken down. In that kind of wilderness, the promise of deliverance—however empty of all practicality—proved tempting and beguiling.

Weimar was heir to all the debts, material and psychic, of the Great War, and National Socialism was nothing more than a continuation of the war and of the war psychosis by other means. Weimar remains to this day the classic example of a polarized democracy gone awry, the embodiment of political dissension, inadequate leadership, and lack of consensus. Only a few were aware that the Weimar Republic—in Gustav Stresemann's time, for example—had weathered great crises and even scored significant successes. After 1930 and in a deepening economic crisis, Germans of all parties were calling for greater governmental authority.

The consequences of the Depression were catastrophic, and the elites were afraid that material misery might explode into political radicalism. What Germany needed then was a DeGaulle who, in a conservative democratic way, could have given the country a new and solid government and at the same time could have made use of resourceful leadership to win respect for that government. But there was no German DeGaulle, or his role was divided among several players. And then on top of Depression and hopelessness came a permanent crisis in public life. At the end of Weimar, feeble governments, lacking popular support, could not stop the ever more pervasive street fighting, which began to approximate a civil war in miniature.

[III]

The National Socialists scored their first great successes—winning, for example, large numbers of students to their cause—even before the Great Depression. The election of 1930 confirmed those successes. It represented the real breakthrough of National Socialism, a breakthrough in which the young played a major role. The new voters at that time were children of the First World War who had had to grow up without fathers. Faced with a new crisis, they turned to a strong leader for safety.[19] But the confidence of the older generations was shaken, too; and in their fears for the future, millions of mature Germans fell prey to National Socialism.

Even after the election of 1930, which made the National Socialists the second strongest party in the Reichstag, a democratic coalition could have tried to master this crisis in government. It would have required cooperation between the Social Democrats and the Catholic Center, but powerful political and business interests wanted to exploit the crisis to establish an authoritarian government and weaken the Social Democrats and the working class. Hitler had been the first politician who had been able to mobilize a mass army large enough to initiate a major shift in the nation's political life. Now, others were hoping to deploy his troops for their own purposes.

For two years the National Socialists had been attracting new votes, and it was only Hindenburg's resistance that had kept them out of power. In November 1932, in the fourth national election of that year amidst electoral weariness, they suffered their first major setback, which left the party in disarray and financial distress, and even as perspicacious and knowledgeable an observer as Konrad Heiden felt that the party's inner splits and the effort of holding its ground would soon bring it down. In a kind of funeral oration, Heiden recognized that National Socialism would not disappear without leaving to the nation a legacy of "political passion." "This passion has given rise to innumerable misdeeds and outrages, but it has also spared our country from an excess of political sobriety. . . . [National Socialism] has done the nation much harm but also much good, even if its only service were to have been to express better than any other movement the German propensity for the absurd. And that it has done in its march without a destination, its inebriation without delirium, its faith without a god, and—even in its worst aspect—its thirst for blood without satisfaction."[20] National Socialism had revived the nation's passion, the same passion that had gripped it in August 1914.

Political passions and economic misery dominated the last years of the Weimar Republic. The extremist parties—the NSDAP and the Communists—worked together in common cause against the republic. The collapse of the Weimar Republic and the rise of National Socialism were two distinct but also related processes. The elite classes despaired of a republic they had never cared for and aligned themselves more and more with National Socialism on its triumphal march.

Tübingen illustrates the successes of National Socialism and the susceptibility of the elite classes to it. We have documentation concerning that city that is instructive; it can serve in what Max Weber called an ideal-typical function. What happened in Tübingen illuminates the complicated process of Nazification. The majority of the professors in Tübingen were opponents of the Weimar Republic. Their political orientation was nationalistic, which meant at the time that they rejected and despised the existing government. To be nationalistic was to be against democracy, against the party system, against the so-called November Revolution, and, of course, against the Treaty of Versailles and the humiliation of Germany that had been brought about by the notorious stab in the back. In addition to all that came a rejection of Marxism and Social Democracy and a mortal terror of Bolshevism. More often than not, there was also a touch of anti-Semitism, an unpleasant feeling that the Jews represented an un-German element, disorderly, pushy, divisive. Theodor Eschenburg, who came to Tübingen in 1924, recalls the "antidemocratic attitudes" and the "scorn for the Republic" that the leading historians blithely passed on to their students in their lectures. "This combination of scholarship and vindictiveness was a dangerous thing. . . . Anyone who confessed allegiance to democracy and affirmed it, even in private, was regarded by most of the faculty as socially suspect."[21] It is therefore not surprising that in 1932 the Tübingen National Socialist Student Association, founded in 1926, had won as much as 50 percent of the seats in the student parliament and that the faculty senate's dealings with the National Socialist Student Association were characterized by "nervous opportunism and elaborately disguised sympathies."* And as the university went, so went the city. In July 1932 the National Socialists won 40 percent of the vote in Tübingen, a somewhat higher percentage than they captured in the country as a whole. Many of the prominent Protestant ministers of the city had also gone over to National Socialism.[22]† After January 30, 1933, the university itself fell into line very quickly, and many professors who until then had been sympathizers with the party hastened to join its ranks. At the time, these latecomers were called the March casualties or the *Spätlese* 1933.

But it is part of the contradictoriness of German life that Tübingen was also the university where eleven of the victims of the July 20, 1944, plot studied, among them Klaus and Dietrich Bonhoeffer, Carl Goerdeler, and Berthold Schenck von Stauffenberg. On July 20, 1984, forty years later, a memorial to them was finally dedicated. It reads: "Students at the University of Tübingen in their youth, they and others died for their resistance against National Socialism."

Tübingen was the rule rather than the exception. The great

* Throughout Germany, the student elections of 1928–1930 were decisively pro-Nazi, far in excess of the party's national electoral strength. The students had grown up in the deprivation of the war; their teachers—authoritarian figures—had contempt for the republic, and the young were enthralled by National Socialism. In turn, they infected their teachers as well. The teachers' envy of the young, the admiration for their "idealism," while they were embarrassed by their own bourgeois tenured security, was considerable.
† A theologian recently related an experience of his in Tübingen during the early 1950s. He was a student in Hans Rothfels's graduate seminar on the Third Reich. Waldemar Besson, who was the instructor leading the discussion, came into the seminar one day, and, pointing to each of the students one by one with his great vitality and conviction, he said: If you had been at the critical age in 1933, then you would have belonged to the SA, and you to the Gestapo, and you would have cooperated too, and so on. That is how enthralling Besson recognized the attractions of National Socialism to have been. In any case, it was an extraordinary thing in postwar Germany to speak so openly and honestly about the temptation of National Socialism. None of us is immune to temptation, and that message is all the more powerful when it comes from someone like Waldemar Besson, who, in his character and in his every deed, has been a model German democrat.

majority of German professors rejected the Weimar Republic. Friedrich Meinecke, himself a republican by default, a republican who saw no rational alternative, thought in 1926 to bring together a few university professors willing to proclaim their support of the constitution, not even of the Republic as such or any specific government. He hoped only for a handful of supporters—such was the climate in most of the faculties.

The rejection of the Weimar Republic extended far beyond university professors and the right-wing parties.* The elite classes had suffered both material and psychic losses from the collapse of the empire. The nobility, the agrarian landowners, the military, the church, and the old educated and propertied upper class lost many of their privileges. New forces were in the ascendancy: Social Democrats, workers, leftist intellectuals, and Jews. "Western" democracy had been scorned before the defeat of 1918 brought it to Germany; it was therefore easier to hold the actual in contempt, to renounce the veneration of the state [*Staatsfrömmigkeit*] which had characterized Germans under the old regime. The rejection of the Republic could be turned into an idealistic repudiation of parliamentary divisiveness, mediocrity, corruption, political impotence. No doubt for many it was an aesthetic judgment, but for most of the elite it sprang as well from deep anxieties about status and power. The elites known as the class of *Bildung und Besitz* felt themselves disinherited in the Republic and diminished in a political culture where their a priori claims to preeminence seemed undermined by "vulgar" concern for vote-getting, for all the trappings of "mass democracy." The glorious (and disastrous) authority of the Kaiser was gone. In its place came rather pale though able professional politicians, and at the same time the old imperial civil service remained in place and obstructed the work of the Republic without improving its status in the public eye. The basic mood of

* Independents as well as leftists despaired of the Republic, too. After endless squabbling in the Division for Literature in the Prussian Academy of Arts—in which Thomas Mann did repeated battle with nationalistic writers—Hermann Hesse decided to resign from the division and wrote to Mann in late 1931 about his "deep mistrust of the German republic. This spineless and mindless state arose out of a vacuum. . . . The few good minds of the 'revolution,' which was no revolution at all, were beaten to death, with the approval of 99 percent of the population. The courts are unjust; the civil servants, indifferent; the people, totally infantile. . . . In short, I find myself as far removed from the mentality that dominates Germany now as I did in the years 1914–1918." Quoted by Inge Jens, *Dichter zwischen Rechts und Links: Die Geschichte der Sektion für Dichtkunst der Preussischen Akademie der Künste dargestellt nach Dokumenten* (Munich, 1971), p. 124.

the elite classes was resentment and ill will. These feelings were expressed in the rhetoric of the German ideology, in old anti-Western attitudes, and in cultural pessimism.

Rejection of Weimar did not have to lead to National Socialism, but that conscious rejection along with the often unconscious dissatisfaction associated with the tacitly accepted secularization of Protestantism increased susceptibility to it. At the end of the 1920s most members of the elite classes regarded National Socialism with varying degrees of sympathy and took a wait-and-see attitude toward it. They were uncertain but at the same time impressed and hopeful. Probably many of them were ashamed of the temptation they felt.

Klaus Scholder has described the reaction within the Protestant churches, divided as these were. There was no single authority within Protestantism and no hierarchical order. Still, it is fair to say that official Protestantism felt homeless in the Weimar Republic, deprived of its official standing in the old monarchical order, terrified of the alliance between Marxism and Catholicism. Protestantism was overwhelmingly conservative and nationalistic; the religious socialists were a small, valiant band battling a powerful orthodoxy. By 1930 the question of the churches' response to National Socialism became central. Officially there was political neutrality, but a sect within Protestantism, the Deutsche Christen, espoused National Socialism, sought to repudiate the Old Testament, and thought of themselves as "the SA of Christ." But outside this extremist group, there was much sympathy as well. In March 1931 the largest church publication, *Allgemeine Evangelisch-Lutherische Kirchenzeitung*, described National Socialism as "an uprising of German youth who were deeply affected by the shame of the fatherland, who hated and abhorred the poisoning of German thought by foreigners, and who had emblazoned the old virtues of truthfulness, honor, and loyalty on their banners." A month later the bishop of Mecklenburg declared: "Many members of the evangelical church live today with all their thought and feeling in the National Socialist movement. . . . The National Socialist movement affirms with passion the social commitment, the idea of brotherhood." The bishop admonished the church to "welcome gratefully the great purpose of the National Socialist movement but at the same time, above this purpose, which is human, hence incomplete and broken, it must proclaim the divine will of God."[23]

After the presidential elections of 1932, the authoritative *Neue Zürcher Zeitung* noted that National Socialism flourished primarily in Protestant areas: "Of course the evangelical church as such did not take a political stand. It remains neutral, but still it is a fact that in the entire Reich many of its leading personalities, especially among the clergy, particularly among the younger members of the clergy, sympathize with Hitler or openly work for his party."[24]

Neither Paul Tillich and the religious socialists nor Karl Barth's followers had much success in countering this tendency. Richard Karwehl, one of Barth's students, saw in National Socialism nothing but "baldfaced messianism." But the church had abdicated responsibility: "There [in National Socialism] is where the power, the passion, the piety is now. That is where the martyrs are, even if they are secular martyrs. National Socialism is unabashedly eschatological. . . . The church, on the other hand, cultivates a Christianity of individual salvation along with petty bourgeois ideology and ecclesiastical complacency."[25] In a radio speech on February 1, 1933, Dietrich Bonhoeffer warned against the confusion of Führer and Messiah: "Where the *Volksgeist* is regarded as a divine-metaphysical sublimity, there the Führer who embodies this *Geist* has in the true sense a religious function, there he is the Messiah and hence with his appearance the fulfillment of the final hope has begun, then the Reich which he must bring forth with himself, already comes close to the eternal Reich." If the Führer allows himself to become the idol of his followers, "then the picture of the Führer slides into that of the corrupter [dann gleitet das Bild des Führers über in das des Verführers], then he acts criminally against the led as well as against himself."[26] Bonhoeffer was one of the first to see the incompatibility of Christianity and Nazi totalitarian presumption and racial dogma. Under increasing Nazi pressure on the church, others came to see the conflict as well—and adjusted to it in different ways. Still, Bonhoeffer was an exception in his vision, faith, and courage.

The Catholic world was also divided. The Center Party was an arch-rival of National Socialism, but at the same time, for tactical reasons, had to contemplate a coalition with it. The German hierarchy was reserved, some of the older bishops troubled by the totalitarian claims of the movement, some of the younger clergy swept up by the fervor of the movement and by its fight against Marxism and Judaism. The papacy, with Eugenio Pacelli as secretary of state, flushed by its—illusory—success in concluding the Lateran Treaties with Mussolini, was seized by an anti-Communist fervor. The great authoritarian church did not speak with one voice before 1933—or after.

There were conflicting views in all Christian churches and from none came a resounding declaration that Hitler was the anti-Christ. In all, in fact, there was affinity between Hitler's program and the churches' hopes to extrude "Judaic-secular-Marxist" elements. The churches could have listened to the voices in their own ranks, that National Socialism was a pseudo-religion, hence especially dangerous. But in the early 1930s the churches were devoutly conservative and did not wish to acknowledge the radical quality of Hitler or of fascism. They were afraid not only of Jewish influence or of the Communist danger but of each other as well.* On balance, for all the official avowals of neutrality, for all the misgivings of many clergymen, the power of the clergy favored rather than hindered the avoidable rise of Hitler.

The despair over Weimar and the temptation of National Socialism were pervasive, particularly striking among those men who in 1944 gave their lives in the vain attempt to eliminate Hitler. Thus in the early 1930s, Carl Goerdeler thought that the state had failed, that it was no longer capable of doing its job.[27] Johannes Popitz described Weimar as "an impotent government, alienated from the nation, with an incoherent, polycratic constitution that is a constitution in name only. . . . The only possible path is the path of revolution."[28] Both these men would later join the resistance against Hitler. Hans Mommsen thinks that "the fact of the NSDAP's success in winning adherents from the ranks of the civil service from 1929 on" casts light on "the deep crisis of the republican government."[29] The military was pleased to see in National Socialism a revival of nationalism and a promise to undo the Treaty of Versailles. From 1930 on, General Ludwig Beck, who would later be the key figure in the resistance, saw "a National Socialist assumption of power as the only hope for Germany." He had been delighted with the National Socialist victory in the elections of

---

* In his Easter message of 1928, the General Superintendent of the Kurmark, Otto Dibelius, wrote: "I have always regarded myself as an anti-semite. The fact cannot be concealed that the Jews have played a leading role in all the symptoms of disintegration in modern civilization." John S. Conway, "National Socialism and the Christian Churches During the Weimar Republic," *The Nazi Machtergreifung*, ed. Peter D. Stachura (London, 1983), p. 141.

September 1930. He believed that the NSDAP victory was the first great ray of light since 1914; the army and the party saw eye to eye in many respects: "An authoritarian state, abolition of the parliament, restoration of the people's armed preparedness, the army as the bearer of this national idea, and, therefore, the special role that falls to the army in the state."[30]

That National Socialism could—for a short time—tempt even the most genuinely idealistic youth is exemplified by Fritzi von der Schulenburg. A devout Protestant, he was appalled by the Weimar Republic, by its corrupting and ineffectual character, by "the dark forces"—probably Jews—that stood behind the parties. He believed in an idealized Prussia that had never existed and in the regenerative hopes of the "conservative revolution." In 1932, he joined the NSDAP and asserted: "I believe firmly in the *idea* [of National Socialism] . . . and I will stick by it, unless it should betray the people and their faith." He saw the subsequent betrayal at close quarters, and he recoiled. He retained his belief in Germany's destiny as Europe's hegemonial power and as civilizing ruler over most of Eastern Europe. But in a gradual, painful process, he broke with the regime and became a key figure in the July 20 conspiracy against Hitler. The motives that led him to embrace National Socialism also inspired his repudiation: a man of passionate integrity who had fallen victim to an evil that devoured souls.[31]

Even before 1933, the National Socialists had made deep inroads within the ranks of the German elites. Hitler knew how to cultivate their vulnerabilities, how to reassure the elites that he was a German nationalist, the true redeemer. Most Germans judged National Socialism from the perspective of their own experience and interests; they saw what fitted their needs. Above all, as Karl Löwith noted, the Germans excelled in celebrating the "idea" and ignoring any unpleasant fact. Hence one could embrace the party and bemoan "excesses."[32] Hence also the diverse images of the movement. Adherents and opponents shared one error: They underestimated the power and the violence of National Socialism.

In the crisis atmosphere of late Weimar, where economic disaster was coupled with political bankruptcy, most Germans shrank back to some kind of collective regression. They saw National Socialism which was radically new as an exaggerated version of something old and familiar. The Social Democrats failed to grasp the psychological power of the movement, thinking that it was Bismarckian repression writ large. The Communists have failed to understand it to this very day, and there is nothing in Marxism that explains the psychological power of a pseudo-religious movement.

The politicians of the right-wing parties saw Hitler as their drummer boy. They, too, had given Hitler much-needed respectability, beginning in 1929, when he was invited to join the hate-filled referendum against the Young Plan. Sympathetic to his goals—if not always to his means—they hoped to use his mass following for their own purposes. They thought they could take Hitler captive—and many opponents of his also thought of him as a mere tool of frightened capitalists or of unpopular reactionaries. Most Germans underestimated the radical, socialist wing of the movement, but in his few weeks as chancellor, Kurt von Schleicher hoped to split the NSDAP in order to bring together union leaders and the radical wing of the NSDAP in a coalition that could develop a rational economic policy. But Franz von Papen, the arch-intriguer, engineered his downfall and convinced President von Hindenburg to appoint Hitler chancellor. With the National Socialists a minority in the cabinet, Papen argued, Hitler would be given responsibility but no power. That, of course, was the most brainless illusion of all, the epitome of the often willful, often desperate misperception of Hitler. It was his genius to encourage illusion—until he could crush those who had cherished it.

[IV]

With dazzling dramaturgical talent, Hitler and his men transformed political intrigue into "the seizure of power," celebrated by a triumphant and unprecedented demonstration of national renewal. From the first day of his chancellorship, he knew what he wanted: absolute power and the elimination of his enemies, real or imaginary. He proceeded by stealth, terror, and seduction, and his most astounding talent was the instant exploitation of opportunities created for him by others. His actions reflected his character; periods of indolence and passivity alternated with lightning decisions. His chief lieutenants were well chosen. They too had a flair for theatricality and an instinctive will to exercise organized, sadistic terror.

At first, stealth predominated. Two days after his assumption of power Hitler addressed the nation by radio. His message was reassuring, traditionally nationalistic; he ended with an appeal for the Almighty's guidance. There were three characteristic aspects to those early days:

1. The commitment, repeatedly stressed, to national tradition, to continuity. Then in March, this tradition was celebrated in Potsdam with unprecedented pomp. Now National Socialism was worthy of the responsibility it had assumed. Germans could once again identify with the state and its power—and nourish nationalistic hopes.

2. Cleverly, the National Socialists cojoined tradition with the promise of a new order, of an historic breakthrough [*Umbruch*], of a national revival and renewal. Most Germans—and especially the elites—were impressed by this eruption of national passion, by the unexpected renewal of the spirit of August 1914; only a few remembered that August 1914 was the prelude to disaster. Hitler's own unlikely rise from obscurity to savior seemed a warrant of this magical breakthrough.* In a sense, by promising a "breakthrough" to tradition, the National Socialists dramatized what they hoped to achieve—and, in a measure, did achieve: the restoration of order, hope, decisive leadership, politics as a continuous drama, the feeling, again as during the war, of identification with the *Volk* or the community. One rejoiced in a sense of power and purpose by proxy or projection, while in fact living in—often unconscious—impotence.

3. Terror: the SA cellars where beatings and murders took place; the public announcement in March 1933 of the existence of concentration camps; the beginning of the National Socialist consolidation of power by means of threats, seduction, intimidation.

Within the first few weeks Hitler had established his absolute dictatorship. He did so by that diabolical simultaneity of reassuring the old elites and silencing or terrorizing most would-be opponents. A decisive moment came with the Reichstag fire in late February 1933: in brilliant, improvised response, Hitler persuaded Hindenburg to sign emergency decrees that virtually ended all civic rights

---

* His detractors often referred to his obscurity by calling him "the Bohemian corporal"—in derisive recognition of his Austrian origins, his wartime rank—and in deliberate recollection of another "corporal," Napoleon, who, one surmised, had been an authentic hero.

that the Weimar Constitution had granted. This was the "legal" basis for a terror that was now unleashed, at first against the political opponents of the regime, most especially against the Communists. So instant and decisive was the response that for decades people assumed the Nazis themselves had set the fire; it is only recently—after a long controversy—that it would seem clear that the deranged Dutchman van der Lubbe was the sole culprit.*

The nation was now being whipped into conformity: *Gleich-schaltung†* was the official designation. The work of terror was carried out more easily because units of the SA and SS were formally turned into "auxiliary police." The SA cellars became chambers of torture and murder, the improvised forerunners of the concentration camps that were established in March 1933. At the same time Goebbels was made minister of propaganda, and the regime captured the media and imposed ever more stringent censorship.

But "self-imposed conformity," often unconscious, kept pace with Hitler, and nowhere was this more striking than in the German universities, which had always boasted of their autonomy. This self-surrender of the intellectual elite recalls Sigmund Freud's sense of why in the Great War "the best intellects" demonstrated "their uncritical credulity towards the most disputable assertions. . . . Students of human nature and philosophers have long taught us that we are mistaken in regarding our intelligence as an independent force and in overlooking its dependence on emotional life. Our intellect, they teach us, can function reliably only when

---

* In early March, in this atmosphere of frenzy, elections were held, and Hitler's party won 44 percent of the vote—a result that is still being differently assessed. Some see the result as confirmation of a people's complicity, others emphasize that despite unprecedented pressure, over half the people withheld their vote from Hitler. A few weeks later, only the Socialists opposed the Enabling Law which, still more or less legally, gave Hitler's government four years of non-parliamentary rule. [The Communist deputies were already imprisoned.]

† Gordon Craig writes of *Gleichschaltung*, "literally, 'putting into the same gear'—a word so cryptic and impersonal that it conveys no sense of the injustice, the terror, and the bloodshed that it embraced." Basically it meant the effort to eliminate opposition and enforce conformity, *inter alia*, the elimination—by decree or murder—of any opposition. Gordon A. Craig, *Germany 1866–1945* (Oxford, 1978), p. 578. Of course, most societies generate some such pressure. I was struck by C. Vann Woodward's description of the American South in the 1930s: "Few were able or willing to speak out. Those who did seemed to me to speak in too mild a voice. The thing was that they lived under powerful inhibitions." The outside pressure came from critical Northern stereotypes about Southern roughness. "The outside source of this *regimented conformity* was an outside as perceived and distorted from the inside. . . ." (My italics.) *Thinking Back: The Perils of Writing History* (Baton Rouge, La., and London, 1986), pp. 14–15.

it is removed from the influences of strong emotional impulses; otherwise it behaves merely as an instrument of the will and delivers the inference which the will requires. Thus, in their view, logical arguments are impotent against affective interests. . . ."[33] These "affective interests" had as much to do with the self-surrender to National Socialism as other interests; cold calculation or opportunism offers only partial explanation. It is ironic to think that many German professors would have applauded Freud's assessment of the power of affect over intellect—if only it had not come from the pen of this terrible Jew.

The temptation was to adapt, to participate, to join the party, to support it enthusiastically—and all that despite the SA cellars, the persecutions, the loss of civic rights for some; despite the book burning, despite the elimination of Jews and "the politically unreliable" from posts in universities and other parts of the civil service. Despite these attacks on the traditional rule of law and on the honor of scholarship, most professors—as they had in 1914— immediately and passionately espoused the national cause, the German renewal. This outpouring of support was of course in part a product of human weakness, of fear of reprisal, of careerism. But opportunism alone does not explain this behavior. (Opportunism, moreover, is a thoroughly uninteresting subject.)

We must not forget either that in the first weeks of the new regime the possibility of cautious criticism still existed without the price of martyrdom. It was a period in which the National Socialists themselves were still uncertain, in which the new wielders of power attacked Communists, Social Democrats, and prominent Jews with massive violence but were cautious and experimental in their dealings with "respectable" people. Signs of protest came from various groups. Workers handed out fliers; business leaders grumbled among themselves; conservatives retreated. Some bourgeois newspapers continued their criticism. Wilhelm Furtwängler sent Goebbels a letter of protest in which he complained about the exclusion of Jewish artists. Nothing happened to him. The co-founder of Gestalt psychology, Wolfgang Köhler, published an open letter protesting dismissals on racial grounds.[34] In March 1933, Alfred Weber ordered the removal of the swastika flag from the roof of his Institute at Heidelberg; he was put on leave for the summer semester of 1933, and thereafter retired at his request. But nothing else happened to him.[35]

There were other examples—and all of these must be kept in mind as one tries to re-create the moral atmosphere of the time. In 1933, Ewald von Kleist-Schmenzien, who would later participate in the resistance and lose his life, suggested to Ernst Niekisch an idea for an underground broadsheet, with the text: "The future will say of us: Without character, like a German civil servant. Without God, like a Protestant minister. Without honor, like a Prussian officer."[36] Those words represented a clean break with his own upper class. The conservative industrialist Emil Kirdorf wrote an open letter to the *Rheinisch-Westfälische Zeitung* in which he bitterly protested the removal of his non-Aryan colleague Paul Silverberg from the chair of the Cologne Chamber of Commerce. "I consider the inhuman enormity of this continuing anti-Semitic harassment a crime. A large number of men who have served Germany well . . . have been stripped of their rightful status in a dreadful fashion. . . . The stab in the back administered to this valuable man has struck me, too. My faith, my hopes of ever seeing a new, pure, and proud Germany emerge are now completely dashed."[37] In January 1935, as we have seen, Max Planck, together with Max von Laue, Otto Hahn, and the physicist Karl Friedrich Bonhoeffer, decided to hold a memorial service for the non-Aryan chemist Fritz Haber on the anniversary of his death in exile the year before. The Ministry of Education was enraged and forbade all professors to attend the service. It took place nonetheless in a fully packed Harnack House at the University of Berlin. Planck concluded his speech with these words: "Haber remained loyal to us; we will remain loyal to him."[38] Might they not serve as an admonishment for all the speeches that were not given?

Instances of instant submission were far more typical. Examples abound. It was a "mass" phenomenon that afflicted the elites. The Germans called it *Selbst-Gleichschaltung*, a term that fortunately has no English equivalent. It signifies voluntary, preemptive acceptance of the conformity ordered or expected by the regime. It signifies submission out of a whole range of motives. Bruno Walter was barred from conducting in the Gewandhaus in Leipzig, and from the Philharmonic in Berlin. As Walter recalled, at the last minute Richard Strauss took over: "The composer of *Ein Heldenleben* actually declared himself ready to conduct in place of a forcibly removed colleague."[39] Strauss had his later quarrels with the regime. Ambivalent responses and contradictory conduct were daily occurrences; so were public deference and private decency or some private gesture to appease conscience. Gerhard Ritter, arch-conservative historian, devout Protestant and defender of the Confessional Church, imprisoned in 1944 by the Gestapo, was appalled when in 1935 his former teacher Hermann Oncken was publicly attacked. Privately, Ritter wrote Oncken: "You are being covered with mud because you are the only one of our guild who dared to begin an *offensive* defensive of our discipline and to stand up for the truth while the great mass of our collegial mob waves the incense censer." He lamented "the cowardice of our gentlemen-colleagues," which he thought "a very remarkable fact," but at the same time Ritter himself was filled with a self-acknowledged sense of Lutheran obedience to secular authority. The whole Oncken episode has a symptomatic character. Ritter's effort to write a professional review of Oncken's collection of essays was in effect blocked by various institutional, not personal, threats. The regime had a calibrated sense of how to apply censorship and terror, which encouraged voluntary submission.[40]

The dictatorship was at once novel and intimidating. The response to it encompassed the whole gamut of human and political attitudes. It is relatively easy to fix the extremes: Millions of Germans were devoted and unquestioned followers of National Socialism; a few were principled, unwavering opponents. Not everybody in the Third Reich had to make choices, but many did, especially those in responsible positions, those with earlier contact with Jewish friends or colleagues or those with earlier liberal-democratic inclinations. Many of them were torn between con-science and prudence, beset by doubts and ever ready for little compromises on either side of conformity. There were shifting loyalties, admiration for the regime's decisiveness and successes, misgivings about its excesses, careerism, gratification at having others act out one's aggressive or resentful feelings. There was indecision, equivocation, evasion. The response sprang from con-scious and unconscious, from rational and irrational sources. In itself temptation was a challenge to thought and feelings.

Only those men and women who had some very strong faith of their own could have been altogether immune to the temptations of National Socialism. For most the appeal to German nationalism and the sense of renewed power and purpose reawakened old hopes. Germans were once again a nation to be reckoned with.

Hitler seemed to assuage the wounded pride, the past humiliations, and his promise to end the "fulfillment policy" of Weimar, i.e., the fulfilling of the provisions of Versailles, impressed Germans. There was relief as well that political uncertainty was a thing of the past. People felt "swept up" by a new wave of hope and expectation. Consciously or unconsciously they welcomed the "liberation" from political responsibility. After all, a great many Germans had been taught that "politics" was base; they had been proud of being apolitical. In short, the enthusiasm many Germans felt for the Führer and for national renewal was often genuine, though just as often plagued by doubt as well.

There was fear of power and delight in it. People believed in the new national community and did not want to be outsiders in a country where the hoisting of flags and the wearing of uniforms, where swastika pins on lapels and the greeting "Heil Hitler" were creating a publicly celebrated and apparently classless society. Professors did not want to lag behind their students and were experiencing the usual guilt feelings endemic to their trade, the repressed desire for power and recognition, the need to serve and obey. The desire to belong was immense, as was the fear of exclusion. In his courage and decency, the physicist Max von Laue stood out in many ways; it was said of him that he never left his home without carrying two briefcases—so as not to have to give the Hitler salute. Apocryphal, perhaps, but telling.

The regime's atrocities were well known, and the usual self-deceptive platitudes were rolled out to gloss over them: You can't make an omelet without breaking eggs. You have to go along with things so you can prevent worse things from happening in the future. These are excesses that will disappear once normality is restored; Hitler does not know of these regrettable outbursts. Things will get better. The forces of renewal need us; we can't abandon them now. Art is sublime, not to be polluted by politics. You stay in your job or work toward a better one so you can influence the system from within.

When a friend of one of Germany's most celebrated writers, Gerhart Hauptmann, spoke with him in 1934 about the fate of the Jews in the Third Reich, Hauptmann responded, "A few Eastern Jews—my God, they're not so important." To himself, this friend added, however, "He has forgotten—and wants to forget—that dozens of his former Jewish friends are in concentration camps or are living abroad as emigrants."[41]* When Hjalmar Schacht became minister of economics in 1935, Erich Ebermayer wrote in his journal: "Schacht is no National Socialist at heart, either. . . . Why [this great, indeed this brilliant man] is putting his talents at the Nazis' disposal in such a prominent position is inexplicable, or perhaps it is just as easy to explain as it is in Gruendgen's case: [Is it] ambition, lust for power, for independence, for achievement? Or to work secretly against the regime?"[42]

Anti-Semitism had always been widespread in the German upper classes. In that context, Hauptmann's remark hardly comes as a surprise, and it is understandable how so many found it so easy to put the fate of the Jews out of their minds or to make light of it or to claim that the Jews did not deserve any better, especially since they had always been different. The anti-Semitism of the upper classes was part of good form, part of what I have called vulgar idealism (*Vulgäridealismus*), and for many it paved the way either for accepting the radical anti-Semitism of the regime or for shutting one's eyes to the ever-worsening persecutions.[43]

The universities surrendered quickly. A few deans and rectors were removed from their posts, if for no other reason than to keep the others in line. Martin Heidegger's hymn of praise for national renewal, delivered in his rector's speech in the spring of 1933, is well known but astonishing when we consider how close he had been to his Jewish teacher Edmund Husserl (to whom in 1927 he had dedicated his work "in admiration and friendship") and to Hannah Arendt, whose lover he had been. (When Husserl died in 1938, Heidegger said nothing, either publicly or privately.)[44] There are hundreds, perhaps thousands, of versions of a speech that Ernst Bertram, a Cologne Germanist from the Stefan George circle, gave on May 3, 1933. Bertram's title was "German Awakening," and he declared that with the National Socialist assumption of power "mighty forces [have been] released in our nation. They have worked a marvelous transformation in our people and country. The long awaited battle of liberation from an internal alien rule . . . has been won. . . . And once again, as so

---

* On May 9, 1933, Thomas Mann lamented that Hauptmann, "This man of the Republic, friend of Ebert and Rathenau, who owes his stature and his greatness to Jews," had hoisted the swastika. "I hate this idol whom I helped to magnify, and who magnificently rejects a martyrdom that I also feel I was not born for, but which I am driven to embrace for the sake of intellectual integrity." *Diaries 1918–1939* (New York, 1982), p. 157.

often before, the world is confronted, in hatred or fear, with a Germanic miracle."[45] How often the Almighty was praised and thanked for this Germanic miracle by the name of Adolf Hitler! It was characteristic for Bertram and for that time that after his public espousal of National Socialism he tried repeatedly to communicate privately with his old and close friend Thomas Mann, even though Mann was already living in exile. Finally, Mann wrote to him in November 1933, "Dear Bertram, I wish you well in your nationalistic glass house, isolated from the truth by a brutality that is so utterly alien to you!"[46]

There is ample evidence showing that the pseudo-religious aspect of National Socialism had great appeal. Nationalistic and folk elements had often been surrounded with a religious nimbus ever since the founding of Bismarck's Reich, and this dreadful blending of Hitler's person with the mysterious and the religious had its origins far back in German history. As early as April 1933 Thomas Mann wrote about "this ludicrous tin god [*diesem vergötzten Popanz*] . . . Hitler, who has become a religion for millions."[47]

Carl Friedrich von Weizsäcker wrote me in 1982: "It is true that I could not develop any interest in the Nazis' ideology either before or after their assumption of power. Nonetheless, I was very much tempted after 1933 to join the movement in some way or another. But that had nothing to do with the ideas these people had but solely with an elemental reaction to what Wilhelm Kuetemeyer has called a pseudo-outpouring of the Holy Spirit in 1933. If I try to analyze retrospectively what it was that affected me at that time and what did not, I come to the conclusion that . . . the views of the Nazis were idiotic but the rise of the Nazis a symptom of a process that they did not understand themselves. It is this process that I am trying to trace."[48] Finally, it is important to stress once again that for the elites, National Socialist ideas were probably less important than the appearance of a new ruler, the embodiment of a new national force, of will and energy. It was precisely the irrational aspect of National Socialism that won over the intellectuals and a "horrendously overstimulated population in a state of national orgasm."[49]

Professors and clergy outdid each other in declarations of loyalty to the new government. This particular following, which had been so easy to win over, was important to the Nazi regime, although, given the antagonism of genuine National Socialists toward academies and clergy, the hasty adoption of their cause must have evoked mixed feelings in the party. Elite support of the regime greatly contributed to its rapid consolidation. On January 30, 1934, Erich Ebermayer wrote in his diary:

> During this first year they have been in power, the National Socialists have succeeded—it would be self-delusion to deny this—in winning over the vast majority of the German people, not only workers, farmers, and the petty bourgeoisie, but also the haute bourgeoisie, the artists, the scholars. We few are becoming ever fewer. We are almost alone. Nothing succeeds like success—that English saying fits Hitler like a glove. . . . But it is equally true to say that nothing fails like failure. And it is my side, our side, that is failing. It requires no little courage, some character, and an unquestioning faith in the future and in divine justice as well to stand firm. How easy it would be, and how advantageous, to let oneself be converted, to throw in the towel. How many, who have resisted thus far, are doing just that.[50]

Ebermayer was right. There was much admiration coming from abroad, too. It was an illusion on the part of the Left to think that terror was the prime force keeping the Nazi regime in power. The National Socialists themselves probably overestimated the amount of resistance; all their anxious spying was perhaps exaggerated, even though resistance groups did exist, particularly early on, among workers and former members of the political parties of the Left. But the majority of the people were on the side of the new Reich, and their support was being constantly reinforced by the dramatization of the regime's successes. The party's public style alone was enough to impress people. Despite internal doubts and divisions, it made a show of self-confidence, arrogance, decisiveness. There were real successes as well: at home, the ranks of the unemployed shrank dramatically; a national labor service, with its egalitarian appeal, was introduced, long planned by Brüning but carried out by Hitler; a discreetly visible state terror replaced the earlier, highly visible street clashes and public violence.* In foreign

---

* Even Jewish émigrés visiting Germany were impressed. In 1936, the physicist Max Born wrote Ernest Rutherford: "My impressions in Germany were very mixed. I found terrible

policy, Hitler introduced a new style, a new assertiveness. There, too, he benefited from the weakness and willed myopia of his opponents, who were all too ready to believe the irenic protestations that followed his bold strokes, gradually demolishing the restrictive provisions of Versailles. His first triumph was Germany's resignation from the League of Nations in October 1933, endorsed by a plebiscite in which 90 percent of the German people expressed their approval. There were setbacks as well, but essentially it was a story of ever greater triumphs: In January 1935, the population of the Saarland in what was essentially a free election voted overwhelmingly to return to the Reich, that is to say, to Hitler's Germany (the population could have remained under the League of Nations or—indeed unlikely—opted for annexation by France). There followed the reintroduction of universal military service, and finally, the remilitarization of the Rhineland—the greatest peacetime coup, for it made Germany virtually invulnerable in the west.*

Success is both intoxicating and dangerous. To hold out against success, mass psychosis, and terror is difficult, and most of those who did hold out did so out of a different, stronger faith, primarily a religious one. There were others who rejected National Socialism out of decency, political conviction, and moral imperatives, yet even they were often beset by doubt and temptation.

Friedrich Meinecke, a humane, unimpassioned supporter of the Weimar Republic, was the most respected historian of that time, and remained editor of the *Historische Zeitschrift* until 1936. He was regarded as liberal and tolerant, and Jewish students had exceptional trust in him. In his lifetime Meinecke witnessed all of Germany's great political upheavals: Bismarck's empire, Weimar Republic, Third Reich, lost Reich. He adapted himself—to what-

distress among my relatives who fight a hopeless struggle. . . . But on the other hand there were so many things in Germany which I could not help admiring. The way they have got rid of unemployment seems to me very reasonable." Max Born, James Franck, *Der Luxus des Gewissens*, Ausstellung der Staatsbibliothek Berlin (Berlin, 1982), p. 127.
* All manner of Germans thrilled to these successes. The day after German troops reoccupied the Rhineland, Gerhard Ritter wrote his mother that for his children "who had never seen German soldiers from close up, this is one of the greatest experiences ever. . . . Truly a great and magnificent experience. May God grant that it does not lead to some international catastrophe." Ritter expressed the feelings of many Germans—including the notion that it might take God to protect Germany from any disastrous consequences. None came—proof of Hitler's luck. *Gerhard Ritter: Ein politischer Historiker in seinen Briefen*, ed. Klaus Schwabe and Rolf Reichardt (Boppard am Rhein, 1984), p. 296.

ever extent he possibly could—to every government. But he did not do so for personal, opportunistic reasons, nor did he hesitate to criticize governments; he chose to adapt, instead, out of his conviction that the historian's task was not only to convey an understanding of the past to the present but also, on the basis of that understanding, to interpret present reality. A purely negative rejection of National Socialism or a total retreat from public life would have seemed to him to be an escape, an abdication of responsibility.

Furthermore, he had a burning interest in public life. His political orientation was liberal and elitist, but his views, rather than deriving from abstract principles, were judgments about constantly changing events. During the Third Reich, he was regarded as altogether decent in his private life, standing by his friends and colleagues if they were under pressure. In public life, he was cautious, always struggling to grasp some deeper historic meaning of the moment.* He called himself a "Christian heathen," and in November 1933 he wrote to his friend Siegfried Kaehler: "In one's work, one sometimes forgets . . . everything else and behaves as if one lived outside time. You are right. We defeated ones, to the extent we are bourgeois, are all on the same tossing raft in a stormy sea, and we should learn to get along with one another." In August 1934 he complained, "I vacillate constantly between secret hopes and total despair." In August 1940, after the victory over France, he wrote, "The momentous events we have experienced turn out to be more and more momentous with each passing day. Granted, there is much we have to learn anew, but not everything. We are hearing—and it is beyond any doubt correct—that in Germany's victorious campaign the revolutionary dynamics of the Third Reich are running their course." He continued with words of praise for the German army: "And the recovery of Strasburg! Whose heart does not beat higher at that news!"[51]

In the first years of the Hitler regime, Meinecke repeatedly

---

* And yet Meinecke too made his compromises. "As early as May 1933 Meinecke thought he could avoid open conflict of the *Historische Zeitschrift* with the government by dropping Hedwig Hintze from her regular participation in the review section of the magazine, work she had been doing for years." Hedwig Hintze, the wife of Meinecke's friend and colleague Otto Hintze, was of Jewish background and leftist in her politics. *Otto Hintze und die moderne Geschichtswissenschaft*, ed. Otto Buesch and Michael Erbe (Berlin, 1983), p. 6.

worried the question of whether this was merely an episode or the beginning of an era. Was it something temporary or a world-historical change? He fell into puzzling about the future. This was a typical response, tragic for a liberal historian. This is where the personal and professional realms intersected, and it explains why he showed a certain readiness to compromise. The nation's triumph had seduced many into learning things anew, but Meinecke stuck by his bourgeois reservations. Right after the war, at the age of eighty-five, he wrote *Die Deutsche Katastrophe* without mentioning his own experience of uncertainty.

It was difficult to escape National Socialism. The regime used both the carrot and the stick to attract the elites and force them into compromises. The total state tried to blur the line between the private and the public spheres. For most people—and for the upper classes in particular—a moment came when the government required a public commitment from them, be it only in the form of membership in an organization that had aligned itself with National Socialism. This caused innumerable conflicts of conscience that were often inconsistently resolved. Hitler was a master at exploiting intuited weaknesses; his unbounded misanthropy probably helped. By the blood purge of June 30, 1934, when he liquidated the chieftains of the SA, in part in order to placate the military, he made accomplices of the latter: They had to accept the murder of Schleicher and his wife and of another German general—an unprecedented act. Referring to the much enlarged army, Claus von Stauffenberg once spoke of people who "had broken their backbones once or twice already" and from whom one could not expect "that they would be able to stand up straight if faced with another such decision."[52]

For some there remained nonetheless the path of "inner emigration," a retreat into a constantly endangered private sphere. This was an evasion of danger and temptation. One was neither an opponent of the regime—or one was so only in secret—nor was one a supporter. Inner emigration was an attempt to live in a state of ambiguity and contradiction. The internal drama arose from the fact that the government demanded a *yes* from the individual, while his conscience, and perhaps his family and friends as well, demanded a *no*. The upshot of this internal battle was an eternal *maybe* that was doubtless a kind of unconscious hedge against the future, too. In a country where the private sphere traditionally

enjoyed great respect, this kind of retreat was readily understandable. For writers and scholars, this inner emigration allowed for
the occasional effort at evading censorship, at writing something
in Aesopian language that would carry some faint resistance
message to the like-minded, that would keep alive "the hidden
Germany." Many Germans were groping about in the dark at that
time. For them the world was not black and white but unclear,
shifting, gray. And here too we should muster a certain empathy:
A refusal to say yes was no small thing.

[v]

Thomas Mann's inner struggle has an exemplary importance.
No one understood the temptation of National Socialism better
than the author of "Mario and the Magician." No one knew better
than he the allure of Germany's "special destiny." *The Reflections
of an Unpolitical Man,* like all his works during the First World
War, positively dripped with anti-Western pathos. And that is why
he immediately recognized the danger of this emotion in the postwar years, recognized both its danger and its appeal. In 1922, he
wholeheartedly embraced the new German republic: "Is republic
not merely a name for that national good fortune in which state
and culture are at one?"[53] In the late 1920s Mann was constantly
at odds with nationalistic writers. In the much more difficult
situation of 1930 he delivered a "German Address: An Appeal to
Reason." The title alone was at odds with the times, as was the
burden of Mann's speech, which was "that the proper political
alignment for the German bourgeoisie today is on the side of the
Social Democrats. . . ."[54] This most bourgeois of authors, who was
so much at home in the underworld of romantic and also pathological emotion, recognized the danger of bourgeois *ressentiment*
and—with all his understanding for the irrational—turned his
great prestige to the task of guiding the bourgeoisie onto a path
of practical rationality.

To no avail. By the summer of 1930, reason had become a
feeble reed in German politics. Mann left Munich on February 11,
1933, on a lecture tour from which he did not return to Germany.
In Switzerland, he continued to observe the gruesome spectacle.
He detested the regime's efforts "to produce mass idiocy [*Massen-*

verdummung], utilizing modern methods of suggestion to exert a mechanistic, monolithic control over them. The worst kind of Bolshevism . . . but differing from the Russian form in that it is devoid of any idea." (Stefan George and many others pointed to this affinity with bolshevism.) "How strange," Mann wrote in April 1933, "that no one in Germany feels my outrage and disgust at the truly swinish methods by which this 'people's movement' has won its triumph!" He also feared this "inner Versailles" that he thought "far worse than the external one." In September 1933 he felt that the combination of "vindictiveness and megalomania constitutes a danger to the world that makes pre-war imperialism look like innocence itself."[55] His condemnation was absolute, yet he had doubts, primarily of a personal nature. The journals of 1933–34 are an unceasing dialogue with himself. Did he really have to give up his beautiful home in Munich and his savings? Should he not go back to Germany despite everything, despite the personal attacks on him and his family, despite his Jewish wife? He was deeply attached to the house, and he cited with great pride Gottfried Benn's remark that it "truly had something Goethean about it."[56] We can only hope and believe that when he speaks time and again of his property he means much more than that, namely, the whole mode of life and work he had built for himself and in part fought with himself to achieve. "There still exists, of course, a Germany receptive to me and my intellectual bent."[57] The close bond with his readers, this special tie—would he have to choose exile and leave that behind?

But he had other thoughts as well. A few days after the law on the reestablishment of the professional civil service went into effect, Mann wrote in his journal: "The Jews . . . , it is no great misfortune after all that Kerr's brazen and venomous Jewish-style imitation of Nietzsche is silenced,* nor that the Jewish presence in the judiciary has been ended. Secret, disquieting, intense thoughts. Nonetheless things that are revoltingly malevolent, base, un-German in a higher sense remain. But I am beginning to suspect that the process could well be of that kind that has two sides."[58] Or a few days later: "I could to some extent go along with the rebellion against the Jewish element, were it not that the Jewish spirit exercises a necessary

---

* The reference here is to Alfred Kerr, a prominent and controversial Jewish critic and journalist, who had already been obliged to flee Germany.

control over the German element, the withdrawal of which is dangerous: Left to themselves the German element is so stupid as to lump people of my type in the same category and drive me out with the rest."[59] That is a reversion to the Thomas Mann of "Wälsungenblut," that anti-Semitic story written in 1906 in which the word "Jew" does not appear and which Mann withdrew from publication at his father-in-law's request. Even Mann then sometimes thought the process had its two sides, especially in moments of temptation and of fear that he would lose his property, his money, his home and furniture, all his bourgeois goods. The decision to remain in exile was a hard one indeed. Despite Mann's rather irritating self-preoccupation and his stress on the "special status" that he alone had, his experience reflects a much broader experience, that is, the fate of those who had to go into exile or of those who remained in Germany and—unlike the Nobel laureate and much-translated Thomas Mann—did not have the option of creating a new life in exile.

Mann had probably always believed in his "uniqueness." Particularly after 1933 he felt himself to be the sole individual called to represent the German spirit both at home and abroad.[60] For practical and human—all-too-human—reasons he at first resisted the widespread assumption that he could be identified with the emigration. He wanted to stand between the camps, without commitment either to the politically engaged emigrants or to the regime in Berlin. For many months he did not want to burn his bridges, and his "vacillation between decisiveness and deference" irritated his friends and family and left him uncertain himself.[61] In January 1934 Mann wrote in a frank letter to Ernst Bertram, "My position, my judgments are not dictated or influenced by the spirit prevalent among the emigrants. I am responsible for myself alone and have no contact whatever with the émigré community strewn throughout the world."[62] This was Mann's official position, despite the fact that his children, Klaus and Erika Mann, were among the émigré community's most prominent members. In January 1936, Erika was outraged at her father's attack on Leopold Schwarzschild, editor of the émigré journal *Das Neue Tage-Buch*; Schwarzschild had maligned Gottfried Bermann-Fischer, Mann's Jewish publisher in Berlin, who as late as 1935 had been able to issue a collection of Mann's essays. Erika thought it "sad and horrible" and felt that she would not be able to see her father for some time. Mann explained that Schwarzschild had calumnied his friend, and that for the rest, by keeping aloof from the émigré world, "I constitute a reserve which one day might be useful." Some time, he thought, "without utter delusion," he would sally forth and tell "the world and the Germans: 'It is enough, put an end to it, away with the rabble.' "[63] For a long time, perhaps always, he preferred to remain with "the inner emigration, to which in essence I belong."[64]*

His inner "vacillation" seemed to cease with the blood purge of June 30, 1934, when the state committed murder. Only then did he feel fully clear and relieved. Before, "one was constantly under the pressure of the zealous faith of the fools. One could occasionally vacillate within oneself. But now . . . Hitlerism is beginning to show itself to be what one had seen, recognized, profoundly felt it to be from the very beginning—the *absolute nadir* of baseness, degenerate stupidity, and bloodthirsty ignominy . . . , and one is ashamed of those moments of weakness when one wanted to doubt one's own feelings."[65]

Even in the Weimar Republic, Mann had no doubt felt himself to be a *praeceptor Germaniae*. He knew that his political statements were those of an outsider, an independent, and for that reason they seemed all the more significant to him. He was probably not even aware that they were sometimes eccentric and self-contradictory. Because his fellow citizens were so unpolitical, they were all the more in need of his advice. "But the German does not want to think in economic terms. And he doesn't think politically either; he thinks tragically, mythically, heroically. . . . The dismembering [of Germany] and the forced depoliticizing would be a great psychic relief for this people."[66]

---

* Was the great ironist aware of the irony that none other than he became the symbol of the German emigration, he, who early on had constantly resisted the assumption that he belonged to the emigration? Did he recall his own doubt when his publisher, Gottfried Bermann Fischer, celebrated Mann's seventieth birthday with the first issue of a new *Neue Rundschau* and a dedication in which he mourned the end of the old *NR* as well as the fate of its former contributors, who had either been victims of National Socialism or had fled into an "alien world" where they were regarded as "dubious" figures? "Exile is hard. But then a voice let itself be heard, Thomas Mann's voice. What had appeared to be a mass of uprooted existences had suddenly found a name and a form of expression. Emigration, until then a rather suspect concept, had a visible, admired, and honored representative." Gottfried Bermann-Fischer, *Bedroht—Bewahrt: Weg eines Verlegers* (Frankfurt am Main, 1967), p. 248.

[VI]

We have seen how the National Socialist regime could silence opponents, control all media, dazzle and intimidate the doubtful and uncertain into conformity or ambivalent passivity. But *Gleich-schaltung* found its limits. There remained one institution that lived by tradition and by speech, that possessed an independent moral authority, and that could not easily be uprooted: the Christian churches. There was some affinity between the deep conservatism and authoritarianism of the churches and the proclaimed goals of the Nazis; there was reluctance on both sides to engage in an open struggle. Relations between them were never easy. Within the churches there was conflict and complicity; the churches, too, witnessed individual acts of courage and institutional instances of appalling abdication or indifference. A few churchmen understood what Hitler's regime at first sought to conceal: The inherent incompatibility between National Socialism and Christianity. If Hitler had won the war, he would have attempted to destroy any vestiges of independent Christianity.

In the beginning, however, Hitler would wrap all his pro-nouncements in Christian garb, use every rhetorical device to reassure the right-thinking constituencies—and above all the aged President, the field marshal, whose silent support was still needed. He was successful for a while. At appropriate moments, in turn, the dignitaries of all the churches saluted the national awakening and congratulated the Führer. For their own reasons and traditions, the churches shrank back from challenging the new regime, concerned above all to protect their preserve, the preaching of the gospel and the administration of sacraments. Lutherans moreover had a dogmatic belief that obedience to the state was a divinely ordained command, the consequence of man's sinfulness. The Catholic Church had learned to adapt, to accommodate, to nego-tiate rather than to defy the secular authority. The rampant fear of Bolshevism and of "godless" Marxism reinforced clerical sym-pathy for National Socialism.

At the beginning of Hitler's regime, the divisions within Prot-estantism were enormous. The Deutsche Christen, adopting fully the dogmas of the new regime, had won over a large number of the clergy, especially the younger pastors; they made huge inroads in the congregations as well. With the help of the government, they hoped to gain control over the entire church, and nearly did. The rest of the church, still further divided within itself, tried to defend the church from such *Gleichschaltung*; as was said later, they were forced into resistance against their will. But even the most outspoken opponents of the Deutsche Christen sent their congratulatory telegrams to Hitler—and probably banked on the old President, who presumably shared an uncomplicated Protestant faith.

The Deutsche Christen were the internal foes of the other Protestant groupings. There were external challenges as well: in May 1933, Paul Tillich was dismissed as a "Marxist" professor, as politically unreliable. The other religious socialists were pushed out as well; there were a few protests. In 1935, Karl Barth was removed from his professorship in Bonn.

Above all, there was the inescapability of the Jewish question. The Nazis, after all, not only issued anti-Jewish decrees but introduced a new, racial definition of Jewishness: anyone with two or more Jewish grandparents was a Non-Aryan, hence subject to the same restrictions as were Jews—regardless of whether the person had received a Christian baptism. Race, not religion, determined a person's fate and character; the efficacy of baptism, the membership of the Christian community, were declared irrelevant. This in itself was a direct challenge to Christian dogma and practice—which the churches met by troubled silence. By September 1933, the so-called Aryan paragraph was introduced into the several Protestant churches; it followed the text of the earlier decree removing Jews from the civil service. From then on, no Christian of Jewish descent would be allowed to occupy an office of any sort in any Christian congregation. The ruling affected only a handful of converts; officially the churches complied and institutionally the silence continued.

From the beginning of the regime, some individuals spoke out. On May 2, 1933—the day after Hitler's dramatic speech on what used to be the workers' main day of protest—the well-known theologian Rudolf Bultmann, in a public lecture to students, warned against endangering or corrupting the honest intentions of the national movement: "Shall we preserve the force of the critical perspective and shall we not succumb to the temptations?" Again and again referring to Hitler's own speech and the wildly anti-Semitic statement of the German Student Association "Against the Un-Germanic Spirit," Bultmann warned against excessive optimism about the new order. He apparently sensed the importance of the students' appeal, which within a few days led to the notorious burning of "un-Germanic" books. "Against the temptation of frivolity we must emphasize the seriousness of the task." He condemned the *"Denunziantentum,"* the then prevalent denouncing of other people for their opinions. This poisons the atmosphere and creates mistrust among *"Volksgenossen."* Using again and again the students' slogan "we must extirpate the lie," Bultmann said: "As a Christian I must lament the injustice which through such defamation is also done to German *Jews* now. I know well how complicated the Jewish problem is, especially in Germany. But 'we want to extirpate the lie'—hence I must say in all honesty that precisely the defamation of the Jews which that students' pronouncement contained . . . is not borne in the spirit of love. Keep the struggle for the German *Volkstum* pure, and make sure that noble desire for truth and *Deutschtum* is not disfigured through demonic distortion." There were many like Bultmann who at first thought that the movement could be kept pure or cleansed of its brutal aspects.

Bultmann acknowledged the "Jewish problem" openly; most churchmen would probably have found it difficult—even in their own hearts—to temper their hostility to Jews, their understanding of Nazi measures, with Bultmann's compassion and restraint.

In May 1933, the twenty-seven-year-old Dietrich Bonhoeffer also addressed the Jewish question—in words that have sometimes been misunderstood. His essay—profound and deeply moving—was an early effort to reconcile the teachings of Karl Barth, his mentor and preeminent theologian, with the crisis of the new era. Barth had taught that church and state were categorically separate realms, that the church must sever its (hitherto authoritarian-conservative) ties to the state and devote itself solely to the Word of God; and yet Bonhoeffer realized that the same state was challenging the church in its own realm, in its own principles—and in Bonhoeffer's own family. His twin sister had married a converted Jew. Bonhoeffer conceded that "without doubt one of the historical problems which the state has to settle is the Jewish question, and without doubt the state is justified to choose new paths here." But he also pondered that there might be times when the church needs to confront the state that violates its responsibilities. The various Protestant churches of course conformed to the laws of the state, but under some circumstances the church would not only be obligated "to bind up the victims who had fallen under the wheel but to put spokes in the wheel itself." He immediately related this hypothetical state to the position of Christians of Jewish descent. Their right to remain in the church is inviolable: "Anyone who feels he cannot bear Christians of Jewish descent [*judenstämmigen Christen*] cannot be denied [the option] of leaving this community of the church."[67]

In September 1933, Martin Niemöller, a former U-boat commander, a committed nationalist and previously sympathetic to some aspects of National Socialism, wrote a letter of protest against the Germanic Christians and against the *"Arierparagraph."* In November, together with Bonhoeffer and a few others, he organized a group of pastors (*Pfarrernotbund*) that would seek to defend church and gospel as they understood it. This was the nucleus of the Confessional Church, born in Barmen in May 1934. Even that part of Protestantism, born in the spirit of defense, was divided. The overwhelming majority wanted to protect the church against the heresies of the Germanic Christians and, to some extent, against the cruelties of anti-Jewish legislation, but they never thought of themselves as resisters—and most of them, too, expressed their loyalty to the regime and their anger that foreign observers would view them as critics or opponents of the regime. This position was preserved even after Niemöller, a man of great courage, was imprisoned in 1937—and many other pastors of the Confessional Church suffered a similar fate. Their congregations remained—passively—loyal. In the rarest instances did they do more. In judging their much later silence at the public degradation and deportation of Jews, one must remember their relative passivity in the face of their own pastors' persecution.* Much to Bonhoeffer's dismay, several synods of the Confessional Church refused to utter a compassionate word for the Jews. But then the Protestant hierarchy did little for its own imprisoned members. Even here, an ambiguous legacy: the courage of a few individual ministers,

---

* As a child I knew some of the pastors of the Confessional Church in Breslau: men who despite repeated arrests would deliver their sermons which would in one way or another express the primacy of the Gospel and compassion for the persecuted; there was no single dogma of defiance, but Christian appeals to conscience that would induce the Gestapo, whose members attended these sermons, to arrest the pastors—again and again.

confirmed by faith and fellowship, on the one hand, and the reticence, the pusillanimity of the institution, on the other.

Without National Socialism there would never have been a Confessional Church, there would never have been that demand for courage and that renewed faith in individual conscience; at the same time, Protestant tradition and Nazi intimidation severely limited the role of that church. One fact is incontrovertible: The history of German Protestantism, at least in the early and decisive years of Hitler's rule, bore witness to the appeal of National Socialism, to the power of temptation—and to the fact that individuals, following their own faith and conscience, could resist that temptation and even warn against it. Even the legacy of the Confessional Church is complicated. For a few, Dietrich Bonhoeffer being the most outstanding example, the struggle of the church proved a path to political resistance and martyrdom; for many men and women of the final conspiracy against Hitler, the call to Christian conscience that was at the heart of the Confessional Church provided courage in desperate action and fortitude in facing death. The church, on the other hand, condemned their attempted revolt.[68]

In Bismarck's unified Reich, Catholics were a minority, and after the *Kulturkampf* of the 1870s and subsequent, if unofficial, discrimination, they felt like an embattled community. Weimar was an ambiguous experience for them. The Center Party played the pivotal role in all governments but did so in a secular-liberal world, a world that many Catholic leaders despised.

Catholicism had the great advantage of a unified, hierarchical organization, but within that structure there were separate interdependent authorities. The political arm of German Catholicism was the Center Party, which needed and received the support of German bishops and which did not necessarily conform to the political wishes of the Holy See. Before 1933, despite the affinity of parts of the church with National Socialism, the party and the hierarchy opposed Hitler. Once Hitler had become chancellor, the several groups changed their policies and the Vatican achieved political preeminence. Pius XI and his papal secretary, Eugenio Pacelli, former nuncio in Germany and steeped in German affairs, had concluded the Lateran Treaties with Mussolini in 1929, ending sixty years of ambiguous hostility between state and church. Pius XI and Pacelli realized that Mussolini could make sweeping concessions—on paper at least—that no democratic regime could have done; it would seem that the Vatican harbored the same hopes regarding Hitler, apparently undisturbed by the fact that already by 1931 serious disputes had arisen between Mussolini and the Vatican over the implementation of the Lateran Treaties.[69] For years, the Vatican had wanted a concordat with the Reich and Hitler encouraged these hopes.

In any case, a tacit bargain was struck between the new regime and Catholicism. I say tacit because whether there was a formal understanding or not remains a subject of controversy. The church agreed to withdraw from the political field and in that realm in effect surrendered to *Gleichschaltung*. Thus the Center Party voted for the Enabling Act, thereby violating its own pragmatic attachment to constitutional rule. Shortly thereafter the German hierarchy confirmed the individual statements of church leaders, welcoming the new national awakening and, with minor reservations, withdrew its objections to National Socialism. In early July, the Center Party dissolved itself.

Two days later, a concordat was signed between the Holy See and the new regime. On the face of it, the Vatican had scored a great triumph. No government under Weimar had been willing to sign such a concordat, which would recognize the principal rights of the church—rights that presumably would render it immune from the kind of persecution it had suffered under the *Kulturkampf*. By the terms of the concordat the church renounced all political activities and in turn the state guaranteed the right to free worship, to circulate pastoral epistles, to maintain Catholic schools and property. The Vatican had reason to be satisfied: Catholic rights had been put on a new basis and at the same time a regime had been strengthened that seemed to correspond to the Vatican's sense that Mussolini and Hitler were indispensable bulwarks against Bolshevism.

Hitler had even more reason to be satisfied. The concordat was his first international agreement, and it vastly enhanced his respectability in Germany and abroad. A great moral authority had trusted his word. But did the Vatican, did Pacelli, really believe that National Socialism would abide by the concordat, was there really much likelihood that the regime would leave untouched a rival organization with its own dogmas and with such sweeping power over education? Disputes arose quickly, and the Vatican dispatched countless notes of protest. But the great disputes that involved virulent attacks on the clergy, and especially on the cloistered clergy, took place a few years later, when nearly a third of the clergy was censured or arrested. The church sought to defend itself against these encroachments and at times even protested the racial tenets and inhumane practices of the regime. But it also struggled to maintain a consistent *non*-resistance stance. At the height of his successful campaign against the Nazi program of euthanasia, in 1941, Bishop Galen of Münster declared: "We Christians do not make a revolution."[70]

Within the church, the hierarchy and the laity came to be split on how far to protest. For the church (as for the army and for the judiciary) the events of June 30, 1934, presented a special challenge. The SS not only liquidated the leaders of the SA but took the opportunity to murder one of the most prominent Catholic officials in Germany, Erich Klausener. The church maintained its silence and the best-known Catholic publicist at the time, Waldemar Gurian, already in exile, protested: "*The silence of the bishops* is perhaps still more horrible than anything that happened on June 30. For this silence destroys the last moral authority in Germany, it brings insecurity into the ranks of the faithful, it threatens to lead to an estrangement between bishops and the people, which no longer comprehends this silence."[71] Some of the people may not have understood the silence, but the overwhelming majority accepted and joined in it.

The many priests and pastors in prison or concentration camps were proof that Christianity and National Socialism were incompatible. Political subservience insured institutional survival, but at what many Catholics came to realize was too high a moral price. There were individual Catholics who found their way into political resistance, such as Father Delp, S.J. The Catholic hierarchy stood by its victims and sought to help them to the last.

The stand of the Christian churches has always had its defenders and its accusers. Throughout the Hitler era, there were those who insisted that not prudence but faith and conscience should determine action. As we saw in the previous chapter, Adenauer shared these misgivings. It was a tribute to the Christian churches that the regime was afraid of them; in retrospect, we know that the fear was exaggerated. The churches sought to protect their already embattled servants. A few of those servants chose martyr-

dom and became victims of the regime, the true nature of which
their superiors discovered very late, if ever.*

[VII]

When war threatened in 1938 and defeat in 1942, and, in the
meantime, as the atrocities of the regime became still clearer,
groups of people formed to put an end to this horror. The German
resistance began in earnest—though there had been some resistance all along, much of it by former Socialists and Communists.
It was concentrated in the old army, where traditional ties were
still intact. Some civil servants were involved, some old Social
Democrats, like Julius Leber, and some young men, like Dietrich
Bonhoeffer and Claus von Stauffenberg. Some, like Fritzi von der
Schulenburg, had at first thrown themselves behind National
Socialism with all the fire of youth. Others had at least been
attracted to it. But then came disillusionment, insight, a more
rigorous patriotism, and a feeling of responsibility that oversha-
dowed all else, a need to act—as Dietrich Bonhoeffer put it—in
the nation's stead. In their plans for the future, the men of July
20 were guided by the past. They did not want a rebirth of Weimar
but had various visions, including that of a conservative, Prussian-
socialist future. Justice and a constitutional government had to be
reestablished, but most of the plans for Germany after Hitler were
not democratic; they were instead inspired by a fear that "mass
democracy" might well lead to another catastrophe, particularly in
so inexperienced and uneducated a people as the Germans. Many
of the conspirators against Hitler believed in Germany's special
path that should be neither parliamentary and democratic—that
is, Western—nor totalitarian—or Eastern. They were an unusual
elite, not only by background and office, but also by virtue of mind
and conscience. Their thinking, too, was elitist; but the crucial

---

* In October 1945, in what came to be known as the Stuttgart Pronouncement, the Evangelical
Church formally acknowledged "not only a great community of suffering with our people but
also a solidarity of guilt. With great pain we say: Because of us, infinite suffering has been
visited on many peoples and countries." The church did fight the spirit that animated National
Socialism "but we hold ourselves culpable for not confessing more courageously, for not
praying more faithfully, for not believing more joyously, for not loving more ardently. . . ."
Theodor Eschenburg, *Jahre der Besatzung* (Stuttgart/Wiesbaden, 1983), p. 221.

element in it was moral and religious. In them, conscience rose up
to rescue the nation and its honor. Their willingness to risk their
lives to free their own country and Europe as well from this reign
of terror—that was an event of human and historical significance
unparalleled in German history.

National Socialism was not Germany's salvation but its destruction. There is much yet to be explained about this drama and
disaster, and it is precisely some of the most profound questions
that our discipline, with its propensity for specialization, has thus
far managed to evade. National Socialism as temptation, the drama
of human psychology in the face of terror, the moral atmosphere
of that time—these are subjects I feel committed to, on behalf
both of the past and of our own present. It is a necessary task to
seek out the human fate in the most inhuman of eras.

On July 20, 1954, in Berlin, I smuggled myself into the
memorial service commemorating the plot of ten years earlier,
held in the courtyard of the old army headquarters in the Bend-
lerstrasse, where some of the principal conspirators had been
murdered by the Nazis. Observing the faces of the bereaved,
recalling what the martyrs represented, my own view of Germany
and of our past began to change. July 20—and the martyrs who
came before and after—should be remembered more vividly than
they are in the Federal Republic. Perhaps there is an unconscious
continuation of the nation's acquiescence to National Socialism,
one that perpetuates the silence not only about the martyrs but
also about the collaborators and supporters of the Nazi regime.
Despite all the distance we may now feel between us and the non-
democratic and, for us, obsolete thought of the resistance, and
despite all our regret that so many of them witnessed so many
murders and atrocities without protesting—despite all the objections we could possibly raise, we cannot and should not withhold
our admiration from these men and women. Theirs was a unique
rebellion, a noble exit from the stage of history. What happens to
their memory, what happens to the memory of the others who
took the lonely task of conscience, is a judgment on those who
have come after them. On us.

III

Peace and the Release
from Greatness

In January 1974, in an essay called "The End of the Postwar Era," I argued that the Arab-Israeli war, the oil shock, and Allied wrangling—events inextricably intertwined and all with deep roots in the past—constituted a clear and ominous caesura in the history of Europe after 1945. That article had an unexpected resonance which encouraged me to write further on contemporary events as seen from an historical perspective, particularly developments in Germany, where past and present are inseparable, where the deepest political and moral issues derive from the past.

The Federal Republic had been born at the very beginning of that postwar era, which constituted the most extraordinary leap to prosperity and pacification that Western Europe had ever seen. In the short run, Europe in general and Helmut Schmidt's Germany in particular proved more resilient after 1973 than I had anticipated. Still, I think the autumn of 1973 ushered in a new and more precarious era. Slowly, and not always visibly, the condition of Germany changed within the alliance. It had been common to speak of the Federal Republic as an economic giant and a political dwarf. The Germans had become accustomed to their political weakness and to the American shield; few of them seemed conscious that they lacked full sovereignty, that because of their country's history and present division, they were con-

demned to be loyal to allies who in turn feared any excessive
German initiative. It was also a time when, inwardly, many Germans, satisfied with economic triumphs and general prosperity,
welcomed, perhaps unconsciously, this release—or respite?—from
greatness, this release from the trials of autonomy.

In 1979, while teaching in Paris, I watched the German scene
from close by and came to sense how "uneasy Germans" made
their Eastern and Western neighbors uneasy. In 1980, I wrote
"Germany in a Semi-Gaullist Europe," published in *Foreign Affairs,*
here reprinted in essentially unrevised form.

In the early 1980s, still greater strains in United States–
European and United States–German relations seemed to appear.
The departure of Helmut Schmidt removed a statesman with a
world perspective and a sense of historical responsibility. The
succeeding government seemed to fit into a world of growing
provincialism. The foreign policy consensus in the Federal Republic
became less secure; Germans became more estranged from American leadership, and a negative dialectic between the two countries
threatened to develop. During the Carter Administration, Germans
had worried about American weakness; in the early years of the
Reagan Administration, Germans worried over American mili-
tancy, over the build-up of what many regarded as offensive
weapons—in every sense. At the same time, Germans watched a
conservative American administration allow the country to indulge
in budget and trade deficits that made the United States economically vulnerable, even as the president sought to make the country
militarily invulnerable—through strategic innovations that worried
many Europeans.

"Germany and the United States: Visions of Declining Virtue"
is a composite of two essays, written in 1983 and published in
1984. In weaving them together, I made minor changes but no
attempts to bring them up to date.

All of these essays, beginning with "The End of the Postwar
Era," were written out of fear lest the end of this era would begin
the unraveling of the European-American connection, a connection
that I still think vital to our security and precious to our health.
The essays in Part III reflect my concern about this connection
that I cherish—and my commitment to its central element, the
relations between the United States and West Germany.

GERMANY IN A SEMI-GAULLIST EUROPE

On the all-important question of Germany's future, my mind was made up. First of all, I believed that it would be unjust and dangerous to revise the de facto frontiers which the wars had imposed on her. . . . Furthermore, the right to possess or to manufacture atomic weapons—which in any case she had declared her intention to renounce—must in no circumstances be granted to her. This being so, I considered it essential that she should form an integral part of the organized system of cooperation between States which I envisaged for the whole of our continent. In this way the security of all nations between the Atlantic and the Urals would be guaranteed, and a change brought about in circumstances, attitudes and relationships which would doubtless ultimately permit the reunion of the three segments of the German people.

—CHARLES DE GAULLE
Memoirs of Hope

THE AFGHANISTAN CRISIS has dramatized and intensified antecedent changes and strains in the Western alliance. There was unanimous, if separate, condemnation of Soviet aggression, but there were also divergent, and often acrimoniously divergent, assessments of the causes of aggression and the nature of the challenge. The difficulties of orchestrating a common response or of at least preventing a discordant one suggest a new balance of forces within the alliance and a set of divergent interests.

In essence, the leadership of a weakened America is being challenged by a more independent Europe, led by an ever more important Franco-German condominium. The European, especially the German, commitment to détente is formidable. The Federal Republic, closest ally of both America and France and at the same time the much-wooed, much-threatened, privileged partner of the USSR, clearly emerges as the principal actor next to the United States. With one overriding loyalty—to the Western alliance—it also feels the pull of its other and conflicting ties.

The balance between unity and discord is precarious. There are not only substantive differences between the United States and its European allies; there is—at least on the nongovernmental level—a growing impatience on both sides. The roots of discord go deep; to ignore or underestimate the shifts of power and attitudes might heighten the dangers of drifting apart. In the past, an external threat has always served to unite the alliance. Now we cannot count on the automatic reappearance of solidarity. As the alliance enters a period of likely crisis, it may be useful to try to assess some of the changes of power and spirit that have taken place on the West European side in the recent past.

[II]

The Western alliance is unprecedented in modern history. A voluntary association of unequal nations, it has survived three decades of intense change and crisis. The alliance reflects a fundamental reality of world politics: The USSR presents a danger to Western Europe which only the United States can successfully deter. This has been the heart of the alliance, whatever the strains and competing interests within it.

The edifice of the alliance still seems solid; the political landmarks have proven remarkably stable. Europe remains partitioned between a Soviet-led consortium of malfunctioning and repressive societies on the one side, and an American-protected group of still liberal, still prosperous countries on the other. Soviet prudence and allied deterrence have given Europe a unique respite from war. But the fundamental pillar of that postwar order, weakened for over a decade, was visibly shaken by 1979: the belief in American power, American resolution, and American capability.

My impressions, based in part on what I heard and observed in Western and Eastern Europe in the first half of 1979, would lead me to suggest that a growing European apprehension about America hardened at about that time into a new assessment of this country, an assessment that, to some extent, paralleled changes in our own mood. The coinciding, moreover, of a perceived American decline and a resurgent German strength brought about a brief reemergence of what used to be called, and in 1979 was called again, the German Question, the "whither Germany" that by and large we had not heard for so long because Germany was thought to be inflexibly anchored in the Western alliance, a voluntary captive of it. In some quarters, there was apprehension that German assertiveness bespoke a renewed ambition for finding ways for reunification.

In addition, in many continental countries, including the very ones that we had for so long assumed to be staunch partisans of the alliance, Denmark, say, or Holland, a new sentiment about East-West relations emerged. To its proponents this sentiment is far from appeasement; it connotes a desire that as little as possible should be done to disturb relations between Eastern and Western Europe, that that division in some distant future may yet be healed. These trends suggest a drift of sentiment away from an American-led alliance and toward a growing Europeanization of Europe—though, as we will see, without firmness, without structure, even without clearly defined aim.

We know that perceptions matter, that they inform and shape political decisions. Power, until tested in battle or crisis, is the perception of potentiality. It combines an assessment of capability, which can be quantified, and the assessment of will and cohesion, which eludes exact reckoning.[1] In absolute terms, America today is stronger militarily than ever before; even in relative terms, it has parity and the potential for more. But perception and self-perception have changed radically. In 1979 it was widely believed that what used to be called "American exceptionalism" had vanished—or, to put it somewhat quaintly, that *fortuna* had forsaken us.

In assessing Europe's views, we must remember that the Europeans are anything but disinterested observers of America's fortunes. Their perceptions are distorted by the projection of their own interests and fears. They have grown too strong for their continued weakness. For the time being, they are unwilling to make the costly effort of creating their own credible military deterrent. They resent their dependence on the United States for security; increasingly that dependence is becoming a self-inflicted psychological burden. The unease about one's own ineffectuality or lack of autonomy grows worse as one has doubts about the strength and will of one's protector.*

For the Europeans, the overthrow of the shah, coming as it did on the heels of Soviet-Cuban adventurism in Africa, dramatized America's enfeeblement. Perhaps better attuned to calamity than the Americans, and, in any case, more vulnerable to Middle East upheavals, the Europeans quickly perceived the shah's fall as a political disaster of the first magnitude—which did not prevent the French from playing their own, almost habitual, game of *sauve qui peut*. In February and March of 1979, usually irenic Europeans clamored for some American riposte, for some sign of strength. They were alarmed by what they saw as American passivity. European clamor for action was wrong, I think; the sense of a dramatic change was correct.

And in the face of it, a president who in late February 1979 could say "on balance the trends have not been adverse to our country" invited disbelief. Europeans worried over what they took to be America's post-Vietnam refusal to take risks in defense of vital interests. There was of course a more direct concern as well: If the shah with his immense strategic and economic assets could so easily be washed away, would other friends or allies of the United States fare better?

Apprehensions and uncertainties compounded real differences of interest and policy. In the economic realm, too, perceptions have changed ever since the early 1970s. The United States, it is argued, remains hideously wasteful; it lives off its deficit, flooding the world with depreciating dollars, endangering the world fiscal system, not for its own profit but out of its inability to solve

---

* In 1980, the former British ambassador in Washington, Peter Jay, warned against "this systematic European ambivalence, willing to wound but afraid to strike, tempted by the glamor of status and gestures but shy of the responsibilities and burdens of real power. . . . But it boosted and boosts European morale to spotlight American errors, to sour its failures, to exploit its market, to resent its overseas investments, to have a critic's ringside seat at its global tribulations, to mock its culture, to deride its leaders and to bewail the 'weakness' of its currency." Quoted in *European Peace Movements and the Future of the Western Alliance*, ed. Walter Laqueur and Robert Hunter (New Brunswick and Oxford, 1985), p. 104.

domestic problems. We have done far too little to reduce our dependence on foreign oil or to curtail our disproportionate consumption. It is not only Helmut Schmidt who is outraged by what—in his milder moments—he calls America's abdication of fiscal leadership or responsibility. The United States, once the pillar of the postwar economic order, is now viewed as its disrupter, pursuing policies inimical to itself and to its allies.

At the same time, the credibility of America's military capability is being questioned.[2] At a point of nuclear parity, the old Gaullist suspicion that the United States would not risk its cities for the defense of Berlin or Hamburg has taken on new plausibility. It is generally thought that the Soviet Union has made significant strides in all aspects of its military power, nuclear and conventional, land and sea power, while the United States has lagged behind in modernizing its forces. Its volunteer army is often thought to be deficient in will and training. Most people do not calculate the relative power of sophisticated weapons; they reckon by trends and demonstrated capabilities. The Soviets have demonstrated their capability, especially their capacitiy to airlift large numbers of troops with extraordinary speed and precision.

At the same time, Europeans have worried that a weaker United States is pursuing a tougher policy toward the Soviet Union. They believed that the drift of policy and mood was away from détente, that the Carter Administration had begun with considerable skepticism about détente, and that by the end of 1979 a popular anti-Soviet mood had gained much ground in America. The Europeans have been concerned about this cooling of relations—just as they worry about excessive warmth; basically, they would like to set the thermostat themselves. Europeans are skeptical about our policy toward the Middle East; they see Camp David as a dead end and would like the United States to pressure Israel to meet what they increasingly regard as legitimate Arab demands. Some Third World countries, notably in the Middle East, have tried to tempt the Europeans into a greater show of independence. Too close an identification with a maligned and partially weakened superpower may not be the most popular stance at the moment.

There have been strains in the alliance before, doubts about the steadfastness of American policy. But at the present juncture, divergent interests coincide with a new perception of the United States: Europeans now worry not merely over American policy, but over the polity itself. It is no longer a matter of the often ill-tempered irritation with President Carter's style or inconsistency; in 1979 Europeans worried that America may have become a crippled giant, an imperial power with structural flaws that make consistent policy difficult.

For a decade and a half—since the assassination of President Kennedy—Europeans saw successive crises in America as so many temporary dislocations of American power, temporary distempers of an essentially healthy body. In 1979 Europeans began to worry whether there is a constitutional debility in America in which, for example, the continued malfunctioning of relations between executive and legislative leads to constant stalemates on economic policy. Has the separation of powers become a dissipation of power? Are the strains in civil society—underlying racial conflict, economic malfunctioning, criminality and drug addiction—perhaps signs of a profound disability that could weaken American leadership for years to come?

The change in perspective can also be seen in another light: In the immediate postwar period, the United States was a superpower that excelled in all realms. Its military might was buttressed by unmatched scientific talent, by a dynamic and unsurpassed economy, by a restrained and steadfast statesmanship, and by a naïve effusion of ideals. American power impressed, but so did American promise. America has lost some of the model quality. Today it is looked upon as a superpower, selectively strong.

Europe's leaders today are essentially pro-American; their political attitudes were formed in the heyday of American promise. They are not ideologically estranged from America; indeed, they have an affinity for the dynamic rhythms of American life, for its vitality, its openness. They were pained by Carter's public musings in the summer of 1979 that the country was suffering from some kind of malaise, some crisis of confidence. They too believed in American exceptionalism. Disappointed lovers make harsh judges. The present apprehensiveness of thoughtful Europeans recalls what Richard Hofstadter wrote in 1969: "The nation seems to slouch onward into its uncertain future like some huge inarticulate beast, too much attainted by wounds and ailments to be robust, but too strong and resourceful to succumb."[3]

It is important to recognize that the present criticism of the United States is categorically different from earlier moralizing or

snobbery. It is often the voices of friends who fear for our future—
and for theirs, which is so directly tied to ours. There are Americans
who would respond with some vehemence: If you are so concerned
about our strength, why not pay the price of greater strength
yourself? There will be growing and perhaps self-defeating American impatience at what will be perceived as European reluctance
to assume their share of the burden or indeed to assume their
proper responsibilities. But our first concern here is to understand
European perceptions of America, not to record the strident voices
and often justified complaints in the present transatlantic dialogue.

[III]

The growing doubt about America, the different assessment of
détente, the Europeanization of Europe—all these changes seem
to approximate de Gaulle's vision. It is odd that this man, so
stubbornly rooted in the past, should still cast his shadow across
our path. He had always sought a more European Europe, more
independent of the United States, about whose reliability *in extremis*
he had some real and some feigned doubts. He had hoped via
détente, and by loosening his ties to the United States and creating
his own special ties to the USSR, to widen French maneuverability.
He wanted a Europe of national states, each true to its particular
historic character and destiny, each jealous of its own interests.
This being so, he envisioned a role of leadership for France,
possibly transmuted into a kind of Franco-German condominium;
he abhorred a federal or an Atlanticized Europe. He thought that
France and perhaps the other nations of Europe should seek a
more active presence in the Third World, especially in the Middle
East, and one independent of the United States. He expected that
national interests and historic identity would in time allow for a
new relation with Eastern Europe, despite the enmity of two
opposing social systems. Given his nationalist premises, he had to
believe that Germany could not remain divided forever—though
any revision of the status quo could be pushed to a reassuringly
distant future. He took France out of NATO's integrated command, secure in the knowledge that the survival of the alliance
depended in any case on its will to defend France, however
autonomous or selfish French policy might be.

To speak of a semi-Gaullist Europe today is intended in part as irony. De Gaulle expected that his Europe would be born out of will and ambition, out of his kind of leadership and vision. The changed attitudes of 1979 were more the product of drift and apathy, of circumstances imposing policies rather than of policies being consciously fashioned. De Gaulle's Europe was to be a Europe of strong nations, secure in their material recovery; today's Europe huddles in precarious prosperity, its economic vulnerability demonstrated by the oil embargo of 1973 and OPEC's subsequent decisions. Its political regimes are shaky, its sense of purpose is muted, its youth disaffected—"fragments floating in the here and now," as Stanley Hoffmann has called his somber analysis of Europe.[4] A Europe of creeping protectionism is in the grips of a Gaullism by default, a selective Gaullism, without grandeur, an improvised, depressed adaptation to unfavorable circumstances.

Neither the perception of American weakness nor that of Soviet strength has prompted a new European resolve or initiative. The political construction of Europe has made little progress. The much-touted popular elections to the European Parliament were intended to infuse new life into the European Community, but the campaign itself was marked by apathy or purely national concerns. Even its rhetoric was remarkably restrained. The reality is continued difficulties within the EEC, as the new parliament battles the commission over the budget, as Britain seeks major adjustments, as the forces of protectionism are everywhere on the increase. The EEC, moreover, is threatened by growth: The prospective adhesion of Greece, Spain, and Portugal—whatever the long-term political benefits may be—will further weaken the internal functioning of the community and further complicate the task of coordinating widely divergent national economies. The building of Europe on EEC foundations is not a part of today's agenda or imagination—another symptom of the semi-Gaullist condition of Europe.

Brussels is not Western Europe; it probably never was. What gives Western Europe a measure of cohesion—aside from the well-functioning machinery of political cooperation—is the unacknowledged condominium of France and Germany, symbolized and facilitated by the close personal ties between French President Valéry Giscard d'Estaing and West German Chancellor Helmut Schmidt. Today no major European initiative is taken without prior consultation and agreement between Paris and Bonn. The introduction of the European Monetary System, an effort to insulate Europe from the vagaries of the dollar, is but one example of the close collaboration between the two leaders and countries. The EEC provides needed machinery; the constant contacts between Schmidt and Giscard provide the living impulse. The two leaders have a sense of strategy and destiny; if given time, they may yet devise new structures and new supports, including military measures, for a much more independent Europe.

The personal equation of the two men is important, but the link between the two nations rests on deeper bases: on geography, on common interests, on the historical experience of enmity tried and attendant calamity, and finally, on the fact that the world outside appears fragile or inhospitable. The Paris-Bonn axis, dreamt of repeatedly in the last hundred years and hitherto never achieved, must contend with domestic troubles, with various resentments on both sides, but it does have an historic resonance and will not be easily supplanted by any other arrangement.

The Franco-German condominium has helped to contain a striking phenomenon of 1979: the sudden realization that the Federal Republic has come to play a much more important role, not just within the alliance, but on the world stage generally.[5] Even as the decline of America was incremental and at first not seen in any kind of historic dimension, so the new assertiveness of the FRG was incremental, and it was largely in 1979 that observers became conscious that perhaps a permanent shift had occurred.

The FRG's presence was more fully felt in international organizations, in the councils of the alliance, in the Third World, in the East. In January 1979 at Guadeloupe, for the first time, the "Big Three" were enlarged to include the Germans; it would have been unthinkable not to include them. At that summit they were charged with a special mission in Turkey. German weight increased everywhere—and everywhere was sustained by an economy that seemed impervious to the ills of others. There was talk of "model Germany," of how others should try to emulate rather than resent German success.[6] Somewhere it became clear that West Germany had shaken off its reticence, its embarrassment at its own importance. And once again the Federal Republic had found the perfect leader for the new stance: Schmidt found his role of worldwide authority as natural to his temperament as Adenauer had found his role as reconciler with the West or Brandt his position of contrite authority vis-à-vis the East.

The Germans had not sought this new role. It was Allied, especially American faltering which led Germany to abandon its more modest role, its pretense at being no more than the "paymaster of Europe," the model member of the international scene. There was a vacuum of leadership and gradually the Germans began to discover that they had a role to play. As one diplomat put it: "Greatness was thrust upon Germany." And still the Germans thought to use the French connection in order, at least partially, to conceal that new greatness.

For the first time in history a German state has acquired power in what might be called a fit of absentmindedness. In some ways this still shields Germans from a realization of their own importance. At the very end of 1979, in a public opinion poll, most Germans thought the FRG was still a passive spectator in world affairs, and only 24 percent of those asked expected the FRG to be "the leading power in Western Europe by the end of the 1980s."

But if the German public has not caught up to present realities, its attitude to the past has changed. More and more, Germans have come to feel that the memories of past horrors should no longer constrain them from playing an active role in the world. A few months ago, Schmidt remarked that the memory of Hitler would continue to haunt Germany for decades to come. Most Germans, I think, would hold with Egon Bahr, Secretary General of the Social Democratic Party, who said in October: "Security for the 1980s—that is an extraordinary challenge to master new dangerous developments, already discernible today, and our participation in solving [these challenges] can be all the more active and uninhibited as the Germans incurred no more guilt in creating them than did all the other peoples." A somewhat unpersuasive statement—since history does not begin afresh at a given moment—but one representative of German sentiments. There is an impatience to be rid of the incubus of the past, to tackle the new problems—uninhibitedly.

In fact, today's West Germans are remarkably free of both nationalist sentiments and historical consciousness; given this simultaneous ebbing of once strong sentiments, it is not easy for them to define their identity or destiny. They are not even particularly conscious of the great and successful transformation they have lived through. Their attachment to the FRG is pragmatic; someday a later generation may look back on these first three decades as a period of unprecedented achievement in German history.

The Federal Republic, founded in 1949 as a deliberate *Provisorium*, has developed into the most democratic and the stablest society that the German nation has ever known. Its successes have been extraordinary. Admittedly under favorable circumstances, it has resolved or diminished conflicts at home and abroad that had dogged Germany for the first half of the century or longer. In retrospect one could be tempted to think of this achievement as a triumph of design; in fact, much of it was improvisation, chance, almost somnambulistic success.

The class antagonisms and social divisions of earlier periods have been muted; the belated *embourgeoisement* of a part of the German nation was made possible by the so-called economic miracle of the 1950s, which, when one remembers the availability of foreign aid and of general European recovery, appears less miraculous than the FRG's economic performance since 1973, when its economy had to cope with worldwide contraction, stagflation, oil price explosion, and increased competition. Throughout the thirty years, and on every level of government, the FRG has attracted higher political talent than any previous German regime. There have been scandals and failures; there has been justified concern over the initial response to terrorism; there is, I think, growing disaffection among the young—but the political culture as a whole has functioned remarkably well. And the power and resiliency of the West German economy remain extraordinary—though the Germans are worried lest contagion from abroad may yet decisively weaken it.

Reconciliation at home was paralleled by an unprecedented reconciliation abroad—also under a favorable constellation. By the late 1960s, a firmly integrated FRG, responsive to the Gaullist model, embarked on *Ostpolitik*, and by voluntarily recognizing the inviolability of existing frontiers and acknowledging the de facto statehood of the GDR (East Germany), it attained easier access to the GDR and Berlin. It sought, in the phrase of that time, "to save the substance of the nation."

Ostpolitik did promote reconciliation with the East, especially with Poland. To its proponents, it marked the liquidation of the past; skeptics, including Henry Kissinger and President Pompidou, thought that it could also mark the first step to an uncertain future. As Kissinger has recounted, Pompidou feared subsequent "nationalistic tendencies. . . . . German nationalism might break forth again and, if through calamity it had learned patience, it might prove even more dangerous."[7]

[IV]

In the first few years of its existence, *Ostpolitik* seemed to justify the hopes of its proponents—reconciliation—and not the fears of its opponents, i.e., a drift eastward or a loosening of Western ties.

But success usually imposes choices. Prosperity and power were bound at some point to pose basic questions. What is the national purpose? Can a divided Germany, given its national history, accept a Swiss-like future: prosperous and passive? Is greater concern with its national future not an almost inescapable burden for the FRG—and one that at the moment its neighbors may see more clearly than its own citizens?

In the spring of 1979, there was a sudden rush of speculation about the future orientation of the Federal Republic; it began at home and instantly acquired an independent life outside Germany. Two members of Helmut Schmidt's party, Egon Bahr and Herbert Wehner, both of whom had long favored a still more intensive Eastern policy, again hinted at possible alternatives for German foreign policy and gave their utterances added meaning by mysterious travels eastward. *Der Spiegel* devoted a lead story to "the return of the German question": in a front-page editorial the *Neue Zürcher Zeitung* worried about the many rumors concerning German fidelity. In October, Minister-President of Bavaria Franz Josef Strauss reiterated: "We will never accept the partition of the German nation into two states." Michel Jobert, former French Foreign Minister and quixotic super-Gaullist, warned about the possibility that America's China card could push the Soviets toward granting German reunification in exchange for neutralization—thus maligning all three principal partners of France at once. In November, Raymond Aron devoted a column to "German Unity," which he said "has now come back on the agenda." The signs of concern were unmistakable and endemic. By the end of the year, then, the question cropped up almost routinely in the press and in conversations in Western Europe. I heard echoes of it as well in the Soviet Union and Poland.

It seemed as if suddenly many Europeans had awakened to German power, presence and putative grievance—and sometimes confused greater German assertiveness and independence with some kind of imminent, dramatic reversal, some new premium set on reunification. In that extraordinary interlude in European history, that most recent, perhaps that last halcyon period from 1948 to 1973, one had assumed that reunification was a dead issue; indeed, that European peace was built on a permanently provisional solution of the German problem, i.e., the division of a country which in the seventy years of its unified existence had proven too strong for its assimilation into a European equilibrium. In the last year, more and more people have come to realize that the Federal Republic of Germany is not like any other state in the world. It is in fact the strongest state between the United States and the USSR, and the state with the greatest national grievance. True, the Germans have forsworn unification by force; true also that the grievance has been muted, in part because its origin is inextricably linked to German guilt. National division *was* self-inflicted, but that to most Germans it is a grievous anomaly and some form of reunification remains a distinct, unclear and unarticulated goal—surely that should not surprise us.

In 1979 the outside world speculated on the possible adventurism of the FRG, on sudden reversals of fundamental alignments. At such moments, to make the implausible seem more plausible, the old specters of the Treaty of Rapallo or of the Hitler-Stalin Pact are invoked—to demonstrate that in the past such sudden reversals in Russo-German relations had been possible. This is to conjure up risible analogies, galling to Germans who, in any case, mind having their fidelity constantly suspected. (One German diplomat said to me not long ago: "If you suspect your wife long enough, she will succumb to temptation"—a well-intended warning that somehow came out as an infelicitous threat.) In 1922 and 1939 Germany sought Russian aid against a hostile West; today the FRG depends on its Western allies for its very existence and for its security against Russian aggression.

But to focus on the remote possibility of a radical *renversement* may be to blind people to the incremental changes that are taking place. The FRG will remain the strongest power of Europe west of the USSR. Increasingly, it will use its power to enhance or protect its special interests, and these special interests link it to both West and East, if in very different ways. Other powers need to understand the special role that détente and *Ostpolitik* play for the FRG and the dangers, remote but real, inherent in Germany's relation with the East.

[v]

As the most vulnerable, the most exposed, and in some ways the most aggrieved member of the alliance, Germany had a special stake in détente. The Soviet Union, the sole threat to the FRG, also holds the keys to maintaining its most important national priorities: the safety of Berlin and the preservation and extension of existing contacts with the GDR. The leaders of the FRG can never forget the other Germany nor can they forget that Berlin is their hostage to the USSR *and* to the United States. Berlin marks the limits of independence. It is here that the Soviets can apply pressure which only the Western alliance can effectively counter.

Ostpolitik has succeeded in political, human and material terms, and even the opposition under Franz Josef Strauss has come to accept the substance of it. For the last few years, access to Berlin has not been an issue. More than 200,000 ethnic Germans have been allowed to leave Poland, the USSR, and other COMECON countries. According to rough German estimates, another 3 million of these former Germans remain in the East. (In a very real sense, these are hostages waiting to be freed by continued *Ostpolitik*.) Millions of West Germans have been allowed to visit the GDR, and a larger number of East Germans have traveled west than ever before. In purely humanitarian terms there has been a marked amelioration. Links between the German states on a familial level have grown significantly.

Relations between the two Germanies fluctuate, depending often on the degree of self-confidence that the GDR can muster. The cultural presence of the FRG in the East is an obvious inconvenience to the Honecker regime, which has responded by a policy of "reinforced borders" *(Abgrenzung)* and by new laws in

1979 that were meant to inhibit if not interdict contacts between East German citizens and foreigners. In 1978, trade between the two Germanies amounted to DM8.8 billion.* But the FRG's economic presence was also felt in other ways: Travel between the FRG and the GDR netted the latter a billion deutsche marks, and the projected Autobahn between Hamburg and Berlin will yield the East Germans another billion marks in hard currency. These sums make an essential difference to the functioning of the GDR economy. The FRG's unheralded aid to the GDR gives that country a margin of comfort—above and beyond what German socialism can provide for its own citizens. The FRG's hidden subventions to the GDR (of indirect help to the USSR, which imports some of its advanced technology from the GDR) and its open aid to West Berlin, where Bonn hopes that material largesse will counterbalance adverse demographic and cultural conditions, attest to its economic strength. *Ostpolitik* has made a significant difference to the well-being of both Germanies—and to the relations between them.

The signing of the Eastern treaties also ushered in a period of startling expansion of trade, especially between the FRG and the USSR. Between 1970 and 1976, while West German foreign trade doubled, its trade with the USSR nearly quadrupled in value, while trade with Poland and Hungary increased at almost similar rates. In the first nine months of 1979, its exports to the USSR exceeded those of the United States. In 1979, West German trade with the COMECON countries was almost as large as with the United States.

These figures tell but a part of the story. The expanding trade between the FRG and the USSR follows the old historic character of German-Russian trade. The FRG has become by far the largest exporter of finished products to the USSR of any Western country. In turn, it receives important raw materials from the Soviet Union, including roughly 25 percent of its imported natural gas under a long-term contract of 1974, large amounts of various metals and minerals, as well as 40 percent of its imports of enriched uranium.

---

* By 1986, trade between East and West Germany had nearly doubled, i.e., to DM15.2 billion. In the same year, the FRG's trade with the USSR came to DM18.7 billion, and with all "state trading countries" (including China and excluding the GDR) to DM47.1 billion, while the total trade of the FRG in that year was DM940 billion. The question obviously arises, whether in an approaching period of threatened protectionism the FRG could significantly expand its trade with the East.

In all, more than 50 percent of German imports from the USSR consist of fuel.

For some sectors of the German economy, exports to the USSR have become critically important: in 1973, 48 percent of West German exports of pipes went to the USSR. In 1979, the exports of Hoechst, Mannesmann, and Thyssen to COMECON countries amounted to 4 billion marks. At the present time, a consortium made up of German BP, Mannesmann, and Thyssen is negotiating another long-term agreement for further deliveries of natural gas, and the anticipated cost of such a deal is $11.8 billion. German industry has a stake in the cultivation of the Soviet market—as do its workers. *Ostpolitik* has proven to be profitable and has built up its own broad constituency at home.

Beyond these hard, substantial facts, there is a kind of boundless lure about the possibilities of cooperation; the Soviets have long toyed with the hope of attracting West German technological expertise and credit that would help them unlock the riches of Siberia—in return for which Germany would get secure access to the newly discovered or exploited energy resources. The earlier natural gas contract, which is to run until the year 2000, suggests a pattern of complementarity. The Soviets are dazzled by German know-how, by German efficiency; if anything, they exaggerate German powers. The West Germans, in turn, dream of a vast market, and both sides can draw on memories of earlier German help to Russian modernization. There remains mutual need, and, on the German side, the race to ward off would-be competitors.

There are compelling reasons, then, for the FRG to try to defend its special stake in détente—quite aside from the political consideration that its survival is of great tactical importance for the present government coalition, which claims a kind of paternity for *Ostpolitik*. But the FRG will not seek any dramatic reversals; it will continue to cultivate its several ties, to protect its various interests. There is no group in German society that would favor adventurism or a return to what used to be called *Schaukelpolitik*, the perpetual game of tilting and jilting between East and West that characterized earlier periods of German foreign policy, especially during the 1920s. Geography, history, and deep-rooted economic realities combine to make Germans conceive of themselves as constituting simultaneously a barrier and a bridge to the East. In the period of the cold war and the gradual rehabilitation of Germany, the role as barrier had priority; in a more nationalistic Europe, with a weakening America, the role as builder or guardian of bridges has come to seem more appropriate.

By whatever standards of past or present, the division of Germany is both unnatural and unalterable. The peace of Europe has been built on it; no one is likely to jeopardize the latter in order to repair the former. But in the minds of some there may be a dim hope: The division of Germany which in the past has symbolized and deepened the breach between the two Europes could perhaps also bring about a narrowing or bridging of that breach. For many a European leader, including, I believe, Helmut Schmidt, the eventual emergence of a Europe from the Atlantic to the Urals is a dream—not for today or tomorrow, but as a vision of some future so distant that it can barely touch policies today. But it could inform sentiment, it does represent a hope. The differences in social systems would diminish; the common interest, and, to some extent, the common past would come to the fore. In such a Europe there could be, not the old notion of West Germany annexing the East, but at least a much greater German cohesion.

[VI]

In the international revaluation of the FRG the Soviets have played a major role. For years the Soviets branded Bonn the hotbed of "revanchism." This was part of the prescribed orthodoxy of the Eastern bloc, and probably the one ideological plank that Russians, Poles, and Czechs accepted alike. In the last few years the Kremlin has abandoned that line, and in its more active *Westpolitik*, the FRG has become its central partner. In June 1978 Leonid Brezhnev formally acknowledged that relations between the FRG and the USSR had become "one of the factors of stabilization and détente in Europe." In October of that year, the USSR sent its top German specialist, Vladimir Semionov, as Ambassador to Bonn. Brezhnev's visit in May 1978 and his dramatic appeal from East Berlin in October 1979—announcing a unilateral reduction in the level of Soviet troops in the GDR and threatening the FRG if it accepted the American proposal for theater nuclear weapons— demonstrated the special place that Bonn occupies in Soviet policy.

Both Bonn and Moscow will try to preserve something of that special tie—if only as some hope for the future.

The relationship between the USSR and West Germany is of singular intensity; the Soviets know that they hold many cards in their hands, and perhaps they hope that a more nationally inclined Germany will be drawn ever closer by the play of mutual advantages—until a point of no return is reached. For years the Soviets and the Germans have regarded each other as principal enemies and as possible partners. The Soviets have tried to woo and bully the West Germans, have made finely calibrated use of the carrot and the stick. They have used every opportunity recently to make the stick appear more formidable and the carrot more enticing.

Both partners have greatly benefited from a decade of close relations. For the Soviets, the FRG's economic and technological presence has been of great significance. But there are political considerations as well: By drawing the FRG and its European partners closer to the USSR, the Soviets must hope that the distance between the Europeans and the Americans will widen. In the recent past, the Soviets have emphasized their historic roots in Europe and the common European interests: détente, SALT, trade—as against the hawkish, unpredictable, truculent Americans.

But the Soviets have paid for their revaluation of the FRG, and not only in regard to their own ideological purity. By accepting the implications of *Ostpolitik* they have opened the door to a certain interpretation of the two alliances. They have allowed for a greater presence of the FRG in the Eastern empire, most especially in Poland and Hungary. Above all, they have complicated their own relations with the GDR, which remains their principal outpost and the main military bastion of the Warsaw Pact. The GDR itself is becoming more important to the Soviets (in Africa, in COMECON, in trade), and hence its continued internal insecurities, characterized by flickerings of dissidence and by a faltering economy, must be worrisome to the Soviets. The closer relations between Moscow and Bonn have a certain exemplary, hence limiting, effect on the GDR as well.

Up to a point, the Soviets will exploit every possibility of mischief as regards the Western alliance. But would the USSR really want to see the FRG as the dominant power of a Europe that had regained a large measure of military autonomy, i.e., of a Europe where American influence and American constraints had significantly diminished? The Russo-German relationship has its clear limits on both sides, and there was cogency and historic resonance to the earlier, implicit Soviet-American bargain: You take care of your Germans and we take care of ours.

[VII]

It is not the purpose of this essay to chronicle or assess the complex diplomatic discussions that have engaged the United States and the Federal Republic in the wake of the Soviet invasion of Afghanistan at the turn of the year. One would judge that Helmut Schmidt and his Foreign Minister, Hans-Dietrich Genscher, have from the first acted in broad support of an American position that has itself been unfolding in the face of an extraordinarily complex and difficult challenge. The Germans appear to have been clearly more cooperative than the French on such crucial issues as a united policy on the export to the USSR of high-technology items of conceivable military application. And on the question of the Olympics—despite some German irritation over the lack of consultation before the president committed himself firmly on January 20, and despite some differences in timing—I believe that the ultimate German position has been foreshadowed by Mr. Genscher's statement of early February: "We expect solidarity from the U.S. in Berlin, and we will not deny it in the question of the Olympics."

At the same time, the Federal Republic has joined with the rest of the European community in urging the exploration of Soviet feelers concerning an ultimate neutralization of Afghanistan. Most Germans adhere to the position that détente in the European framework must be disrupted as little as possible. And there seems to be a German consensus that a sensible divison of labor within the alliance could preserve solidarity while recognizing special interests and capabilities.

The FRG has never doubted that an adequate defense is the absolute precondition for détente. Helmut Schmidt has been vociferous in demanding a balance of forces in Europe; to pursue détente under any other condition would be an invitation to blackmail and disaster. Agreement on principle between the Germans and the Americans has never guaranteed agreement on

specifics, and there has often been the suspicion on both sides—
lately particularly on the American side—that the other partner is
not doing enough. For all the temptations of détente and for all
the apprehensions of an eastward drift, the Germans know that
the Western alliance and the American nuclear shield are the sole
guarantee of German security, despite the extraordinary progress
that the Bundeswehr has made. Doubts about the credibility of
the American shield are not going to tempt the Germans to
abandon it. They are not likely to commit suicide out of fear of
death. The continued presence of Allied troops on German soil
embodies Allied determination to preserve the status quo against
any would-be disrupters, à tous azimuts (from any direction). Allied
troops, then, serve many functions and provide a kind of built-in
reality principle that has few historical analogues.

Throughout 1979, the FRG worked closely with the American
government to bring about the NATO decision of December on
the production and deployment of theater nuclear weapons in
Europe, with a large component to be based on German soil. It
was a highly successful and sophisticated diplomatic effort, and
demonstrated the strength of the alliance in military matters and
of Germany's commitment to sustain allied power. The West
German government had to fend off opposition from within its
own ranks and it had to withstand the most insistent threats and
blandishments from the Soviets. For the Soviets it was a critical
decision. They are genuinely fearful of nuclear weapons on
German soil aimed at Soviet targets. But the FRG's decision was
unambiguous and a portent of its likely attitude on other defense
matters. The German public seems to understand the simultaneity
of contradictory elements in its relation with the USSR: détente
and defense, cooperation and resistance.

Ostpolitik has built up its own momentum. To most Germans
it has ceased to be an option and has become a national necessity.
But its successful pursuit depends on continued Western integration. It is once again a complicated hand that history has dealt the
Germans. They must have Western support in order to carry out
a policy that at times will bring them into disagreement or even
conflict with their Western protectors. Since the Afghan crisis
broke, the German Question as such has faded temporarily into
the background. But the FRG will not go back to the cold war
denial of the reality of the GDR, to any effort at isolating it. At

most, the Germans will put the pursuit of closer contacts on ice, waiting for a phase in which the USSR would once again and on acceptable terms allow a policy of greater flexibility.

It is perhaps an irony of history that the greatest calamity that could befall the FRG today would be a collapse or even a decline of the West. Of their own accord the Germans are not likely to drift into an Eastern orbit or to succumb to what has been infelicitously called self-Finlandization. Only a West in disarray could make such adventurism or such defeatism plausible.

So in the end the question of Germany's future is inextricably related to the success of the United States, and of the West as a whole, in meeting the Soviet challenge. The task of coordinating Allied policies at a time when the nature of the challenge is in dispute and when the principal Allies, the United States, the FRG, and France, are responding to different pulls will prove hard, perhaps uniquely hard. It is already clear that the United States, deeply alarmed at the Soviet threat, will increasingly look to its allies and will find them uncertain, of many minds and tempers. Whatever common strategies can finally be agreed upon by governments, it is likely that in the public realm, including, in American terms, in congressional quarters, a certain impatience with lagging allies will build up. It does not require "the imagination of disaster" to think that a semi-Gaullist Europe could confront a sullen, exasperated America—to the (foolish) delight of the Soviets, who have always banked on a conflict among their enemies.

Of the centrality of German-American relations there can be no doubt. But these relations have changed as well: The United States has lost some power and the FRG, pushed into responsibility, has learned to exercise it. The agenda of potential disagreements is long. But at some point, the FRG will always support a steadfast America—with whatever misgivings. It is likely that the Germans will remain our strongest partner, and Helmut Schmidt our best ally, not despite but because of his often uncomfortable candor. But we must not confuse solidarity with an absence of tensions. We need to remember that the Germans have hostages in the East that none of the other Allies has. The United States must continue to assess realistically Germany's interests and options; it must reckon with Bonn's ties to Paris and Europe—and with the narrowness of the majorities that both Schmidt and Giscard must put to the test of elections in the fall of 1980 and the spring of

1981 respectively. Washington cannot afford the presumption of instant assent by Bonn—nor can the Germans indulge too much in procrastination. Perhaps better means of consultation can be devised so that substantive disagreements are not gratuitously exacerbated; but consultation can also be a prescription for paralysis.

We helped to fashion this uniquely successful German polity; we remain its principal defenders. Both sides need to tend these relations at a time when the FRG's new prominence will make them more difficult and potentially more rewarding. But beyond these generalities lies a more awesome charge. We must recover our credibility, not measured by military means alone, but by the implementation of an energy program that goes beyond rhetoric and minutiae, by the adoption of an economic strategy that will effect radical reforms. Nothing would sustain and benefit the alliance more than a domestically strong America; nothing would endanger it more than an enfeebled America. Credibility, too, begins at home.

EIGHT

GERMANY AND
THE UNITED STATES:
VISIONS OF
DECLINING VIRTUE

[1]

EVEN IN OUR CENTURY of upheavals, the turbulence of
German-American relations stands out as exceptional, swinging
twice from desperate enmity to spectacular amity. In 1917, Germany, recklessly reaching for world power, brought America to
Europe; American troops turned the tide in the Great War, and
in the same year that America entered on the global stage, the
Bolshevik Revolution challenged America's claim to moral leadership. In the intervening decades, German ambition, American
power, and the Soviet challenge have dominated world politics. In
1941, German power, driven to still greater frenzy and perfection,
once more brought America to Europe, this time to liberate it
from the Nazi terror and in alliance with the Soviet Union. It was
an alliance of rivals that only Hitler's Germany could have brought
about.

In the 1920s partially and fitfully, and since 1947 consistently
and forcefully, the United States turned from being Germany's
enemy to being its chief friend, ally, and protector—and the
reversals of role, from enemy to friend, brought a reversal of
sentiment. Both countries are unusually adept at sentimentalizing
foreign relations. When the United States was fighting Germany

in World War I, caricatures of the brutal Hun and the evil Junker abounded; in the second war, the reality of Nazi horror exceeded Western imagination. But at war's end, the Soviets became our chief opponent, and our image of the Germans grew more benevolent. Moreover, a defeated Germany fell under America's spell in a reversal that began a celebration of friendship and harmony that lasted until recent times.

I believe that the German-American alliance has lost the overexuberance of the immediate postwar years. It has become normal, and the new relationship has turned sober, *sachlich,* except at moments of national celebration. Lord Palmerston once said that Britain had no permanent friends, only permanent interests. In 1849, after the Russians had helped Austria to crush the Hungarian revolt, an Austrian statesman vowed: "By our ingratitude we will astonish the world." Seven years later, the Austrians attacked Russia. Palmerston's dictum is memorable and misleading: Even interests are rarely permanent, and for nations, as for individuals, the recognition of true interests is not always easy. But Palmerston's main concern was to warn against sentimentalizing politics and against assuming permanent congruence in a world of change.

For decades we assumed, on both sides of the Atlantic, that the United States and Germany were permanent and exemplary friends, held together by a common threat from the USSR. The United States, moreover, assumed that the Germans would be permanently grateful and compliant. I believe we are now discovering that we are allies bound by common interests and threatened by divergent ones, that the rhetoric of sentiment will not dispel the reality of conflict, and that we had best recognize the differences among ourselves and search for means of coping with them. We are allies with differences, friends with reservations.

By claiming that the alliance is turning normal, I do not for a moment wish to suggest that sentiment plays no role in statecraft; it does. At times nations do sense a special affinity or a special distance and even hostility for one another. In the nineteenth century the British felt a great enthusiasm for Greeks and Italians, and their poets were partisans of liberation. At the same time the British harbored the deepest suspicion of the Russian bear, who was forever pawing at the gates of India; it was an historic moment when British suspicion shifted from Russia to imperial Germany.

Sentiments rise and fall, and the new German-American alliance after 1945 was burdened by an exceptional baggage of feelings.

A special bond between the United States and the Federal Republic of Germany has lasted for nearly four decades. In this period there have been immense changes, and we now view the alliance more coolly; it has become an alliance among more equal partners, under more critical conditions, with increasingly divergent interests and perceptions and mounting suspicions. It would be dangerous to allow special occasions or extravagant rhetoric to becloud reality.

[II]

The Germans have called 1945 *Stunde Null*, and, however inappropriate was the implied suggestion of a complete break and a new beginning, that year did mark the moment when Germany was at its nadir and the United States at its zenith: The new friendship between victor and vanquished began at a time when Germany was in shambles, morally devastated, economically ruined, intellectually bankrupt—and America was at the height of its power. It was not only the victorious world power, unchallengeable by any other power, but it was self-confident that it excelled in all realms; it had no peer. At that point the Germans were enraptured by all things American; they looked upon America as sole protector and provider, as model and as guide. Never again was the gap between the two countries to be so great—or the effort to overcome it so intense. Germans came to the United States in droves, as students, as tourists, as vagabonds; they came for their requisite year in America, and it was in America that the true reeducation took place. Our efforts inside Germany were largely unsuccessful and often risible. But by and large—despite clouds of misunderstanding or lingering prejudice—Germans were enchanted by the United States, by its Care packages and its music, by its material power and its writers. It was inevitable that sooner or later enchantment would turn to disenchantment, that the German fascination with America would turn to excessive disillusionment. In a recent book describing changes in America over the last three decades and hence in the perception of America, Marion Countess Dönhoff, the most respected writer-editor in the FRG, recalls how, after the [German] collapse and the long years of moral perversion, intolerance and spiritual emptiness, the United States, with its modern, open society, with its unfettered debates, its optimism and its confidence in the future, appeared to those of us who at that time had the chance of getting to know America more closely almost as a revelation. . . . Students, scholars, politicians who in those years got to know America returned with the impression that that society was nothing less than the model of the modern society.[1]

Postwar Germans had no doubt whatever that their country was Western and that the long tradition of anti-Westernism had died with Nazism.

Perhaps President Kennedy's *"Ich bin ein Berliner"* had such an electrifying effect because it reciprocated the tacit identification of so many Germans with America. (Even today, one of the Greens said: "We have all become Americans.")

I am suggesting here that Germans did us or themselves no favor by embracing us so uncritically; their need was clear, and they saw us not as we were, even then, but as how we wanted to be and how they would have liked us to be. To be sure, America was self-confident, but in the year of our most constructive statesmanship, 1948, a young American historian, destined to become the greatest of his generation, Richard Hofstadter, wrote that American "culture has been intensely nationalistic and for the most part isolationist; it has been fiercely individualistic and capitalistic."[2] By 1948 America was facing an unprecedented historic challenge: to assume—more or less suddenly and by default—world leadership while preserving and enlarging democratic practices at home. To reconcile global imperium and isolationist, democratic tradition was a gargantuan task that could never be mastered, only fitfully attended to.

At the height of our power and political will, we helped to create the Federal Republic. Our success in promoting a new German democracy seemed proof of our strength and virtue. Under the threat of our new and mortal rival, the USSR, which has rattled this country ever since its creation in 1917, we quickly switched from a Morgenthau spirit of vengefulness to the generosity of the Marshall Plan, a splendid act of practical, self-serving idealism. We liked "our" Germany; successively, millions of GIs served in West Germany and found it uniquely congenial. In turn, we liked being liked, and Germans, distant and impoverished, were our European claque.* The liberal Establishment in America took a strong, almost proprietary, interest in the alliance and most especially in German-American friendship.

For the last decade or longer, the special glow by which Germany saw the United States has faded. The United States is no longer seen as the model society. Indeed, for many Germans— and for many Europeans—the United States and the USSR have been reduced to a moral equivalency: Both are superpowers that evoke fear and distrust. Americans resent this charge and see it as politically and morally reprehensible. To a large extent, however, after Vietnam and Watergate, after the faltering of so many of our domestic programs and hopes, the Europeans are only echoing the doubts that pervade America itself. Do we think of ourselves as we did in 1945? Americans revel in self-criticism, but as a nation we resent foreigners who echo such criticism. For a global power, we are remarkably, prohibitively, thin-skinned.

For decades we have assumed that even within the alliance we have a special relationship with West Germany. The Federal Republic was an American offspring; we fathered and protected it. It has been the most exposed member of the alliance; America was the guarantor of its endangered security. Under our benevolent protection, the Germans created miracles of their own. The economic miracle, a product of inherited skill, hard work, and the influx of foreign aid and refugees from the East, ushered in a quarter of a century of unprecedented growth and prosperity. With that growth came the pacification of German society; the much-vaunted class conflict was transmuted into new collaborative schemes and into a general *embourgeoisement,* and the old working class, still discriminated against, especially in access to education, lost its embattled sense of isolation. A kind of cultural miracle occurred as well: a young German elite embraced an American and Western orientation. That generation of Germans turned its

* It was a time of great patriotic pride in America—despite McCarthy, perhaps even because of McCarthy: one realized that a great tradition was being threatened. Yet some observers sensed the dangers of this new mood. Thus C. Vann Woodward recently recalled his response: "Unparalleled power, unprecedented wealth, unbridled self-righteousness, and the illusion of national innocence—it all struck me as an ominous combination full of potential dangers to the republic." C. Vann Woodward, *Thinking Back: The Perils of Writing History* (Baton Rouge, La., and London, 1986), p. 103.

back on that old German dream, that Germany should describe something different from Western soul-destroying capitalism and Eastern youthful barbarism, a dream that under Hitler had finally been realized—as a gigantic nightmare. Konrad Adenauer represented the beginning of what I have called the political miracle, Bonn's only briefly broken succession of effective and responsible leaders from Adenauer to Helmut Schmidt, each appropriate to the historic demands of his time. Chancellors were matched by political talent at other levels as well and it seemed as if the FRG— for all its faults, beginning with its purposely bungled de-Nazification policy—sought to make up for past calamities. Politicians had an almost Weberian sense of vocation, and thus Bonn gradually earned the respect and trust of its own citizens and of most of the outside world. In the fall of 1982 conditions changed, and *The Economist* noted at that time: "The West Germany that is preparing to get rid of Helmut Schmidt is a more worrying place than it has been at any time since 1945. In acquiring one sort of self-confidence—as western Europe's economic giant no longer in need of having political allowance made for it—it has lost another: the sort that goes with knowing exactly who you are, and where you stand in the world."[3]

The United States has watched with mounting apprehension as its most compliant client pursued its own détente policy, its own *Ostpolitik*—even as the United States backed away from détente. Both the United States and the Federal Republic tend to have expectations for each other's foreign policy that often ignore the realities of domestic pressures. So successful was Germany's integration and so close its relations with the United States that many people in this country forgot that German interests—beyond the fundamental interest in the preservation of peace—were necessarily dictated by geopolitics, by the presence of nearly 3 million *Volksdeutsche* in Eastern Europe, and 17 million East Germans, all of them in some sense hostages to détente. Their fortunes are linked to Soviet-German relations with an immediacy that many in the United States fail to understand. The well-being of Berlin also depends on the faithful execution of the Four-Power Agreement, and trade with Eastern Europe has become ever more critical in a period of protracted recession. But above all, many people in the United States—and perhaps some people even in the Federal Republic—forget what Germans could never forget: that Germany is the one country in Europe, perhaps the one major country in the world, with a deep national grievance. That the division of Germany was self-inflicted, the consequence of Hitler's war, does not lessen the German hope that someday—in the framework of a general pacification of Europe from the Atlantic to the Urals— the German nation will be reunited or that in an era without blocs the two German states will eventually forge special and permanent ties. Until recently, the issue of reunification was muted; it was almost as if the Germans had adopted the old French slogan from the post-1871 period concerning the loss of Alsace-Lorraine to Germany. The French followed the injunction: "Speak of it never, think of it always." No FRG statesman can even for a moment forget the tie to the German Democratic Republic or the ultimate hope of reunification. It is striking that Chancellor Kohl on the occasion of his trip to Moscow in July 1983 brought the issue openly to the fore. Franz Josef Strauss has also learned to fish in Eastern waters. Helmut Schmidt's admiration for the Poles was partially shaped by his awe for a people who regained statehood after 125 years of extinction. The dream of a German nation no longer divided is not going to disappear, regardless of which party is in office. It is the ultimate reason why the Federal Republic favors détente; but there are many more immediate reasons for preserving a policy that once had its wise analogue in Washington.

A chief difference between the Federal Republic and the United States—even on the governmental level—was and is a divergent perspective on the power and intentions of the USSR. The Germans tend to minimize the Soviet threat, the Americans periodically to exaggerate it—the vision of each influenced by respective interests. A divergent perspective necessarily leads to differences in policies, the latter also being attuned to divergent interests.* There have been many U.S. officials who are convinced that the USSR is bent on an aggressive course, as exemplified by the relentless advance in its armaments and by its aggressive conduct in various parts of the world. Convinced of Soviet power and fearful of Soviet

---

* An American historian, reflecting on this country's style in foreign policy, recently wrote that there has been a "persistent irrationality in [U.S.] postwar foreign policy. A central element of the American response to the outside world in this period has been an unthinking anticommunism," which he attributes to domestic strains and pressures in a profoundly changing society. Robert Dallek, *The American Style of Foreign Policy: Cultural Politics and Foreign Affairs* (New York, 1983), p. xvii.

intentions, these officials seek ever greater armaments and favor a tough course against the Soviet Union.

President Ronald Reagan probably does see the Soviet Union as "the source of all evil," and believes that détente gave it a chance to build up military superiority. In this view the Soviets are sneaky and strong, aggressive and expansive, ever on the prowl; they are godless to boot, and not like us. Their every move in the Middle East or in Central America is seen as yet another tentacle or part of some nefarious scheme to spread their odious influence into ever new areas. Early on, the Reagan Administration decided to restore the military balance that had existed before détente, to challenge the Soviets to a new arms race, which, it was hoped, would ruin them economically. Meanwhile Washington looked for ways to punish the Soviets for all kinds of transgressions, whether in Afghanistan or Poland, whether in the Middle East or in the shooting down of a Korean plane. American bellicosity in rhetoric— fortunately not matched in action—aroused fears everywhere, and American attempts to place the Soviet Union in some kind of moral quarantine—well provided with American wheat, however— seemed to Europeans a dangerous and ultimately immoral variant of a moralistic policy.

Many Germans—following general European perceptions—are more impressed by Soviet prudence, by the Soviets' efforts always to expand their power with minimal risk. Most Germans see the Soviets as heirs of Russian history and imperialism, still backward in all respects save the military realm. They see the regime as marked by essential conservatism and rigidity. They are much more impressed by the fears the USSR is prey to: fears that go back to the devastation of the Second World War, with the loss of 20 million Soviets, fears of a country that sees itself "encircled." (Germans should know that countries seized by this apprehension can act most irrationally, as German policy before 1914 demonstrated.) The Germans, in addition, have become apprehensive lest their protectors have come to speak loudly but carry a weak stick, a fear that first hit them at the time of the overthrow of the shah of Iran. They see a paradox in America's insistence that the Soviets are immensely powerful and immensely dangerous—but that their system could be toppled by imposing an arms race on them. The Germans see further selfish contradictions in U.S. preaching of economic restraint while concluding essential grain deals with the USSR and demanding of its allies greater military preparedness, especially in conventional weapons, without itself building a citizen army.

Like many Europeans and Americans, the Germans regret President Reagan's rhetoric; at best, they think it imprudent and dangerous. They are appalled by the return to political Manichean-ism—with the Soviets the incarnation of evil and the United States presumably, by definition, the source of virtue. Many critics also fear that the rhetoric either is intended to bespeak a defiant policy or will result in one as a self-fulfilling prophecy. Not a wild member of the peace movement but the eminent physicist-philosopher Carl Friedrich von Weizsäcker wrote in 1981, "While Soviet policy is uniformly concerned with power, American policy moves in waves, with swings of the pendulum, and the present pendulum swing aims at the recapture of America's hegemonial position in the world."[4] There is a widespread apprehension in Germany that the United States is pursuing a provocative course. Despite Helmut Schmidt's insistent warnings, many Germans have failed to notice that in the 1970s the Soviets augmented their military potential far beyond Western efforts.

[III]

We know that one dramatic issue dominated the recent past; the implementation of the double-track decision, the deployment of new American missiles of intermediate range on German soil. In the life of nations as of men there occur moments of crisis which jolt people into greater awareness of self and into greater recognition of earlier, barely noticed subterranean changes. Deployment was such a moment.

The debate over deployment brought so much to the fore: the prominence of the peace movement and the fear of so many West Germans that an uncontrolled arms race could lead to the incin-eration of both Germanys, a fear fed by a growing distrust of America's capacity for leadership; a recognition of uniquely Ger-man, of uniquely national, interests, about which one felt less and less inhibited to talk. Deployment stirred up thoughts of national destiny, and West Germans lived through what Freud called "the

return of the repressed." In 1983, the German question reap-
peared—in all its intractable complexity.

The Reagan Administration seemed largely oblivious or scorn-
ful of these changes, as it was of the general deterioration of the
alliance. As deployment began in November 1983, and did so
without the oft-predicted violence, Washington thought that good
sense had triumphed over some kind of politically tainted wooli-
ness, that the Soviets, so anxious to stop deployment, had suffered
a major defeat.

But deployment dramatized the deepest issue. It suddenly
made Germans realize their dependency, the limits of their autonomy, the extent of their vulnerability. It also made them feel a
certain chilly isolation: Many Germans feared that the new missiles
added to Germany's insecurity rather than security.[5] They thought
that to deploy the Pershing II missiles—which can reach to the
suburbs of Moscow, where the Germans were once before—was a
provocation to the Soviets. To them, deployment suggested a
further escalation of hopelessness and helplessness, an abdication
of human and political responsibility. They thought themselves
misunderstood: as they became more conscious of the special
vulnerabilities of the FRG, they thought that the great protector,
the United States, was heedless of them—and that circumstances
had left the West Germans exposed and dependent.

In the 1980s it became ever more acceptable to speak of
German interests, to emphasize German needs, and above all to
speak with a new urgency about German-German relations. In
muted form these themes had been there since the mid-1970s; in
the election of 1983, the Socialists ran on the slogan: "In the
interest of Germany."[6] Disappointed in the West, disturbed by
economic dangers, many West Germans turned to the other
Germany and the consciousness of partition has become ever
greater. A chronic, half-forgotten pain suddenly became sharper
and less tolerable.

None of this was necessarily ominous. None of it could be
understood in isolation. In part the Germans were responding—
along with many Europeans and Americans—to the new emphasis
in American policy under President Reagan.

America is not historically minded—the Europeans, who once
were, have also lost much of their historical sense. But an America
that is ever ready to celebrate something new is sometimes blind

to change. Thus with our relations with the FRG. Many assumed that the FRG would forever remain our most compliant client; they did not see that Helmut Schmidt's critical, sometimes contemptuous style was a kind of world-historical metaphor for the FRG's maturity and increasing assertiveness. The last two American administrations assumed the status quo *en permanence*. The alliance would remain the guarantor of peace; we accepted that it would always be "a troubled partnership," but never doubted that the alliance—already unique in its longevity in peacetime—would continue because it corresponded to the national interests of all concerned.

We assumed that the West Germans were "ours," even as the Sovietized East Germans were "theirs." We knew that the Germans needed our protection for their security. And in the process we forgot that Bonn was intended as a *provisorium,* that the federal constitution anticipated the time when the two Germanys would be reunited "in peace and freedom." We also forgot that NATO was originally intended to contain the Soviets openly—and the Germans, discreetly. We forgot to reckon with changes that were occurring in the FRG, in its place in the world, both in absolute terms and relative to our own standing in the world.

For several decades we forgot "the German question," as did so many Germans. We assumed that Adenauer's original option for Western integration and indefinite postponement of reunification would last forever. We did not anticipate that once the FRG had become the most powerful country in Europe west of the USSR, that once it had become somewhat disenchanted with the dream of Europe or the model of America, it would recall Germany's historic unity, it would remember that it uniquely is a powerful state with the deepest national grievance. People assumed too readily that the division of Germany had become a tacitly accepted fact—and one of great convenience to Germany's neighbors and allies. Tacit renunciation of reunification inspired other forms of preserving "the substance of the nation," and *Ostpolitik* gave the FRG the chance and context to improve German-German relations. These relations are growing ever closer—and on every level. At a time of overall contraction, trade between the two Germanys is increasing, as are various forms of close economic cooperation. To a surprising extent they are insulated from the coldness between the superpowers—at times, indeed, the coldness has strengthened collaboration between the two Germanys. The process of collaboration has built up its own dynamic, with risks and rewards for both sides. German-German relations have entered an entirely new and fascinating phase.

Most non-Germans probably underestimated the permanence of the German question. We were unprepared for "the return of the repressed," for the reappearance not only of German concern for the "other" Germans, but of the brooding that has set in about German identity, about German destiny, a blend of *Realpolitik* and dreaming, of wishing for a purer past and a deeper future. In 1983, Richard von Weizsäcker wrote that "curious ambivalence marks this German question. On the one hand, it has existed with ever greater vitality. There is hardly a serious political controversy in which sooner or later this question does not emerge."[7] In his book *German History Has Not Stopped*, Weizsäcker argues that the overcoming of partition is not the same thing as unification. It is, however, an effort to diminish the barriers of partition, and he himself has done a great deal to demonstrate the possibilities of German-German contacts. Like many other West Germans, he attended the celebration of Luther's 500th birthday which was held in East Germany, in the Marxist-Socialist state, which in recent years and with some success has tried to appropriate some of the German historic patrimony. Luther was symbolic; the GDR's debt to the West amounting to nearly $8 billion is symptomatic, as is the fact that from 1980 to 1983 West German exports to the GDR rose by nearly 25 percent. The two Germanys are closer today than they have ever been, and some West Germans have come to think that the GDR, that curious amalgam of old-fashioned, small-town life with socialist exhortation and drab austerity, is perhaps more "German" than the Americanized consumer society of Bonn. The appeal of austerity—from a safe distance—is still great.[8]

"The return of the repressed" reflects a change of mood. West Germans are disenchanted with America; they feel alone—and a pervasive, contagious *angst*. In December 1983, Helmut Schmidt defined the sources of *angst*: "It is a fear of unemployment, of the natural conditions of life. . . . There is a growing fear that our total society, that our state or its leadership might not have the necessary understanding and the needed decisiveness to deal with these dangers, to circumscribe them and to avoid them. . . . [The rise to great power of] inexperienced people or, worse, of dilettantes . . . arouses further fear. In me, too." This fear, present everywhere in the West, is worse for Germans because they lack a clear sense of national identity and still suffer from the legacy of Hitler.

Schmidt calls today's fear irrational: "It sits in our soul, it does not come from reason." It is spreading in the FRG and it alarms Germany's neighbors. "Once again 'the restless Germans'—thus speak many Frenchmen and other European neighbors." If Germans allow this impression to spread it will become a self-induced political liability because it will lead other nations to contain "German freedom of action and legitimate German interests."[9]

"The restless German, the incalculable German": these are epithets that Germans use as taunts for their political opponents. A critic of the alliance is quickly dubbed "restless"—and warned that too many critical voices will make the rest of the world nervous and thus will jeopardize the trust so carefully built up during years of loyal obedience. In his defense of deployment to Parliament, Hans-Dietrich Genscher warned that the Western neighbors were troubled by "a new kind of unpredictable German neutralism. . . . Theirs is the concern that in a state of somnambulence we Germans might proceed to withdraw from the Western community, captivated by the illusion that we can best solve our national problems through neutralism."[10]

The fear of the "restless" German could have salutary effects, too: the specter of a neutralized Germany already prompts greater French solicitude for the FRG. A new Franco-German condominium—far closer than anything we have seen so far—could evolve in the next decade, based on common needs and on a common mistrust of the two superpowers, a condominium that would establish an entirely new pattern of military and economic integration. More or less secret talks on greater military cooperation have been underway for some time. A much closer Paris-Bonn entente that would prove the basis for a more independent Western and Central Europe is a distinct if remote possibility—especially if the European community should fade into ever greater insignificance.

"A reunited, neutralized Germany"—that has been a recurrent dream of some Germans—and a nightmare for Germany's neighbors. It seemed an option in the early 1950s (Stalin's famous note of 1952), Henry Kissinger feared it in the beginnings of *Ostpolitik* around 1970, and it has resurfaced now. Most Germans and most Europeans would reject it—if for different reasons. The Germans would reject it because it is improbable and unwelcome: A neutralized Germany would be too vulnerable to Soviet threats or blandishments, the Austrian example notwithstanding. Europeans reject it because a united Germany, with its immense economic strength, would pose too great a threat to Europe's stability. Still, there is a vision that attracts a growing number of people everywhere: the dissolution of both blocs and a reintegration of Europe, a Europeanization of Europe. Germans hope that in the wake of such a reintegration some closer bond between the two Germanys could emerge as well. For the time being—and in the absence of any sign that the Soviets would want to play so daring a game— neutralism is a kind of dream. German interests, economic and political, would argue against neutralism, but sometimes people act not out of interest but in pursuit of some kind of collective national dream and such dreams must also be taken seriously. Heinrich Heine recognized the role of dreams:

> *It's only when dreaming his ideal dreams*
> *That a German boldly expresses*
> *The German thoughts he bears so deep*
> *In his loyal heart's recesses.*[11]

Many Germans are anxious and some are angry. They resent their own dependency, especially at a moment when they wonder whether this imported security may not actually be a concealed risk. In their dubiety and anger they rediscover that they enjoy only limited sovereignty; the Allies withheld certain normal attributes of sovereignty from a state which has yet to have a regular peace treaty. The Allies, for example, retain their rights in Berlin, and the West Germans forswore the development of their own nuclear weapons. The FRG's formidable Bundeswehr is entirely integrated into NATO. As Germans begin to think of alternate strategies for themselves, as they begin to spin dreams about the dissolution of both blocs and the Europeanization of Europe, they discover that the prohibitions on sovereignty correspond to still deeply rooted apprehensions about the Germans. The Soviets are not the only ones in Europe who would resist a reunited Germany;

the Western nations have similar reservations and memories. In short, the Germans are discovering all sorts of things about themselves, and to generations that have been brought up largely ahistorical, these reminders are especially perplexing. In their present mood and after the agitation over deployment, a strident tone is sometimes struck. I recently heard a leading German writer lament the fact that Germans were still living under an occupation power, that the United States was the *Besatzungsmacht*—a term that to his generation and mine instantly recalls the German occupation of most of Europe during the Second World War. Rhetoric matters, and these are deliberately wounding epithets that express anger and resentment.

In their apprehensions, the Germans are not alone. But in a newly felt estrangement or isolation, in the absence of the earlier comforting miracles, the Germans, like so many other Western nations including the United States, have turned more inward, thereby augmenting their fears and estrangement. Some Germans, as I mentioned earlier, dream of a new dispensation in Europe. In September 1983, Rudolf Bahro, a popular figure who left the GDR and is now a leader of the Greens, spoke of "our aims—to withdraw both parts of Germany and Europe from the two military blocs and to neutralize Europe."[12] In December, Rudolf Augstein, publisher of *Der Spiegel*, wrote "that if the Soviet Union, contrary to every expectation, offered authentic unification of the two German states—not merely a loose confederation—we, the West Germans, like the Germans of the German Democratic Republic, would respond to our submerged national impulse. The problem, meanwhile, is to survive until we get to that point."[13] Survival is threatened, he believes, by the possibility that the two superpowers would, in a confrontation, "use German soil as their battlefield." Other nations have also turned inward and seek to protect their immediate interests; in a similar mood the Germans turn to the other Germany.

For the time being, most Germans affirm that the alliance remains an historic necessity, but as public opinion polls show and as private conversations confirm, there is little passion behind the commitment either to Brussels or to the Atlantic Alliance. Many Germans probably see the inevitability of existing ties, but it would be myopic to assume that the same number would subscribe to

Richard von Weizsäcker's assertion that the FRG's political order demands the closest association with the other Western democracies—and that that tie is "final and irrevocable."[14]

In Germany, as elsewhere in Protestant Europe, much passion has been invested in the peace movement. In the FRG, as elsewhere, it is a response to the new cold war and the new arms race, though the fear of nuclear power in any of its guises is real enough. But in the FRG there is the added fear that the two Germanys would become the battleground of the two superpowers. The Greens overlap with the peace movement; their anarchic concern with ecology, with the defense of nature against the mindless greed of a driven, achievement-bent society, is neither new nor exclusively German. But both these movements have a specific German element to them; they speak of a new concern for *German* interests.

The peace movement has attracted a following in the other Germany as well—and again largely through the agency of the churches, the only possible forum for opposition. (The GDR is predominantly Protestant and hence it has been the Protestant churches that have spoken for peace and thus encouraged a peace movement in a country where "peace" had been the monopoly of state propaganda.) Here is an additional tie between the two Germanys and an element of what might be called a new common consciousness of the German nation. Many Europeans speak of the two superpowers as if the term connoted not only equal power but some rough moral equivalence as well. In the two Germanys this sense of being at the mercy of the two superpowers (one of which, no doubt, is still held in far greater fear than the other) is probably spreading.

Perhaps something else was repressed and is now returning: the German soul, that indefinable, unquiet spirit so full of a kind of nostalgic longing for a vague future. I believe there is such a thing as the reappearance of the German soul in world politics, at present in domestic politics and fastened on the overriding necessity for peace. That soul—those strivings of the German spirit which in the past have fused idealism and nihilism with little room for practicality—has often had a calamitous effect on the outside world. This time the German soul combines a universalist appeal—against war, against nuclear lightheartedness—with a nationalist note that speaks to the division of the country. German preoccupation with self may be the contemporary analogue to nationalism, and the world is leery of anything that resembles German nationalism because of its aggressive past, its unsatisfied present, and its unpredictable future. History would suggest that an FRG that feels itself isolated abroad and beset at home is most likely to be volatile or unpredictable.[15]

[IV]

In the United States—in the government, among some members of the Congress, and probably in a growing section of public opinion—there is a sense that the Europeans, but most especially the Germans, are showing ingratitude and political myopia; the United States expected a permanently compliant Germany. There is an American impatience with what is viewed as inadequate military efforts on the parts of the Europeans, again with a particularly high standard for the Germans. Why should the Europeans not make the supreme effort to defend themselves conventionally or at least do much more in that direction—even at the huge social sacrifice that that would entail?* Just as American speeches are taken as bellicose, so German speeches and marches are taken as signs of incipient appeasement, of creeping neutralism—and there is no doubt that a small but growing German minority would favor a bloc-free, more or less neutralized Europe. A tiny but ever-growing minority of Germans favor unilateral disarmament. The overwhelming majority of the Germans continue to favor NATO.

The two countries trust each other, and yet within each there are groups that view the other with deep apprehension. Americans are afraid that the Federal Republic might drift away from the alliance in an Easterly or neutralist direction, and there are Germans who fear that the United States is seeking to regain its hegemonial position, trying to force the Soviets to their knees, or conversely that the United States might return to a sullen, protectionist isolationism. Specific events, when seen in the perspective

---

* In 1984, a French Foreign Ministry official, Bernard D'Aboville, told an American audience that "making the world safe for conventional war is not at all appealing for Europeans." Quoted in *Securing Europe's Future*, edited by Stephen J. Flanagan and Fen Osler Hampson (Dover, Md., 1986), p. 42.

of fear, can be read as confirmatory evidence: German *Ostpolitik* or an American Senate that threatens to cut off funds from the United Nations. Beneath the still friendly rhetoric between governments, misperceptions, parochialism, and polarization seemed on the increase; a negative dialectic was beginning to be at work, a reciprocity in mistrust, which no amount of intergovernmental harmony could fully banish. The rifts in the Alliance were greater than ever before.

Fears are exacerbated by ever-growing difficulties. Is it too much to say that for the Federal Republic the economic and political miracles have ended all at once? The protracted recession signals the end of an unprecedented period of prosperity. The political scene in the Federal Republic may also turn less stable, and however much some Americans find Chancellor Kohl's amiability more pleasing than Helmut Schmidt's always instructive acerbity, they will find that he speaks for a more troubled polity. The emergence of the Greens as a fourth party, or rather the emergence of a fourth party that claims to be an antiparty, the leftward drift of a Socialist party in opposition, the difficulties that Chancellor Kohl will encounter in balancing demands for social services, for investment, and for military purposes—all of these elements will complicate the political scene in the Federal Republic. The Kohl government began with great promises, but inspires little confidence; the Germans have acquired a kind of *Unlust* (dissatisfaction) with their present politics, and the only hopeful sign is the choice of Richard von Weizsäcker as the president of the FRG; he at least will again present the FRG—and, in time, perhaps the world beyond—with a voice of the greatest integrity and intelligence. For thirty-five years the FRG has benefited from greater political stability, better political leadership at all levels, and a higher degree of social cohesion than any other regime in German history. But now the Federal Republic may also be turning more normal.

The context within which alliance issues have to be resolved has grown more difficult. In the economic realm—as in so many others—the two countries need each other, have common international interests and aims, and benefit from the open markets they both believe in. But there are divisive issues as well: The Germans are troubled by America's ever-growing fiscal deficit, which a conservative administration is amassing; their economists, as ours, see in that deficit the cause either for continued high interest rates or for renewed inflation. The Germans are not alone in wondering how future historians will judge a nation that could recklessly and with seeming oblivion defy economic prudence and tacitly admit that the immediate political price for fiscal responsibility is too great to pay—hence burdening an unknown future with present debts. The United States in turn is apprehensive about Germany's Eastern trade. The two countries are competitors in some fields, and both are threatened by the appearance of new rivals, especially in East Asia, where capitalism, unexpectedly, has apparently found its last and most congenial home. Unemployment is the most serious challenge in the Federal Republic today.

We need to acknowledge as well that we live with what is often called the successor generation—a generation that hardly remembers the halcyon days of the Alliance, the early days of America's abundance. Its political education was formed in Vietnam, and its fears focus on American involvement in Lebanon and Central America, in the Philippines and Chile. Of their own past, many young Germans are relatively ignorant; Hitler's crimes are distant in every sense. In truth, they are an unhistorical generation and know nothing of John Dos Passos's warning that "In times of change and danger when there is a quicksand of fear under men's reasoning, a sense of continuity with generations gone before can stretch like a lifeline across the scary present. . . ."[16]

The younger generations on both sides are drifting apart and have no a priori sense of affinity. The governing elite of America is also changing, and the predominance of what we called the Eastern or liberal Establishment is a thing of the past. We can no longer count on an automatic affinity or on people feeling at home in each other's country.

[v]

Both sides have to recognize the profound changes in mood and political designs that have developed despite the surface normality. The alliance cannot be saved or served by amiable rhetoric. A troubled FRG and a divided Germany in the heart of Europe remain a permanent challenge to the status quo. The Europeans must recognize America's global interests, especially its ever-growing involvement in the Pacific Basin, and American impatience with Europe's lagging contributions to defense. To speak of the possibility of a new American isolationism is not a scare tactic vis-à-vis the Europeans. It is part of a realistic assessment of the possibilities of estrangement.

The Europeans must understand the depth of irritation that many Americans feel at European passivity. They cannot ignore the recent speech by Lawrence Eagleburger, then Undersecretary of State and an old Europe-hand, who warned that continued European parochialism would force a shift in U.S. foreign policy toward greater concentration on the Pacific area and toward still greater collaboration with Japan. Henry Kissinger's call for a radical restructuring of NATO also reflects the fear that the continuation of the status quo, including the self-injuring European dependency on American protection, could encourage an American neo-isolationism, a new kind of backlash. He has harsh words for all; his analysis of the present inadequacies will dismay only those who wish to live in ignorant comfort, but whether the Europeans will respond to these appeals or to what the French like to call the logic of events remains to be seen.

The core of the alliance—and of German-American relations—is security. There is general agreement that in the immediate postwar period the United States unilaterally, and after a few years the United States in NATO, provided the necessary shield for Europe—and for thirty-nine years preserved the peace. (The earlier record for lasting peace in Europe was forty-four years—and ended in 1914.) Containment and deterrence remain the goals of the alliance, but the credibility of nuclear deterrence has become ever more controversial. In its present state and with its present strategic plans, the alliance—according to some of its critics—provides risk and security in roughly equal measure. The presence of 200,000 GIs in Germany also provides unambiguous evidence of America's resolve to defend Europe. Many Germans would want even more men—and fewer missiles, or none. On the other hand, if European carping persists, if the Europeans fail to make a greater defense effort, then the United States, divided in its views and taxed by the increased use of its military all over the world, may decide to reduce or withdraw its European contingents.

The Europeans are more aware of the German question than we are; they worry about "whither Germany," and thereby deepen

Germany's sense of relative isolation. Our bilateral relations are both separate from and an integral part of the alliance: if the latter drifts apart, if it slides into a "progressive divorce," as the French foreign minister remarked, then German-American relations will suffer as well. Bonn has always striven to avoid conditions in which it would have to choose between Europe and America. Its ties to Europe grew stronger as its trust in the United States diminished, but the crisis in Brussels complicates relations among the European allies. The trouble is that Europe's search for greater autonomy, its much-vaunted wisdom that comes in the form of *Realpolitik*, is not accompanied by the political will to construct a credible autonomy, to become truly independent. A carping Europe with the pious wish to be equidistant from both superpowers, is going to succumb to semi-Gaullism, i.e., a Europe that has the wish but not the will to be independent. Gaullism as a reverie rather than as a summons to action is a prescription for resentment. Gaullism on the cheap is worse than the whole of the general's audacious vision.

Reason and collective self-interests prescribe a different course. But material difficulties and new fears could induce irrational responses, to the detriment of all. In democracies generally and in the United States in particular, foreign policy is not an insulated charge of a few, and hence both in the FRG and in the United States, there will have to be a greater commitment to the alliance by all the groups of a civil society, i.e., by business and labor, by the professions, by scholars and writers. The message should be clear: Our values and our interests demand that the remaining, embattled democracies hold together and learn to live with their differences; they must aid other nations who seek to escape the clutches of authoritarianism. Interest and sentiment should tell us that there is no escape from our friendship, that at present there is no alternative to an alliance that protects the future. To our German friends one would want to say that between the 1890s and Hitler's end, their penchant for utopianism, their restlessness, has in some fields been one of their most attractive traits; in politics, it has been calamitous. To which Germans might reply that American moralism has been attractive and dangerous as well. By and large, in the last four decades, the two countries have shown a healthy sense of realism and prudent self-interest—with a dash of intermittent generosity rare among nations. They need to cling to that recent, undramatic achievement.

IV

Historians and
the German Past

AMERICANS AND THE GERMAN PAST: A CENTURY OF AMERICAN SCHOLARSHIP

In 1984, the American Historical Association celebrated its centenary and at its annual meeting devoted special sessions to the history of American scholarship in diverse fields. What follows is a revised and enlarged version of my lecture on American writing on Germany.

The topic combined two abiding interests of mine: the history of historiography and the writing of German history. It also gave me a chance to ponder the development of American scholarship of Europe, at once akin to and yet quite different from Europe's own efforts. I was struck by the simultaneity of America's becoming a world power and its historians acquiring world status. I enjoyed studying—even if in a narrowly focused manner—the work of several generations of American historians; I relished returning to themes I had once discussed with my friend Richard Hofstadter. Americans were shrewd commentators on the Germany of their time; Thorstein Veblen devoted a book to Germany, others formulated their views on the current political or cultural scenes in letters or articles. In short, my subject touched not only on historical writings per se but on the temper of German and American life as well. The two World Wars and the arrival of European émigrés had a profound effect on American scholars: The topic demonstrated again the openness of our discipline, the responsiveness—at once enhancing and endangering—of historians to the public drama during their own lives.

This essay appeared in *Central European History* in 1986.

THE FOUNDING of the American Historical Association a hundred years ago invites these reflections on American scholarship, even as we know that there is something arbitrary about chronological exactitude concerning intellectual endeavors. American involvement with German historical thought did not begin with the founding of the AHA. It started earlier, it started, like so much else, with Leopold von Ranke and with the founding of his historical school. The establishment of the AHA and of the *American Historical Review* reflected American efforts to emulate German and European professionalization. Americans, too, came to recognize the importance of academic—or, as it was then put—scientific history. In what has often been called an unhistorical country, an uphill battle began.

We are commemorating a century in which American historians in their relation to Germany moved from dependency through a kind of academic emancipation and political antagonism to equality and collaboration. It is a story that begins with German preeminence when overeager American students transplanted German institutions and methods to America and hoped to write American history in the German style. By 1903, a new generation of American historians sought to free themselves from the German model; the Progressive historians misinterpreted and partially repudiated Ranke in order to foster a "new history," designed to serve the needs of a new America. Some American students found Imperial Germany far from congenial, but, whether pro-German or troubled about Germany, hardly any of them ventured into the *writing* of German history.

The Great War and America's involvement in it posed the German problem and altogether brought us closer to Europe. During the war, some leading historians took an early, often a crude anti-German stance; Germans now paid for the excessive admiration they had exacted, encouraged, or accepted, and many Americans turned unreflective admiration into uncritical antagonism. After the war, American historians, imbued with a new sense of commonality with Europe, started to tackle European history and gradually achieved international recognition. When defeated Germany turned into a monstrous tyranny, we became the guardians of German history; from 1933 to 1945, German history was being written here and in England or not at all. The German problem proved an immediate political and historiographical challenge; the latter was made evident by the arrival of German exiles, German-trained historians who came to an America that was at least partially receptive to their presence. The Second World War and America's postwar role of Western leadership fashioned a younger generation of American historians who were at home in Europe and its intellectual life and some of whom contributed important, original interpretations of the German problem.

The postwar generation—my generation—had its share of undeserved good fortune. We grew up—whether in the United States or in Europe—at a time when Europe was the center of passionate political and ideological conflict. Europe was dramatically inescapable. We became historians of Europe when the field was enriched by that unprecedented mixture of indigenous and foreign, especially German, talent.

In the last twenty-five years, American and German historians have collaborated as never before; our works are divided not along national lines but by substantive orientation, by differences in style and method. We have reached a rough equality in achievement. Both sides suffer from a tendency to ever greater specialization, while at the same time the immediate political impetus has diminished. "Why National Socialism?" no longer grips a younger generation with the immediacy that it gripped its predecessors. In short, the framework of 1933 has become less compelling and more controversial. Nor have the days of German preeminence returned: American historians of American history are more likely to know the work of French or British historians than of contemporary German historians.

In what follows I shall dwell on the earlier period, on the distant beginning and the dramatic phase when greater intellectual sophistication and political upheavals coincided, and historians saw the past in greater complexity and with some moral urgency. I shall say less about the most recent past or the living present because presumably it is more familiar and in any case most of the contemporary work has become too minute and too multifaceted to allow even for classification. It is also true that historians prefer to deal with the past rather than the living—and this not only for prudential reasons.

The growth of American scholarship in the German field touches on some of the great themes of our time and discipline. It demonstrates the openness, the malleability of history. It illustrates the responsiveness of historians to changes within and without the discipline. The history of history, as exemplified by our topic, is a study in changing cultures; at times, why historians write the way they do may be as revealing and important as what they write. The ideals and practices of historians, the material conditions of research and publishing, have changed—and so has the class and cultural milieu of American historians. Patrician scholars presided over the professionalization of history; at the beginning of the twentieth century a different breed of men arrived, self-made, mostly from the Midwest, attuned to a Progressive America, grappling with the problems of an industrial civilization. They set forth new principles of American historiography. The Progressive historians were revised in turn. American historians of Germany were affected by these changes, just as they were affected by the changes in German historiography and above all by the radical transformations of Germany itself. At the founding of the AHA, the United States and Germany were distant countries; they became rivals, enemies, friends by turns. Twice in the twentieth century, America battled German ambitions; in both wars, a great divide was opened. Most Americans regarded the Third Reich as a challenge not only to the security of the West, but to our basic values and assumptions. Certainly historians had to view it that way. Fleetingly after the Great War and enduringly after the second, the United States sought to bridge that divide by measures of utilitarian beneficence. German history was being written in the shadow of catastrophic events.

There is a picture, idyllic in the eyes of some, of the lonely scholar, buried in the archives, reconstructing a past by dint of the critical sifting of surviving evidence, insulated from the storms outside, from passions inside. No doubt such scholars exist, but I doubt that there are many. I think of the great Theodor Mommsen, of whom such a legend was forged. His political testament taught us otherwise: The world did impinge on most of our colleagues.

Many knew that it did and still sought to write dispassionate history; those who did not know it were more likely to write partisan history. I hope I can at times catch something of the drama that was an essential part of our seemingly sedate, scholarly story.

To return to the beginnings: In 1884, American historians founded our association—a professionalization that lagged behind Germany's by a generation. But then the whole temper and experience were different. In Europe, the French Revolution and Napoleon had forced a new sense of history on people, and the ever-growing cult of the nation demanded knowledge of a nation's past as well. Americans were less affected by these upheavals, and their nationalism was not so competitive; Americans had not so much a common past as a common future. The systematic study of the past was less of a cultural-political imperative in America than in the rival nation-states of Europe.

Richard Hofstadter once remarked that "in the common American opinion, the heroic conduct that made the Revolution and the wise statecraft that made the Constitution showed that the country was launched under the leadership of men who were virtual demigods and under institutions that were close to perfection." But Americans also believed in the Whig interpretation of history, "in which the idea of progress is a central tenet. How can a people progress if they have started near to perfection?" Still, the belief that one could move from near perfection to ever greater heights was a recurrent, happy, contradictory tenet of American exceptionalism. But of course America *was* different, it was—to quote Hofstadter once more—the "first post-feudal nation, the first nation in the world to be formed and to grow from its earliest days under the influence of Protestantism, nationalism, and modern capitalist enterprise."[1]

If the United States was and thought itself remote and unique, if it believed in its own exceptionalism, there would be less reason to study the past of other nations, dissimilar and malevolent and bigoted as these nations were. In the nineteenth century, when gifted amateurs still dominated the field and thought history a branch of literature, there might have been reasons for studying edifying subjects, such as the Revolt of the Netherlands, that either resembled or affected America's struggle for independence, but indifference and deference made Americans shy away from writing about the European past.

In nineteenth-century America, European history, in Leonard Krieger's words, was prenatal American history, hence marginal.[2] There was little incentive to study about Germany, but every reason for studying *in* Germany. The German university, as reformed by Humboldt, was a magnet for foreigners; between 1820 and 1920, some nine thousand American students attended German universities.[3] George Bancroft was the most illustrious American student in Berlin and Göttingen, where to boot he formed a lifelong friendship with Bismarck. Others flocked to the mecca of knowledge as well; they attended the lectures of Ranke and Johann Gustav Droysen, later of Heinrich von Treitschke and Karl Lamprecht. There were no native equivalents to these giants. A hundred years ago, there were some four hundred colleges and universities in the United States and about twenty full-time historians.[4] The Germans, on the other hand, had enshrined history as a discipline central to all *Bildung* and had given learning a special nimbus, had invested it with a special kind of awe.

Many American students were impressed by the scientific ideal, by the assumption that historians had to re-create the past according to verifiable sources; some assumed that the scientific ideal also demanded the strictest objectivity. They came to accept the notion that history was a cumulative body of knowledge, built up fact upon fact, monograph on monograph. Some thought it was an inductive science and inferred historical laws from empirical facts. Above all they realized that history was a serious profession, to be taught in special courses in universities. They sought to transplant the characteristic German institution, the seminar, to American universities; as early as 1869, Charles Kendall Adams introduced a Rankean-type seminar at the University of Michigan, in which independent research was collectively criticized. Amateur history became academic history. Now whether Clio on tenure is a good idea or not—that is another question altogether. It certainly has not been a cost-free change.

The German influence on American higher education is well known, though it probably was less important in its intellectual substance than in its institutional or rhetorical form. (Substance was to come with a later transplantation.) Several German-trained

American historians contributed greatly to this earliest academic borrowing. Two leading exemplars were Herbert Baxter Adams and John W. Burgess, both great organizers of American scholarship who thought they were importing the historical method of the great German teachers, the institutional means for teaching *Wissenschaft*—an oft-misunderstood word that signifies systematic knowledge in any field rather than exact science.

A graduate of Amherst in 1872, Adams subsequently studied at Heidelberg and Berlin, under Droysen and, more importantly for him, under Johann Kaspar Bluntschli. Droysen's dictum "The essence of historical method is *understanding* by means of *investigation*" became Adams's own lifelong motto.[5] In 1876, Adams became the first teacher of history at Johns Hopkins and also set up an historical seminar.

Shortly after Adams's death in 1901, Woodrow Wilson recalled his former mentor as "a great Captain of Industry, a captain in the field of systematic and organized research."[6] In 1882 Adams inaugurated and, until 1900, edited the Johns Hopkins University Studies in Historical and Political Science, a series in which the characteristic form of American scholarship, the monograph, appeared. Adams of course was also the principal mover in the founding of the AHA and its first secretary for fifteen years. In 1885, the AHA resolved to make Ranke its first—and for the time being only—honorary foreign member. George Bancroft as president wrote Ranke: "We wish for your benediction. . . . We have meant to make this a special homage to yourself as the greatest living historian."[7] Adams's efforts to enlist the aid of the federal government in support of historical work proved futile. European governments subsidized the needs of historians, recognizing their importance; not so the American government. Governmental indifference had no benign cause, but it may have had some benign consequences. It left American historians freer of official ties, and it is possible that our profession, especially in its beginnings, had more examples of what Hofstadter ascribed to Beard, "hardboiled iconoclasm."[8] In any case, considering the dependency of American higher education on private and public funds, I think one of the great achievements of our academic life has been the acquired habit of biting the hand that feeds us.

For all his public utterances about German scholarship, Adams retained no connections with German colleagues. He was responsible for Johns Hopkins's acquisition of Bluntschli's library and on the occasion of its formal delivery the president of the Hopkins Board of Trustees, Judge Dubbin, once more celebrated German learning in the ritualistic fashion: "For what problem of science, what question in literature, what disputed point in history, can be considered as satisfactorily examined before the results of German research have been availed of?"[9]

John W. Burgess was another German-trained organizer of American scholarship. In his enthusiasm to convert Columbia into a German-type institution, in which research and scholarship would predominate, he sought to abolish the College, the undergraduate part, in favor of a single Graduate School. In this he was fortunately unsuccessful, but by founding the Faculty of Political Science, he helped to make Columbia a major research university.[10] He trained the next generation of historians in what he called the scientific study of history and politics. His Germanophilia was boundless; in 1908 he still insisted that "in ethical, moral and intellectual qualities, the Germans stand nearer to the genuine Americans than do the people of any other European Nation, even of the English Nation." He tried to explain to himself why he, of English descent, should always have felt as much at home in Germany as in England, and he arrived at this ingenious answer: "The Englishman is a German with a Norman-French veneering; the conditions and experiences of American life tend to remove this veneering and to bring the German element in the English character again to the front."[11] Burgess of course urged that racial affinity should govern political alignment as well. He thought himself a scientific historian and probably hid from himself the fact that that cloak covered extravagant prejudices.

Burgess, the several Adamses, and many others wrote their monographs on American history in what they assumed was the German style. Their very admiration for things German inhibited any inclination to compete with Germans on their own turf.[12] They did adopt from German and English historians of the time the so-called germ theory—the very term of course bespeaks scientism: The germ of local institutions in England and America was found in the Germanic forests. American patricians readily embraced this Teutomania. In 1883, Albert Bushnell Hart of Harvard, also with a German doctorate, set down "the fundamental principles of American history," maintaining *inter alia* that "our institutions are Teutonic in origin: they have come to us through English institutions."[13] Primitive forests had little to do with American institutions, modern German universities a great deal. At a time of mass immigration to the United States, this Teutonism was more than some kind of scholarly idiosyncracy; it was racism disguised as historical science.

Piety informed practice. In 1896, the AHA created a commission to consider the study of history in secondary schools, even then in a lamentable state. Herbert Baxter Adams, Albert Bushnell Hart of Harvard, Charles Homer Haskins of Wisconsin, Andrew C. McLaughlin of Michigan, Henry Morse Stephens of Cornell, Lucy Maynard Salmon of Vassar, and George L. Fox of the Hopkins Grammar School made up the commission. It fell to Lucy Salmon to inspect and report on the German school system—principally of course on the Gymnasium. "It will be seen," she wrote, "that of foreign countries Germany is the one that offers to America the most lessons," including the centrality of historical study; it was the unifying element in the German curriculum. She also thought that "every teacher of history is an absolute master of the subject taught," an enviable condition—if true. But she also quickly saw the limits of adaptability: "The German [teacher] believes that until the boy reaches the university he has no judgement to be appealed to." The German lives "in a military atmosphere, where obedience is the first law of men. . . . [He is] a boy who, from his earliest recollections, is taught that everyone obeys someone else." She warned against concentrating exclusively on American history in our secondary schools; such concentration would stunt the minds of students in later life. "American history is in the air—a balloon sailing in midheaven—unless it is anchored fast to European history."[14] We have gone through periods of anchorage—and of drift.

From 1907 to 1910, another AHA commission examined the same question, without mentioning European models, and concluded that American schools should have four years of history, two of which should be devoted to European and English history. The later report bespoke a greater degree of American self-confidence and makes for elegiacal reading when compared to the recent government report, entitled *A Nation at Risk*.[15] The past is richer today than it was eighty years ago, but our teaching of it has become still more parsimonious.

Americans had mixed responses to their German experience. In 1867, William James wrote a sketch of what a German scholar is like; he happened to pick one of the greatest, Wilhelm Dilthey—the picture would have been still more damaging if he had chosen a lesser figure. The American scholar, he wrote, remains a citizen, a man in society, "whereas this cuss seemed to me nothing if not a professor . . . as if he were able to stand towards the rest of society *merely* in the relation of a man learned in this or that branch—and never for a moment forget the interests or put off the instincts of his specialty."[16] Other students began to complain after 1870 of "crotchety, opinionated, illiberal" professors.[17] At the very end of the century, William E. Dodd studied in Leipzig under Karl Lamprecht and Erich Marcks; he wrote his German doctoral thesis on the origins of the Democratic Party in the United States, a subject that his German masters couldn't have known much about. Dodd, too, was divided in his impressions of Germany: he delighted in its cultural life and found its militarism appalling.[18]

With the new century a new breed of American historians emerged. Frederick Jackson Turner, Charles Beard, James Harvey Robinson, and Carl Becker came from the Midwest, less inhibited by New England pieties and more attuned to the new America, an industrial America, which in the 1890s suffered a great depression. Hence the new generation was aware of economic injustice, of poverty and corruption, of greed, of the problem of the new mass immigration. They wrote history with different passions, more concerned with immediate grievances than with past glories. Like Robinson, Beard had studied in Germany and wrote his dissertation there; what he took to be Ranke's historical-scientific principle haunted him all his life precisely because he was torn between his wish to be objective about the past and his commitment to present needs. Robinson assumed both could be done; Beard brooded about it. Meanwhile the slightly older Turner spoke for the entire younger generation when he proclaimed, "This new democracy that captured the country and destroyed the ideals of statesmanship came from no theorist's dream of the German forest."[19] This younger generation of American historians, so much concerned with specifically American issues and shortcomings, could not have been insulated from the subtle psychological effects of America's ever-growing imperial power, of her new place among the powers of the world.

Robinson and Beard took a more critical view of German scholarship—not only, I suppose, to emancipate themselves from Teutonic tutelage but to distance themselves from their immediate patrician predecessors.[20] They called for "a new history," a history consonant with the ebullient spirit of the Progressive Era.[21] A new critical nationalism arose in the United States, while German historians developed an ever more strident nationalism and a methodological narrowness.

James Harvey Robinson, exact contemporary of Frederick Jackson Turner, also of Midwestern origin, studied at Harvard, where William James had been the only teacher who had truly impressed him. In 1888, he began his studies in Germany, in 1891 he published his doctoral dissertation on the Bundesrath, a conventional topic, conventionally executed. He came to Columbia in 1895, as the first professor of European history. Beard joined the Columbia faculty in 1903, and the two formed a close friendship. In 1902–3, as a forty-year-old, Robinson pleaded for a new approach in history—and attacked what J. R. Green long before had called "drum-and-trumpet history" and what Robinson no doubt associated—erroneously—with the Rankean legacy. He called for a broader history, a history that would take account of economic and intellectual developments, that would transcend and at the same time explicate the political history of states and institutions. He also demanded that the past should serve the cause of future progress; antiquarianism was anathema. His own widely used textbooks exemplified the new approach.

He was also a critic of German scholarship; in a major review essay, "The Study of the Lutheran Revolt," which appeared in the *AHR* in 1903, he noted that most German historians were still perpetuating "the party rancor," the confessional struggle of an earlier time; he thought that the religiously inclined overlooked the determining secular elements in the Reformation. Historians should practice toleration, accept that no one faith was correct or incorrect, but that each served a particular interest. He noted that "the development of political economy and sociology has attracted our attention to a new class of historical sources and is influencing our interpretation of those that have long been familiar to scholars." "The old issues"—by which he meant clerical partisanship—were by no means dead, especially in Germany, "to which we have become accustomed to looking for constant aid in solving the historical problems of the time." Robinson wrote of "the admiration which German scholars always express for Ranke, and which to some of us nowadays appears exaggerated and rather inexplicable." He added that "the brilliancy of Ranke's work has paled by reason of the very success of the reforms which he did so much to establish in the writing of history."[22] It was an odd and unconvincing thing for Robinson to say: If anything, Ranke's work, if read, should have shone the brighter because his successors and epigoni had very little of his breadth and literary talent. Robinson's article, however, did double duty. It criticized prevailing, especially German, scholarship and pointed toward his programmatic call for a "New History," published nine years later.

Robinson was a justly famous teacher, first at Pennsylvania and then at Columbia, where in 1904 he introduced his standard course on the Intellectual History of Western Europe—and thus established an American specialty, i.e., the discipline of intellectual history, which differs from its more abstract German analogue, *Geistes-* or *Ideengeschichte*. His influence at Columbia was immense— and enduring. It was Robinson who inspired Lynn Thorndike, Preserved Smith, C. J. H. Hayes, and James Shotwell to embark on broad studies of Europe's past. Thorndike became an internationally renowned historian of medieval science and a teacher of monumental dullness. In 1920, Preserved Smith wrote *The Age of the Reformation*, which a present-day German historian calls "the single most important American contribution . . . to Lutheran studies."[23] It is still an important work today. Hayes in turn founded a formidable school of intellectual historians and his doctoral seminar must be counted as one of the most productive in American historiography of Europe. That school included one of the first important American historians of modern Germany, Eugene Anderson, and also Jacques Barzun, who was my teacher; hence I can claim some form of descent—I use the ambiguous term deliberately—from Robinson.

The New History—and the new spirit that inspired it—had little use for Burgess's Teutonic delusions. Some American scholars became quite critical of the Kaiser's Germany even before the war and their views came to inform their work. In 1911, Bernadotte Schmitt, a 24-year-old scholar who had been one of the first Rhodes Scholars in Oxford, wrote in *The Nation* that "fear of Germany" was "the primary cause of bloated armaments." That is why liberal hopes for an end to war were in jeopardy. He saw the Agrarian Party in Germany as dominant, and "these men are notoriously reactionary . . . [they] are born and reared in the traditions of militarism . . . they thrive on the habit of dictating to other nations their line of action, and they have no desire to lose their occupation." In order to banish war, "the world at large must proclaim that no one nation shall disturb the peace to protect supposed interests or to satisfy the whim of a privileged class, and a self-confident monarch."[24] All his professional life, Schmitt was accused of being anti-German and pro-British; perhaps he was "prematurely anti-German." His years in Oxford no doubt had their effect, but German conduct or at least German rhetoric seemed determined to bear him out. Schmitt's book on Anglo-German relations after 1740 appeared after the outbreak of the war and was one of the first examples of American diplomatic history of Europe. Another in the new generation of Anglophile American historians—very different from earlier patricians—was Roland Usher, who in 1913 published *Pan-Germanism*, again a warning signal against German expansionism.

The first great American analysis of modern Germany was written by a non-historian. Thorstein Veblen's *Imperial Germany and the Industrial Revolution*, conceived and begun before the war but published in 1915, is a complicated work, of quirky brilliance. It was also a tribute to Veblen's capacious mind and to the new spirit that animated American inquiry; Veblen was interdisciplinary by intuitive logic. In his analysis of why Germany had overtaken Britain, he examined the different characteristics of capitalism in Britain and Germany and drew upon anthropology and sociology to explain the divergent political developments of the two countries. He stressed the discrepancy in Germany between the triumph of modern capitalism and technology, and its outdated "dynastic state," its feudal society and atavistic drives, its old forms of class rule. Industrial society does not bring about identical political cultures. He thought Germany's "cultural scheme . . . is out of date and touch with itself, in that it is part archaic and in part quite new. . . . The resulting want of poise is not to be accounted an infirmity, perhaps." He wrote, memorably, "that this spirit of subservient alacrity on which the Prussian system of administrative efficiency rests is beneath the dignity of a freeman; that it is the spirit of a subject, not of a citizen; that except for dynastic uses it is a defect and a delinquency; and that in the end the exigencies of civilized life will not tolerate such an anachronistic remnant of medievalism, and the habit of it will be lost."[25] That it served the dynastic state and the industrial economy superbly well was also true. Like Marx, Veblen was at once diagnostician and moral critic; like Marx, he abhorred servility. Veblen was a homespun American Max Weber, and in breadth of understanding and in civic courage the two men had much in common.

Veblen's book was little noticed. During the war, the government's propaganda agency wanted to encourage its distribution; however, the U.S. Post Office banned its circulation under the Espionage Act. Veblen's diagnosis proved correct, and the discrepancies he noted persisted even beyond the life of the empire. Germany was unstable; her industrial development did not produce an English-type society. Many years later, Talcott Parsons wrote a perceptive essay, "Social Structure and Democracy in Germany," but this also had little influence among historians.[26] Historians operated from narrower, but empirically more secure assumptions. Veblen's analysis found a clear echo in the important work of another scholar of comparable breadth, in Ralf Dahrendorf's *Society and Democracy in Germany*, published in 1967.

For most Americans, the Great War ended the romance with Germany—John W. Burgess being a notable exception. A certain moralistic strain in the American mind or in American foreign policy may help to explain why Americans seemed to make up their minds quickly and determinedly on the question of war guilt, on the question of who started the horror. Let me cite three exemplary cases. By late August 1914, Bernadotte Schmitt noted that "apart from our citizens of German birth or descent, the public opinion of the United States seems to be decidedly against Germany in the struggle ushered in by her own declaration of war against Russia." The Kaiser had started the war because he had "felt the moment opportune to attain certain long-cherished ambitions"—a piece of "midsummer madness," thought Schmitt, caused by the Kaiser's fear of internal subversion, of the steadily growing power of Social Democracy. In effect Schmitt argued that Germany had sought war and external victory in order to escape "internal difficulties," an old device of governments.[27]

For Schmitt, the Kaiser was the chief culprit; he anticipated what public and professorial opinion would drum into the American and Allied mind. The Kaiser became not merely the symbol of villainy but its actual cause. This excessive, and, as we now know, erroneous concentration on the Kaiser probably influenced Wilson's insistence that the Kaiser's abdication constituted a precondition for an armistice.

Consider as well a letter written by Arthur O. Lovejoy, on September 9, 1914, from London and also published in *The Nation*. Lovejoy, an Anglophile philosopher from Johns Hopkins, was rebutting a German pamphlet signed by leading academics including Harnack, Lamprecht, and Wilamowitz-Moellendorff, and called *Truth About Germany*.[28] He rejected what he called the falsehoods which "several of the greatest scholars in Germany" had accepted; Americans, he recalled, had "learned much from German scholars about historical 'objectivity.' . . . This scandalous episode in the history of the scholar's profession" should instruct American scholars: "it seems . . . to show that the professional class, in the country where it has played the greatest part, has signally failed, at the most critical moment in German history, to perform its proper function—the function of detached criticism . . . of insisting that facts . . . be known and faced. It appears to be shouting with the rest for a wholly avoidable war of which, in nearly all non-German eyes, the moral indefensibility seems exceeded only by its fatal unwisdom from a purely national point of view."[29] Lovejoy could not have imagined that still greater failure was to come thirty years later—or that the American professoriate would not be shielded from unreflective chauvinism either.

In 1917 Charles Beard resigned from Columbia because the trustees and President Butler had dismissed an instructor for some critical remarks about the war effort. Beard actually favored America's participation in the war and thought that a German victory would "plunge all of us into the black night of military barbarism," but he was appalled by his colleagues' conformity, expected and delivered, and his letter of resignation is full of enviable defiance: "Having observed closely the inner life of Columbia for many years, I have been driven to the conclusion that the University is really under the control of a small and active group of trustees who have no standing in the world of education, who are reactionary and visionless in politics, narrow and medieval in religion."[30] By and large this kind of civic courage among academics is a rare quality in the best of times, and there was little of it during the Great War, probably more in the Anglo-American world than in Germany.

American scholars—no less than their European counterparts—contributed to the war effort. Many of them did so by indulging in the most extraordinary anti-Germanism—not least those scholars who had studied in Germany. William E. Dodd—in the 1930s Roosevelt's ambassador to Germany—wrote in the first month of the war to his wife: "Germany is the enemy of mankind in this war and I am almost ashamed that I have my doctorate from such a people."[31] In 1917, Albert Bushnell Hart and Arthur O. Lovejoy edited *A Handbook of the War for Readers, Speakers and Teachers*, dedicated to "informing the understanding, of awakening the moral vision and the moral passion, of the entire people. . . . It is essential to bring to the mind of every honest and loyal citizen the momentousness of the present crisis; to bring all to feel that America has never entered upon a more just or more necessary war." The two scholars adduced the "facts which establish . . . the responsibility [of the present German rulers] for this greatest catastrophe of modern history." "Democracy is the normal political order for civilized peoples," Lovejoy wrote, but when a democracy goes to war, it must modify its normal processes, it must for the duration "accept loyally innumerable restrictions of individual liberty which in time of peace it would deem intolerable."[32] Perhaps Lovejoy had forgotten his own strictures of three years earlier; how short is our memory, especially under the commands of collective passion.

The Great War ended America's isolation and renewed its ties, material and spiritual, to Europe. The postwar interlude of willed normalcy did not destroy the memory of shared fate. In fact the war had a lasting and beneficent effect on American education: In 1917, the War Department asked Columbia to prepare a course titled "War Issues," to be administered in all colleges which housed Students' Army Training Corps. Columbia scholars prepared such a syllabus and two years later Columbia College inaugurated a successor course, soon to be called Introduction to Contemporary Civilization—the assumption being that American history was a part of Western civilization, that the educated citizen needed to know at least the elements of that civilization and the great moments of its intellectual life. Columbia's course became a model followed by most American colleges and universities.

In so many ways the war had brought America and Europe closer together. Americans discovered both difference and proximity; as one soldier remarked in surprise: "There's a hell of a lot of difference between Trenton, New Jersey, and Paris, France. . . ."[33] The very notion of "the West" became a central idea in American thought and education, more so than in a divided and embittered Europe. It restored the sense of linkage with Europe and facilitated the historians' supranational approach. When Carlton Hayes changed the title of his immensely popular textbook from *A Political and Social History of Modern Europe* to *A Political and Cultural History of Modern Europe*, he called Europe "the set of that continuous high civilization which we call 'western'—which has come to be the distinctive civilization of the American continents as well as of Europe."[34]

The war invigorated America's sense of its connection to the European past and present; the American story was not simply a story of separation and rejection. American scholarship reflected this new sense. Robinson's student James T. Shotwell conceived of a typical American enterprise, *The Economic and Social History of the World War*, to be written by foreign scholars and financed by the Carnegie Endowment for Peace; earlier titles such as "The Teutonic War" were abandoned, as was the original plan to investigate the causes of the war. That subject, it was decided in 1919, was too controversial. The intent was to "describe and, where possible, to measure the displacement caused by modern war in the process of contemporary civilization."[35] Shotwell's hope was that the project would strengthen the resolve for universal peace. The one book most relevant to our purposes is also the least quantitative: I am referring to the poignant work by Albrecht Mendelssohn-Bartholdy, *War and the German Society: The Testament of a Liberal*, a study of the moral effects of the war. It was one of the last volumes in the Carnegie series, published in 1937, after the author's death in exile, an exile imposed on him by political and spiritual upheavals that had begun with the Great War. The national boards of editors included distinguished historians, economists, and public servants: Henri Hauser, Henri Pirenne, John Maynard Keynes, and Charles Rist as well as William Henry Beveridge. In 1937, the project was completed; 150 volumes comprising 300 monographs had been composed, almost entirely by foreigners. The enterprise, so expressive of American ideals and wealth (the total cost was

$879,448.26—an exactitude that would have pleased Andrew Carnegie), was symptomatic of a time when our interest in Europe and the world was still greater than our own competence in dealing with these areas.[36]

In the decade after the Great War, American historians of Europe became more and more professionalized, more and more conscious of their own identity. In 1922, Charles Homer Haskins, in his AHA presidential address "European History and American Scholarship," said: "We may at times appear more mindful of Europe's material indebtedness to us than of our spiritual indebtedness to Europe; we may in our pharisaic moods express our thanks that we are not even as these sinners of another hemisphere; but such moments cannot set us loose from the world's history." American historians should not simply translate and appropriate the work of European historians; they should make their own efforts, collect their own material, offer their own interpretations, make their distinct contributions to historical knowledge. Also, there was a public service to be rendered: "It is the historian's business to tie Europe and America together in the popular mind."[37]

American historians did have certain advantages over their newly divided European colleagues: Because of the war, they had acquired a new mixture of involvement and detachment. We were separate and not equal. We were at once creditor and debtor. Europeans began to take note of American cultural achievements. At the same time, seen from America, Europe seemed more unified than it appeared to the nations so recently at war with each other. In our teaching, this "Western" perspective was already established; in our writing, it was in the process of being attained.

The condition of Europeanists in America changed, as had America's place in the world. The Great War, the Bolshevik Revolution, the new order devised at Versailles had given Americans a new sense of Europe's uncomfortable importance. We began to pay attention to the historic record of these upheavals.

Chester P. Higby of Wisconsin University was the main promoter of European studies; he estimated that in 1926 there were some 250 American historians of Europe; in the same year, the total membership of the AHA was 2,868. In 1929, primarily for the European scholars, the *Journal of Modern History* was established, of which Higby has been called the "father."[38] In the 1920s, the

Hoover Library was created at Stanford, a unique repository of war and postwar archives.

The list of Europeanists grew longer and more distinguished: Carlton J. H. Hayes, Sidney B. Fay, Bernadotte Schmitt, William Langer, Carl Becker, Louis Gottschalk. They in turn trained graduate students and the field began to flourish.

Many of the graduate students went to Europe, but no longer to sit at the feet of great German or French historians—though some may have done so. Their principal purpose was to work in the archives, to prepare their dissertations as equal workers in the same vineyard as indigenous historians. I wish one knew what enticed students in the 1920s to opt for European against American history. No doubt, there was the pull of outstanding teachers, and Prohibition must have been a propitious time to go to Europe. But there was the language barrier as well as the intimidating lure of something foreign, something exotic. America and Europe were more distant then than now: A journey took eight days, not eight hours. One had to work hard. A return trip to the archives was difficult to negotiate, and the reproduction of archival sources was primitive and expensive.

I wonder whether young American Europeanists realized the ambiguity of their position. Unlike the Americanist, the doctoral student who went into European archives had to contend with two traditions: he had to reckon with his own master in America and with the indigenous European tradition of scholarship, itself often divided. In some ways, our Europeanists stood on the shoulders of giants, of Albert Mathiez and Marc Bloch, of Otto Hintze and Friedrich Meinecke, but it was not an easy climb to get there.

In those days, as today, the Europeanists worked side by side with their far more numerous Americanist colleagues. The latter had masters and material at hand, but ease does not necessarily attract or produce excellence. John Higham spoke of the "amiable mediocrity" of Americanists of that period, and some twenty-five years ago, John Lukacs remarked that "it is a curious condition that American historians of Europe . . . have been consistently better than American historians of their native country. . . ."[39] If ever true—and Europeanists are in an awkward position to judge— it ceased being true in the 1950s, when as Hofstadter both noted and exemplified, "our historical writing" experienced "the redis- covery of complexity in American history."[40]

Let me, despite my barely repressible Luddite instincts, introduce a quantitative note. Ours is an age of grants, not of laurels, and of all the grants, none is as long established or as much sought after as the Guggenheim. The record of awards is revealing: in the very first triennium of Guggenheim existence, from 1925 to 1928, European historians received 11, American historians 4 awards. From 1925 to 1956, Europeanists—excluding medievalists—received 122, Americanists 94 grants—and this at a time when the proportion of Americanists to Europeanists must have been very high. From 1957 to 1980, the trend is reversed, and by 1990, Americanists end up ahead by 7 grants. The foundation does not have the number of applications in each field, but even these scant figures suggest that in the first thirty-year period the Guggenheim judges must have been impressed by the disproportionate promise of the Europeanists.[41]

America's role in peacemaking had been preeminent—despite its late entry into the war. The League of Nations was America's most celebrated contribution, but the ultimately most pernicious provision of the treaty was probably also of American origin. Reparations had been a major unresolved issue; the opening clause of the Reparations section of the Versailles treaty was article 231, asserting German responsibility for the war, thus providing the moral justification for economic calamity. The article, apparently drafted by John Foster Dulles, was intended not as an assessment of guilt, but as a compromise assertion of acknowledged responsibility so that the actual amount of reparations could be settled later, at a more propitious time.[42]

The war guilt clause, as outraged Germans quickly dubbed it, intensified the historians' search for the causes of the war, a search at once political and historical in motivation. European governments issued great collections of documents, and historians wrote more or less national accounts. It was in this field that American Europeanists first excelled. Sidney B. Fay and Bernadotte Schmitt published their massive studies on the causes of the war in 1928 and 1930 respectively; their books established American scholarship as being equal to that of Europe. Fay and Schmitt held divergent views—Fay stressed that he had suspended judgment before he studied the sources, while Schmitt remained silent about his prior assumptions. The revisionists rebutted the notion of Germany's sole or even principal guilt. Fay and Schmitt wrote with no particular flair or originality, but with complete mastery of the sources, and with a fine balance between involvement and detachment.

American studies of diplomatic history obviously included German politics—hence they deserve brief mention. At the end of the 1920s, the most distinguished of American diplomatic historians, William Langer, published his first book, a study of the Franco-Russian Alliance, 1890–1914. In 1917, Langer was teaching modern languages in a boarding school; he responded to an appeal that the army needed someone with a knowledge of French and German; he ended up with a unit in chemical warfare and with the advice of his company commander: "All you need in the Army is a strong back and a weak mind."[43] At best, Langer was half-qualified, but the experience of Europe turned him into a European historian—and one with an unmatched influence on the profession. His studies of European imperialism and politics became classics, and the series which has always borne his name established the excellence of American Europeanists and their characteristic strength: the supra-national perspective.

There was no great American migration to postwar Germany. London and Paris were the powerful magnets. Weimar did not acquire its halo of distinction until after it was gone; in retrospect, one recognized its greatness. As Haskins acknowledged in 1922, little work had been done by American scholars in German history, except for the Reformation era. I doubt that American historians were much concerned with the response of German historians to the overthrow of the imperial regime. A few followed the work and political thought of their German colleagues, but there was little contact or collaboration.

Three historians specializing in German studies deserve mention: Eugene Anderson, Walter Dorn, and Raymond Sontag. A student of Hayes, Anderson began with a book on the First Moroccan Crisis, published in 1930. In 1935 the *JMH* published his exemplary essay on "recent works on German unification." It is sometimes forgotten just how important the art of reviewing is: The profession depends on what Robert Merton has called "socially organized skepticism."[44] Anderson notes that German historiography of the entire nineteenth century "lacks a Mathiez. The determined avoidance of social data has restricted German scholars to political history or its idealistic refinement, Ideen-geschichte."

He celebrated the history of nineteenth-century Germany in four volumes by the liberal Catholic Franz Schnabel, and called for their translation: "They would afford the American public an understanding of modern German history which cannot be obtained in any other study."[45] At that time Schnabel was far from being a popular figure; as he said to me in 1950: "It took two wars to get me a professorship at a regular university." In 1939, Anderson published his *Nationalism and the Cultural Crisis in Prussia, 1806–1815*, a book that reflected his earlier stay in Berlin, where he had met Meinecke, and also his anxiety over the nationalism of the Nazis. Walter Dorn studied with Otto Hintze and published two important articles on Prussian state-building, which together with his fine *Competition for Empire* bear the mark of Hintze's influence. In 1938, Raymond Sontag published a work on Anglo-German relations, while Pauline Anderson wrote a major volume on the background of anti-English sentiment in Germany.

The Andersons and Walter Dorn had been inspired by the young, brilliant maverick of the German profession, Eckart Kehr, who in January 1933—at a time when his professional chances in Germany seemed dim—visited the United States. Not yet thirty, he had already challenged every orthodoxy in German historical writing. A student of Meinecke, he had defied the accepted categories; he wrote neither *Geistesgeschichte* nor the history of the state, and he wrote out of a deep commitment to a progressive, democratic spirit. He paid the penalty of the dissident, and he paid it by suffering pain and, when possible, by inflicting it. In a way he was the missing Mathiez that Anderson referred to; he saw political decisions as reflecting conflicting economic and social interests. Not for him the much-fabled *Primat der Aussenpolitik* (primacy of foreign policy); he was enough of a German to turn thesis into perhaps too facile an antithesis, but as with most innovators his work opened up new perspectives on what had been assumed was a familiar past. Champion of an unpopular search for reality, for the bedrock that was class or group interest, not some disinterested sense of statecraft or patriotism, Kehr found an early echo in this country, when in 1931 his *Schlachtflottenbau und Parteipolitik* was hailed by Charles Beard, who had been introduced to the work by his son-in-law Alfred Vagts, himself a German-trained historian and author of works on militarism and U.S.-German relations. The affinity between Beard and Kehr was clear, and Kehr must have been a riveting presence to young Americans. He died in May 1933 in Washington. In the 1970s, to quote Gordon Craig, "the influence of Eckart Kehr has become perhaps the strongest reforming force in German historiography, and the one that has been largely responsible for curing the myopia that affected its vision of the past."[46] Meanwhile the Kehrites have been attacked in turn; it is hard to be permanently revisionist.

Kehr's visit to the United States—just before the Nazis seized power in Germany—had something paradigmatic to it. He was the accidental forerunner of the Great Migration, of that celebrated moment when a totalitarian regime in Germany forced some of the best scholars to leave their country and careers and to begin anew in a wildly different climate. The Nazis had an instant sense of the centrality of history; they sought control, most especially of modern history, and Jews automatically, but liberal- or democratic-minded historians also, were banished from totally acquiescent universities. The story is too familiar to be rehearsed again: Germany's articulate talent came here or to other havens, but mostly here; the remaining talent in Germany embraced the new dispensation, gradually made its compromises, or fell silent. Beginning in 1933–34, Hajo Holborn, Felix Gilbert, Theodor Mommsen, Hans Rosenberg, Franz Neumann came—and many others. Some of them, like Holborn and Gilbert, had been the most promising and most prodigious of Meinecke's students; all of them possessed an astounding breadth of knowledge and a burden of experience that must have impressed their American colleagues. The arrival of this talent from Germany brought home to Americans the fragility of civilization, the refugee scholars embodied a deep moral and intellectual challenge, their presence was a reproach to whatever lingering indifference there may have been.

The time was at once difficult and fortuitously propitious. America was steeped in the same unprecedented economic depression that had shaken Germany. In the wake of crisis, Americans, too, questioned all manner of assumptions and ideological and intellectual controversies flourished. The émigrés also discovered that a largely unacknowledged anti-Semitism still governed elite universities, and that Jews found it difficult, if not impossible, to attain professorships, especially in the humanities.

And still the effect of the migration was immense. The émigrés came when the indigenous profession had become strong, rich, and mature, and therefore receptive to foreign scholars. The encounter of American and German learning—despite the obvious handicaps of the newly arrived, with their uncertain prospects and their uncertain English—was triumphant because it represented reciprocal learning. The refugee scholars became more empirical, less dogmatic, more attuned to the social realities that their former traditions had tended to neglect; most of them also held a critical view of their own past traditions since these traditions had proven so fragile, so debilitated vis-à-vis the Nazi onslaught. American scholars became more philosophical, deeper, more speculative—and each group learned from the other, learned from the other social sciences, and learned from the inescapable experiences of the 1930s: the ideological struggles, the threat and temptation of totalitarianism, the approach of yet another European war. Certainly the 1930s brought home the centrality of the German problem, the unavoidable question about the relation of German past to Nazi present—and how tempting it was for many to see the German past entirely in light of the Nazi experience, and thus in a sense to copy Nazi efforts to twist the past to their thousand-year destiny. How difficult for the émigrés to grasp what had gone wrong in that past without jettisoning all; how difficult for Americans and émigrés alike to understand the failure of democracy, the triumph of a regime that violated every liberal-democratic principle they had grown up with. And how difficult and yet probably how relentlessly stimulating to carry out scholarly tasks in the face of ever-intensifying political crises. But these same crises steeled a younger generation of American students who had begun during the depression and who were carrying on their graduate work as the world approached catastrophe. Great teachers and terrifying events fortified this new generation of American students.[47]

Scholars, established and beginning, were divided on the question of isolationism or interventionism. Some of the most influential historians were opposed to intervention, fearing the inevitable cost to life and liberty. Pearl Harbor changed all that, and America's inextricable involvement in the world was now accepted; the destruction of Europe—save England and the Soviet Union—had already imposed new responsibilities on America. The fruitfulness of forced cooperation between American and émigré scholars, between established scholars and young graduate students, was demonstrated by that wartime institution, the research and analysis branch of OSS, headed by William Langer. Sherman Kent of Yale and Langer of Harvard recruited the best talent available, much of it from Yale and Harvard, and brought together Holborn, Gilbert, Franz Neumann, Herbert Marcuse, Otto Kirchheimer, Crane Brinton, and some of their students: Stuart Hughes, Carl Schorske, Leonard Krieger, Franklin Ford, Henry Roberts, and, as the ultimate Benjamin of the group, John Clive. The list is not complete. Leonard Krieger has called the veterans of the Research and Analysis Division "the one identifiable cohesive group among the American historians of Europe."[48] In that seminar *en permanence* there were differences, but the imperatives of war taught the group the reciprocity of historical and political analysis, the complementarity of the social sciences, the urgency of scholarship. They were all philosophical historians, they were all political beings. After 1945, this group returned to the universities, wrote truly influential works on modern history, and trained yet other generations. Clusters of talent working under crisis conditions have often produced exceptional work—but the mixture of people, generations, experiences made the OSS unique.

After 1933, there was no escaping the centrality of German history. For twelve years or longer, we were, as I have said before, the guardians of German history; in 1945, we returned to Germany as conquering reeducators. It took some time for German historians to recover from the inner and the outer emigration, from the ready submission of so many of them to the dictates of National Socialism. By the early 1960s the Fritz Fischer controversy over Germany's role in World War I signaled a renewed vitality among German historians and a willingness to challenge the prevailing conservative consensus.

I first taught German history at Cornell in 1951: what a dearth then of usable texts. There was A. J. P. Taylor's mischievous *Course of German History,* which illuminated the subject with devious, angry clarity. There was Arthur Rosenberg's *The Birth of the German Republic,* written even before the National Socialists had come to power, and stressing the desperate resistance to democracy in the Second Reich. There was S. W. Halperin's *Germany Tried Democracy: A Political History of the Reich from 1918 to 1933*—a work that very much corresponded to its subtitle. In 1952 appeared Alan Bullock's superb *Hitler,* but I am concentrating here on American scholarship and thus have largely ignored English works, some of them important and influential, beginning with W. H. Dawson and continuing through John W. Wheeler-Bennett and beyond. And still the field was sparse as compared to now.

Beginning in the 1950s, American historians have concerned themselves ever more with German history, and a multitude of monographs has appeared; there have been so many that even classification has become difficult. In 1968 the first issue of *Central European History* appeared "in response to a widespread demand for an American journal devoted to the history of German-speaking Central Europe." The editors hoped for "works of broad synthesis and . . . specialized research," also for works in traditional and experimental genres. In quality and quantity these monographs have become more impressive; they also cover hitherto neglected areas, such as the early modern period. Between 1968 and 1978, 231 books on German history since 1740 were published, which put German studies in fourth place among European countries.[49] At obvious risk, let me cite a few studies.

In the early 1950s, diplomatic and military history achieved new distinction. In 1953 Gordon Craig and Felix Gilbert published their collection, *The Diplomats*; the volume was largely an OSS operation in mufti. But it also set a new standard of analysis; it represented a new genre of diplomatic history, broader still than Langer's earlier work. In some ways, Craig's career has been paradigmatic for the study of German history in this country. In 1955, he published his *Politics of the Prussian Army,* a path-breaking work that helped to transform the picture of Prusso-German military history. At the very beginning, he spoke of the "German problem" itself, and rebutted the then still popular notion "that the Germans are by nature subservient to authority, militaristic, and aggressive. . . . The basic assumption of this book, however, is that these things are not inherent in the German character but are rather—as Franz Neumann has written—'products of a structure which vitiated the attempts to create a viable democracy.' "[50] More recently, Craig gave us a synthesis of modern Germany in the Oxford *History of Modern Europe* and a more intimate portrait, *The Germans,* in essays that probe the cultural habits and hidden assumptions of a literate and complex people. Craig's trajectory gives us some idea of the breadth to aim for.

Klaus Epstein also helped to define the field. His book on Matthias Erzberger used biography to integrate politics, religion, and culture; his work on German conservatism was a thick study of a neglected strain in German life. But I want to pay tribute to this colleague, tragically killed at an all too early age, for another reason: Epstein belonged to that relatively small band in our profession who take the art of reviewing with the utmost serious-ness. Meticulously fair, he often thought beyond the bounds of the book. He reviewed with intelligence, empathy, and imagination, and in this fashion, too, he enhanced American scholarship; his reviews were collected after his death and published in German— as testimony to a scholar who was one of the first to be effective in both countries.

In 1955 appeared Ludwig Dehio's collection of essays *Germany and World Politics*. The Rankean demand for writing history "as it actually happened," Dehio thought, should be transposed to show "how was it possible," and that question understandably haunted much of our work. The perspective of 1933 or 1945 was an inevitable consequence of events. It allowed for many answers, and in a few instances a scholar radically revised his own judgment. Franz Neumann's *Behemoth: The Structure and Practice of National Socialism* appeared in 1942, a brilliant, Marxist-oriented analysis and profoundly influential. He inferred much about the regime that we discovered later in the historical record. He also thought that the regime would become increasingly terrorist and could be destroyed only by outside force. In 1954, weeks before his tragic accidental death, he delivered a lecture entitled "Anxiety and Politics," in which he applied Freudian categories to several his-torical processes, including the rise of National Socialism. Collective anxiety, caused by economic distress, sharpened paranoid feelings and facilitated the triumph of National Socialism.

Implicit in so much of our work of that time was the question whether and why German history had diverged from the Western path. The question was mostly answered in facile and polemical form. The first historian to transpose it from the polemical to the philosophic-historical plane was Hajo Holborn in his 1952 article in the *Historische Zeitschrift* on German Idealism in the light of social history. "The split between Germany and the West will of necessity always be an important theme for historians."[51] He analyzed the divergence between German and West European developments in thought and society in the last two hundred years. He elaborated on themes developed by Ernst Troeltsch and Friedrich Meinecke. Here was what seemed like an irrefutable warrant for asserting that Germany had followed a *Sonderweg*, a separate path, that indeed some of her intellectual giants had welcomed it, as Thomas Mann, for example, made clear in his writings during the Great War. Other studies went beyond Holborn: Leonard Krieger's exacting work *The German Idea of Freedom* was a further historic-philosophic elaboration of this theme. I have already mentioned Ralf Dahrendorf's influential *Society and Democracy in Germany*, which elaborated Holborn's theme in altogether new ways.

Holborn's own massive and unmatched reconstruction of the German past, his three-volume *History of Modern Germany*, is more than a monument to a great historian. The work is a tribute to the successful blending of two traditions; the perspective from America, Holborn wrote, can give "many events and ideas of German history . . . their proper proportions."[52] But Holborn's work also attests the growth of monographic literature that informed almost every paragraph of his synthesis. His influence transcended his books and many essays; what he did for German history in this country, for history in general, is incalculable. He trained his own students, who in turn became important scholars; I think of Theodore Hamerow, Otto Pflanze, and Henry Cord Meyer. Unfailingly, he helped younger colleagues, by kindness and ineffable example. Finally, it was Holborn more than anyone else in this country who built the first postwar bridges to German intellectual and public life; in many ways he *was* German history in the United States.

There were others, of course, émigré and native historians. Hans Rosenberg contributed decisively to the development of social and economic history, especially of the underdeveloped earlier period of German history—and again Rosenberg did this on both sides of the Atlantic. His influence on younger historians in the Federal Republic was very great. Carl Schorske has written of Felix Gilbert's "gently emendatory spirit of erudite criticism which has made him the prime post-graduate educator of so many historians of my generation and the next."[53] In Gilbert's case, too, the influence has been equally strong in the United States and in Germany. In the last two decades or so, in the period of partnership, the influence has been reciprocal: American scholars have learned a great deal from their German colleagues, and we have incorporated the work and help of scholars like Thomas Nipperdey and Hans-Ulrich Wehler, Jürgen Kocka and Hans and Wolfgang Mommsen, Knut Borchardt, Karl-Dietrich Bracher, Reinhart Koselleck, H. A. Winkler, to mention but a few.

The dividing line is no longer national. Controversies have become international. The question of the German *Sonderweg* has never disappeared. In one of the most original works on German history written in the last decades, Mack Walker's *German Home Towns,* I detect a certain impatience with one aspect of the literature about the much-vaunted *Sonderweg*:

> A commonplace of German history is to say that "Germany lacked a strong liberal bourgeoisie," one of those negative comparisons that plague the interpretation of German affairs. This book, though, is not about the liberal bourgeoisie that Germany did not get, but about the hometown *Bürgerschaft* that Germany preeminently did get. . . . Yet the German home towns between the Thirty Years' War and the Second Empire represent a certain social style and character in the purest historical form I can think of, and one especially amenable to historical examination; and if there is any place to explore the meaning of social community it is in modern German history, in many ways a caricature of all our histories.[54]

To speak of a caricature is to suggest that German history has much to teach us about the life of other nations.

Most recently, this putative *Sonderweg* has been the focus of yet another controversy. We are rich in talent and in controversy, and given the existence of a third historical school, one that I have not had a chance to mention, that of the German Democratic Republic, our field must be adjudged as dynamic and likely to continue its agitated rhythm.

In 1922, in his AHA presidential address, Charles H. Haskins said: "The present state of European history in the United States calls neither for self-satisfaction nor for discouragement."[55] The last sixty years allow for some satisfaction at the work of our predecessors, but earlier successes create their own problems. German history has become an industry, both here and in the two

Germanies; I am reminded of what William McNeill said, that
professionalism in European history in America had become "an
end in itself. . . . The result was that the study of European history
in this country tended to cut itself off from the mainspring of
human curiosity that ultimately, in any society, must undergird
whatever historical investigation occurs."[56] There is some discour-
aging truth to this—and not only for one branch of history or for
one country.

Haskins also raised the question of our potential audience and
spoke of "an Anglo-Saxon tendency to think overmuch of the
general reader even in our works of erudition, with the result that
too many books fall between scholar and the public, fully serving
the needs of neither."[57] I would have thought that in the intervening years we think undermuch of the general reader—and in
some way have contributed to society's indifference to history. Noel
Annan's caricature points to another reason for the loss of audience: "Social scientists have depersonalized acres of human experience so that history resembles a ranch on which herds move,
driven they know not why by impersonal forces, munching their
way across the prairie."[58] Again a caricature, but a dash of truth,
as Annan hints at the absence of a larger vision of historical
meaning or framework.

Of course, the discipline dictates or rewards certain directions
and styles, but we owe the world something as well; we owe it our
sense of the complexity of the past. The world is inundated by
tempting simplifiers. Consider the history of National Socialism as
an illustration; surely here is a subject that demands the greatest
clarity. How was the public informed? One hundred and twenty
million Americans saw the TV film *Holocaust,* a meretricious and
distorted version of reality. Between 1960 and 1975, William
Shirer's readable but historically primitive *Rise and Fall of the Third
Reich* sold nearly 3 million copies. On the other hand, Bracher's
German Dictatorship, probably the most authoritative account, has
sold around forty thousand in the fourteen years since it appeared
here. Most monographs sell tiny fractions of Bracher's total.[59]

It is not our task to compete with the trivializers and the
simplifiers. Quantity is not an end in itself. There are subjects and
occasions that warrant our addressing ourselves solely to our
colleagues. More: to be an historian's historian is a supreme
achievement, but there are few of those among us. But we must

not use the fact that we are living in a culture increasingly indifferent to history as a further justification for a retreat to professionalism. We do not have to resign ourselves to marginality or abet it by indifferent style. In choice of subject and of style we can aim at greater intellectual appeal. We need not forget that the past is a great "social drama," as Fernand Braudel said when he was talking of the price of wine and real estate. He also cited Edmond Faral, who in 1942 said: "It is the fear of History, of history on the grand scale, which has killed History."[60] In our own field, we have examples of sovereign, beautifully crafted scholarship that has found a wider audience: I think of Gordon Craig's *The Germans*, of Thomas Nipperdey's *German History*, or Theodor Schieder's *Frederick II*.

The development of German history in the United States has had its dramatic aspects. Certainly German history itself has been terrifyingly dramatic, rich in ambiguity, in continuities and discontinuities, in creativity and nihilism, in poetry and truth. The most recent book by Richard von Weizsäcker is entitled, not altogether undefiantly, *German History Has Not Stopped*.[61] As that history evolves into the future, a new past will beckon as well.

TEN

CAPITALISM AND
THE CULTURAL
HISTORIAN

This essay was written in 1976 for a *Festschrift* for Jacques
Barzun as a tribute to a teacher, Columbia colleague, and
mentor over four decades. In writing *Gold and Iron* it
seemed to me that the complex and contradictory culture
of capitalism had not been adequately grasped, and I tried
to suggest in this essay that appropriate to such a task
would be the kind of cultural history that Jacques Barzun
himself had practiced. If I were to write the essay today,
I would do it quite differently, benefiting from such
recently published works as those by Albert O. Hirschman.
It is here reprinted, virtually unrevised.

*"[W]e must assert what no one questions in theory and every-
body violates in practice, namely that the complexity of life,
taken both quantitatively and qualitatively, is greater than
our documentary, chronological, and critical schemes allow
for. The clues and witnesses are, to begin with, very numerous, taken as brute facts by themselves. But they are, even
so, a vast oversimplification of the past. . . . But huge as
this harvest of clues may seem, it is not enough. The Ariadne's*

thread is missing. It is found in no letter, no archive, no encyclopedia. It must be spun from one's inner consciousness, at great risk of error and on guard against cocksure superiority. Hence the need for a priori *sympathy, in the exact meaning of that term:* feeling with.

" 'Feeling against' is sure falsification, for life is lived by everyone on the assumption that it has meaning, that he who lives it is a rational being, honest, worthy, and human."

> JACQUES BARZUN, "Truth in Biography: Berlioz,"
> *The University Review: A Journal of the*
> *University of Kansas* (Summer 1939)
> and in *Biography as Art*, ed. by
> James L. Clifford (1962)

TALK OF CAPITALISM is endemic and in most areas of the world contemptuous. The detractors of capitalism are legion, its defenders few and uncertain. Stereotypes prevail: Capitalism involves alienation, exploitation, class conflict. Historically it is seen as the triumph of a corrupt and spineless bourgeoisie, ruthless in its pursuit of profit and in its repression of the class it lives off; faithful followers of Marx still expect that this same class, the proletariat, will some day inherit the earth and establish at last a just and egalitarian society. Such is the simplified drama, as suggested by compressed accounts and sweeping systems and as believed in by a multitude of people. Increasingly, historians have dealt with discrete, often highly technical aspects of capitalism so that the simpler version could prevail.

It is paradoxical that the longer we live in capitalism the less we seem to understand it. In the nineteenth century, when capitalists promoted and profited from the ever greater application of industrial power, the understanding of the dynamism of capitalism—of its immense power, of its revolutionary character—was deeper than it is today. In the first half of the last century, poets, novelists and critics understood the magnitude of the upheaval and saw in it a force that was changing the physiognomy of the world, most notably through the railroads, and transforming the social and moral conditions of life. They perceived man's changed relation to nature, to his fellows, and to the self; his painful mobility; the "purse-proud impertinence" of the bourgeoisie, as

Balzac called it—the psychic vulnerability and the vulgarity of the newly risen and their monumental callousness; and new class antagonisms exemplified not by the clash of abstract classes but by the lives and sufferings of individuals. They wrote of peasant sons seeking their fortune in a Paris that was at once enticing and corrupt; of love denied by convention or economic calculation (how vivid are the torments of love and class for Bradley Headstone, infatuated with Lizzie Hexam); of aristocrats who saw their world denied and bourgeois who saw theirs sumptuous but empty, and who had to pay for their achievements with repression and denial of self. (The antagonism between Thomas and Christian Buddenbrook is fed by their contradictory responses to the demands of repression and to the psychic cost of success.)[1]

The artists and writers of the last century not only understood the nature of the new society but inveighed against the greed and the hypocrisy of the new age. They felt the changes, and hence their accounts are memorable, whereas "value-free" renditions, once again in vogue today, are neither vivid nor memorable. Jacques Barzun has often referred to the impact of the earlier generation: "Carlyle," he wrote, ". . . denounced the mounting tide of poverty, disease, squalor, and vice in words which make Marx's sneers look boyish in comparison." Or again: "The swearing and cursing against the burgher-at-large by Beethoven, Berlioz, Liszt, Flaubert, and Shaw are simply peacetime bombs and bayonets."[2] Marx converted the moral outrage of his predecessors and his own into a system which, so ran the promise, would lay bare the laws of capitalist development with the same objectivity as obtained for the laws of nature, and these would likewise operate independently from human intentionality. Marx's laws also signaled the direction of capitalism: Mankind would move forward to a preordained stage of socialist equality. In the wake of Marx and Marxism, the analysis of capitalist society lost some of its subtlety and acquired a harsh, lifeless quality which at times falsified Marx's own complex thought and brilliant insights into the interconnectedness of social phenomena.

At present, capitalism is mostly studied by economists and economic historians who develop ever finer abstractions and mathematical models for the behavior of the market but who tend to forget in print what they know in fact: that the economic order and the social and cultural realms are linked in countless vital and non-quantifiable ways. The one important book of our time which is fully cognizant of this interplay is characteristically entitled *The Unbound Prometheus,* the very title harking back to ancient myth and poetic truth.[3]

I came to understand the impact of capitalism—and some of the inadequacies of general abstractions—in a study of Gerson Bleich-röder, born in Berlin in 1822. He was the son of a Jewish money jobber, a trader in foreign currencies, who only gradually came to be known as a banker. Gerson was the first of the family to have been born into a world that no longer imposed legal restrictions on Jews. In 1830, Gerson's father became an agent of the Roths-childs, that fabled dynasty which by the 1820s already was recognized as the embodiment of a new power. (Heine, an occasional guest at Baron James de Rothschild's, proclaimed that "Money is the God of our age, and Rothschild is his prophet.") From 1830 to 1855, the Bleichröder Bank prospered, by virtue of its ever closer ties to the Rothschilds and its own shrewd exploitation of the railroad boom. By 1859, the Frankfurt Rothschilds recommended Gerson to the departing Prussian minister, Otto von Bismarck, and thus began a relationship which ended with Gerson's death in 1893. Bleichröder became Bismarck's private banker and counselor, his *homme de confiance* and secret agent at home and abroad. Because of his many roles in Bismarck's life, Bleichröder had immediate access to him; with no one else outside his family did Bismarck have an equally long or close relationship. Bismarck and Bleichröder: an unlikely combination, representing an old and a new world, and yet their collaboration was symptomatic of the energies that shaped the new Germany.[4]

I was attracted to the prospect of writing on Bleichröder by two considerations: the lure of an unexploited Bleichröder archive, which on first inspection seemed to promise a new perspective on Bismarck and his era; and the cooperation of an economic historian who would handle the story of the great banking house, a story which I would have been incapable of writing. The archive proved a tantalizing beginning, but no more; it contained private letters to Gerson but almost none from him, and hence was inadequate as a guide to his career. It had to be supplemented by material from the most diverse private and public archives of Europe. After a few years, the economic expert withdrew as well, and the task of writing about Bismarck and Bleichröder fell on me alone.

My first day of work in the Rothschild Archives on the rue Laffitte I came across a receipt for 1,000 taler, debited by Bleichröder on the Rothschild account, and signed by Cosima von Bülow, née Liszt. A few years later, of course, Cosima was to become Wagner's mistress, later mother to his children, even wife, and, after his death, guardian and exploiter of his heritage, musical and ideological. I had once written an essay on this formidable creature, so noble, so greedy, so idealistically anti-Semitic, for a seminar given by Jacques Barzun, and through many years of labor, I remembered Cosima's draft as a talisman, a sign that even a cultural historian could find sustenance in the complicated travails of a banker.

Bleichröder was a representative man, an exemplar of the *homo novus* who shaped the life of the nineteenth century. His beginnings were modest; he died the richest man in Berlin. He demonstrated the enormous power of wealth—and all the limitations and ambiguities of wealth as well. A close study of his life offers insights into the mentality—the ambitions, values and fears—of the capitalist class in Germany, and his intimate relations with Bismarck, with Bismarck's entourage, and with the old aristocracy reveal something of the complicated response that the older class, based on birth and honor, had to the new class, based on wealth alone.

Bleichröder amassed a fortune; this was the obvious condition for his success, but it was never enough. He was indefatigable in ferreting out economic opportunities; he came to have an intuitive sense of where to place his funds, on what terms, with what associates, and against what rivals. He cultivated his close ties with officialdom and had important clients among the fourth estate. He was not a demonic entrepreneur but a prudent banker who knew how to play the market; he financed railroads, helped build the St. Gotthard tunnel, floated companies, served foreign governments as banker, and made a profit on every transaction.[5] And yet he was anything but an "economic man," that abstraction of the textbooks which would lead us to believe that businessmen, with lightning speed, are able to gauge the opportunities of the market and make their decisions accordingly, rationally, and with an eye to maximum profit. For Bleichröder that activity became routine; he excelled at it, even if in his later years he may have eschewed profitable risks for the sake of respectable security. But his incessant striving showed that the accumulation of wealth, which no doubt at a certain stage of his life had been an end in itself, became essentially a means. He knew how to make money, but money could not buy—at least not entirely—what he most desired: a recognized place in society, prominence and influence.

The social ambition of the bourgeois is one of the great themes of the nineteenth century. In Bleichröder's case we have the documentation of this ambition and can reconstruct the maneuvers by which he sought to realize it. In a few cultures, notably in North America, the epithet "self-made man" became a badge of distinction. Not so in Europe, and least of all perhaps in Germany. Traditional society defined a man by his birth and bearing, by his honor. Wealth was rarely considered a moral asset; more likely it bespoke character traits of dubious morality. In the face of such prejudice against Mammon—prejudice that was at once moral, religious, and self-serving, since it was a defense precisely against the presumptions of a Bleichröder—it was hard to gain acceptance. Money talks—but it talks in different tongues in different countries and at different times.

Bleichröder's struggle for acceptance was an extreme instance of a common experience. It was made extreme by his Jewishness— he had to contend with prejudice not only against Mammon but also against a race that for long had been suspected of being uniquely gifted in materialistic, that is, evil, pursuits. His special ties with Bismarck gave him a unique advantage which, in turn, quickened his desire for admission and status. A Bleichröder had to forge his own role, as his old identity as a marginal man in society and a pariah became invalid. For Bleichröder, this search for a new identity was made even more imperative when in 1872, at Bismarck's personal behest and for services rendered to the state and its financially embarrassed paladins, he was formally ennobled. No other unconverted Jew had had such an honor bestowed on him in Prussia. Now Bleichröder had to fashion a life that would be consonant with his new position as Herr von Bleichröder, or Baron von Bleichröder, as he was often called.

It called forth an extraordinary effort. By dint of great feasts at which the diplomatic corps and the local élite, including the Princess Bismarck and her sons, dined and danced in the company of handsome officers from the best regiments, Bleichröder established his social presence in Berlin. The feasts were opulent—and painstakingly prepared. One enjoyed at Bleichröder's the best food, the most celebrated musicians, and always and above all the choicest company; fellow Jews or fellow financiers were usually excluded, as were Bleichröder's relations. Neither host nor guests could have felt at home. Bleichröder's social role—so solid on the outside and so fragile in reality—caused endless tongue-wagging. As Princess Radziwill once wrote: "Berlin society is divided into two camps—those who go to Bleichröder while mocking him, and those who mock him but do not go."[6]

But most went, because social gatherings had long since ceased to be celebrations of congeniality; they had become a reflection of the market. Likewise, Bleichröder was assured of the gratitude and friendship of many leading figures, and the protestations marked the decline of the ideal of friendship. Bleichröder craved acceptance and his social fortunes epitomized the triumph of utility—he was a presence because of his unsurpassed usefulness and because, as an intimate of Bismarck's, he was a dangerous man to snub. The Bismarck entourage, suffering under the moody inconstancy of the genius-autocrat, suspected Bleichröder of having a mysterious hold over the chancellor and of having the power to make and break careers. Since Bismarck had to be humored, Bleichröder had to be humored and the élite had to go to his house, vilifying him the more as it went.

Bleichröder also "modernized" impoverished members of the old élite, seeking to salvage the fortunes of men who had fallen on evil days. He helped men who had succumbed to the great capitalistic greed of the time by placing them in lucrative directorships. His services were legion—quite aside from providing the routine advantages of a reliable and accommodating banking house with the most excellent connections in Europe.

In his search for acceptance, Bleichröder sought to impress the world by his intimate knowledge of all that went on in Europe. Everybody came to Bleichröder—officials, diplomats and fellow magnates—to solicit his advice and receive his news. Like the Rothschilds, he discovered the usefulness of instant intelligence, and he built up a network of informers so that he was probably the most knowledgeable man in Berlin. He was especially knowledgeable about Bismarck, whose fortune he invested and who therefore had to keep him properly informed. Bleichröder collected secrets as other plutocrats collected *objets d'art,* and for the same reason—to dazzle people and to exalt his own importance. As in most things Bleichröder did, the functional and the psychological coincided: Being in the know was an inestimable advantage in the market and in society, and served as well to augment self-esteem.

The drive for acceptance was the lodestar of his later life. In the pursuit of it, he distanced himself from his own people. He still interceded for the Jews and used his power in Berlin to lobby for his coreligionists in Eastern Europe; had he done less than that, his valuable connections with the Rothschilds would probably have snapped. But gradually he moved away from the Jewish community; at most, he served as a kind of ambassador of Jewry to the dominant culture. The police report of 1874—two years after his ennoblement—may have maliciously exaggerated, but it has a ring of authenticity, and many variations on the theme were current in Berlin in the 1870s:

> Mr. von Bleichröder, who since his elevation to nobility almost bursts with pride and who publicly no longer entertains his former friends and associates, keeps himself apart from them even in his walks: on his promenades in the Sieges-Allee [Berlin's fashionable avenue along the Tiergarten] he walks on the western side, instead of on the eastern with the great majority of promenaders, who are almost all Jews. Asked why he walked on the other side, he is supposed to have answered that the eastern side smelled too much of garlic. Several of Bleichröder's former acquaintances heard of this remark and a few days ago took him to task for it on the promenade, and things did not go too smoothly then.[7]

The police report depicts the classic case of the *arriviste*—who never arrives. Bleichröder's life was an attenuated form of deferential dissembling; as such it brings to mind Lionel Trilling's observation that there were societies that seem to favor dissembling:

> We cannot establish by actual count that there were more villains in real life at one time than another, but we can say that there was at one time better reason, more practical use,

for villainous dissembling than at another. Tartuffe, Blifil, *la cousine* Bette, Mme Marneffe, Uriah Heep, Blandois, Becky Sharp—these wolves in sheep's clothing are not free fantasies, and it is a misapprehension to think of them as such. The possibility of their actual existence is underwritten by social fact.[8]

Bleichröder's social climbing was a form of dissembling and forced a similar dissembling on the elite he sought to emulate, for the latter had to conceal its true feelings. Most aristocrats, contemptuous of such climbing and such disloyalty, were bemused at Bleichröder's efforts to emulate them. And he tried hard. Shortly after his ennoblement, he purchased the large estate of Field Marshal Roon, an old landed seat near Potsdam, which in the early nineteenth century had been remodeled by the great Prussian architect David Gilly. Here he led the quiet life of the landed elite. But if it was a genuine retreat for him, it was also the spot where his royal neighbor, William I, once called on him after the most intricate preparations for the event.

Bleichröder had decorations, titles, connections. Yet nothing—not even a royal parchment—could prevail against ancient prejudice. The Junker nobility still drew its living and its dignity from the land, but agrarian pursuits were threatened by overseas competition and by the rise of new wealth at home. The Junker feared that the new plutocracy would buy up their mortgaged estates, that wolf or Jew was forever waiting at the door. They thought themselves in a mortal struggle for survival, and in that struggle they were not about to give up their ancient prejudices against business and unproductive wealth, or their traditional sense that honor, service, and unpretentious living and piety defined human worth.

Money, so the saying went, was something one had, but did not talk about. Under the new system, exemplified by Bleichröder, the Junker stood in danger of not having money, and so they were condemned to talk about it, at least in private, while publicly maintaining their stance against Mammon. The more capitalism altered the social physiognomy of Germany, the more the Junker were forced to do battle in the material arena, to mobilize their political power in order to defend their declining economic interests. All of this hardened their prejudices against the grasping money-man who had but one value, that of ruthless profiteering. If only there had been a Marxism for nobles. As it was, they had to make do with their own harsh mixture of the idealization of rural life and the denunciation of urban, rootless capitalism, for which Jews seemed to have a most uncommon penchant.

It is not surprising that by the end of the century the old classes were trying to reassert their higher status, their more honest and authentic life, their superiority in virtues that were decisive for the state, such as self-denial. (These virtues came generally into vogue as the military spirit spread through society, aided by universal conscription and chauvinism.) What was less predict-able—and certainly ran counter to the expectations of Marx and liberals alike—was the willing submission of the upper bourgeoisie to these same values. That submission Bleichröder exemplified in a hundred ways, perhaps none more poignant than his carefully orchestrated petition to William I to restore his son, Hans, to his position as a reserve officer (lost when, on the day the emperor was shot, he appeared at the royal castle with a *cocotte* at his side). In his petition Bleichröder begged for his son's reinstatement, because the continued humiliation might drive the father to leave Germany; not all his millions, not all his proximity to eminence, could balance the shame of having a demoted, denuded son. The emperor showed some clemency, and Bleichröder's other sons fared somewhat better. But the descent of Bleichröder's progeny into sloth demonstrates the terrible risks of success. The father's labors paid for the children's license. Spoiled from the beginning and also desirous of belonging, they converted to Protestantism, while abandoning the Protestant ethic. They lived a life of decad-ence, and Thomas Mann's "Blood of the Walsungs" conjures up something of the suffocating atmosphere.

Bleichröder's career demonstrated the lure of wealth and the yearning for what has been called "status," but the term does not suggest the anguish that the long climb involved. Quantifying or latter-day scientific historians tend to neglect this side of capitalist striving. Adam Smith, who discovered "economic man," also knew that there was no such reality. "The rich man," he wrote,

> glories in his riches, because he feels that they naturally draw upon him the attention of the world, and that mankind are disposed to go along with him in all those agreeable emotions

with which the advantages of his situation so readily inspire him. At the thought of this, his heart seems to swell and dilate itself within him, and he is fonder of his wealth, upon this account, than for all the other advantages it procures him.[9]

A recent critic, aware of the discomfort that terms like "fame" and "honor" would cause his scientific brethren, has jestingly spoken of such "ultimate desires" as "obituary-enhancing activities."[10] The rich have always striven for more than wealth. That more may have been ostentation or pomp, may have been morally and aesthetically less creditable, less genuine than their search for wealth; but the yearnings have existed and have further unsettled society.

In imperial Germany, the striving for these "higher things" was both peculiarly necessary and peculiarly arduous. If Bleichröder's life shows anything, it is the strength and dynamism of capitalism in practice and the pervasive power of anti-capitalism in spirit. The aristocratic classes—but not only they—looked upon the new system and its profiteers as an insiduous evil. Capitalism offended their code and their social standing, and however much they may secretly have embraced capitalistic techniques or capitalistic greed, their public stance and private views were still contemptuous. (In this, as in so much else, Bismarck was the exception. But although he was a modern Junker, quick to recognize the utility of capitalism for the state and for the individual Junker, his unease at his link with Bleichröder can be gauged by the fact that his memoirs mention his banker and long-time confidant only once, and then in an inconsequential role.)

The social disdain of the aristocracy was matched by the anger and resentment of the lower classes, whose lives had been placed in jeopardy and whose self-esteem had been destroyed by the relentless pressures of "a free economic society." Artisans who had once found their economic security and their dignity in guilds felt themselves estranged and disadvantaged in the new society. In the late 1870s, these groups were attracted to a new ideology which blamed their lot on Jews because Jews had fastened an alien economic system on unwitting Germans. The proof of the charge was Bleichröder: his wealth and pretensions, his connections with men of power, his widespread and pernicious influence over press and parliament. The early anti-Semitic movement was also anticapitalistic, and Bleichröder was the chief witness to the validity of its assertions. If he had not existed, it would have been impossible to invent him; he found, moreover, that it was impossible to defend himself against charges that combined the obvious with the venomously fanciful. The proletariat, imbued with the Marxist faith, held not the Jews but the capitalistic system as such culpable, and lived and worked in the confidence that the eventual overthrow of exploitative capitalism and its replacement by a humane socialism was historically preordained.

Imperial Germany, as seen through Bleichröder, affords the extraordinary picture of a triumphant capitalism spiritually devalued. The psychological premises of capitalism were obviously incompatible with the pretensions of German idealism and nationalism: The German ideal of self-cultivation was hardly consonant with an insistence on material self-aggrandizement, and the glorification of state authority in German nationalism can be seen as a rebuke to economic selfishness. Capitalism became widely discredited in the 1870s, when a great boom, fueled in part by speculation and corruption, gave way to a great collapse, and when serious economic dislocation was followed by Bismarck's abandonment of free trade—that classic ingredient of early capitalism or Manchesterism—and his adoption of protectionism. By the end of that decade, unfettered capitalism was thought morally bankrupt, and gradually a new kind of cartelized capitalism, at times in collusion with the government, replaced it, while popular sentiment continued to denounce a system of private greed.[11]

The notion of devalued capitalism may also help us to understand the prevalent hypocrisy of Imperial society. The new system was a special spur to dissemblance. It condemned everyone to hide or deny his true role: the *Bürger* sought the trappings of nobility, and the nobleman, so contemptuous of any system that assigned rank by wealth, needed to modernize his ways or lose his ancestral seat. It is customary to speak of the alliance between upper bourgeoisie and nobility which governed Germany after 1879, and in a political sense there was an alliance between landowner and industrialist; but, like most alliances between unequals, common interests and common foes barely hid a deep suspicion and antagonism.

The life of Bleichröder makes this clear. Everybody used him and nobody acknowledged him—Bismarck partly excepted. A list of his clientele reads like a selection from the Almanach de Gotha; but these clients came to him stealthily or wrote him letters about their material needs with the injunction: "to be burned." Perhaps it has always been so, yet the degree of involvement and concealment seems to have been unusual. Thorstein Veblen commented on the discrepancy in Germany between capitalistic reality and older cultural survivals long ago in his *Imperial Germany*. But it is only fair to add that the German reaction to capitalism—a subject so infinitely complicated that it still deserves to be examined in all its aspects—was conditioned by more than the survival of premodern customs. The hostility to this bustling, ever innovative and restless force was also affected by a collective nostalgia, part genuine and part nurtured, for "The World We Lost," for a preindustrial world of communitarian harmony in smaller cities and amidst guild structures that regulated morality and economic pursuit in one insulated system. Wagner was the greediest of artists; his people were uplifted by the *Meistersinger von Nürnberg*, which they took to be the epitome of their true heritage.[12]

For many Germans of the mid- to late-nineteenth century, the dance around the Golden Calf was the more revolting because it coincided with a falling away from true worship. None of this was unique to Germany; churchmen—and not only churchmen—of the nineteenth century railed against the replacement of God by Mammon, of faith by indifference and greed, of duty by utility. In Germany, however, the degree of resistance—and hypocrisy—may have been greater than elsewhere; the unrecognized social reality poisoned the political atmosphere for decades. (It has of course always been thought that devotion to material objects would diminish devotion to spiritual commands: "Having food and raiment, let us be therewith content. But they that will be rich fall into temptation and a snare, and into many foolish and hurtful lusts, which drown men in destruction and perdition. For the love of money is the root of all evil" [1 Tim. 6:8–10]. But the race after the goods of the world has mobilized human energies, and the race itself constituted a goal. In contemporary society, the dance around the Golden Calf is once again in great disrepute, but what other dance will mobilize the same energies? Or will an increasing number of affluent young devote their energies to subduing that drive in order to embrace what Nietzsche warned against as the worst form of nihilism: European Buddhism?)

Bleichröder's desire for acceptance manifested itself in ways other than the emulation of the forms and values of the older classes. He also embraced the new secular faith, nationalism, and did so with the special passion that so many Jews, hitherto homeless, displayed. Bleichröder's special tie to Bismarck proved a kind of personal bridge to patriotism, which by the late 1860s and early 1870s had taken on the emotional hue of a new, exuberant nationalism. At times he exuded this overweening pride in the new Germany even to the Rothschilds, who reacted with predictable chill. As a banker, he remained a man of pacific and cosmopolitan leanings; like most bankers, he thought himself an instrument of peace. But for the rest he cherished a demonstrative loyalty to the new nation—and for his estate, ordered a collection of stones from all the battlefields in France where German troops had fought victoriously. It was a bizarre demonstration of faith and taste, but not out of keeping with the monumental architecture which at the time glorified German arms and unity.

The rich needed to show their munificence in many ways, and Bleichröder became a patron of the arts and sciences. He commissioned Germany's foremost portrait painter, Franz von Lenbach, to paint a portrait of Bismarck; years later, he asked Lenbach to paint his own portrait as well—which Lenbach did, at twice the fee. As Bismarck liked to tell the story, Lenbach, when asked about the discrepancy, explained that he had *enjoyed* painting Bismarck. For his own portrait, Bleichröder had to pay 30,000 marks.[13] One is reminded of Jacques Barzun's apt definition: "the really paying patron of art in our society [is] the passionate snob—C. Snobius Maecenas."[14] Bleichröder also commissioned Reinhold Begas, the most celebrated sculptor of the day, and the perpetrator of many a monstrosity in Berlin, to design a family mausoleum. Begas suggested a large, ornate structure in Carrara marble, at a cost of 75,000 marks.[15]

But Bleichröder had also to show his largesse while alive, and his giving was truly ecumenical. He contributed to the poor and sick of all denominations—from Catholic hospitals to the Hebrew Orphan Asylum in New York. He helped to build an Anglican church in Berlin, a synagogue in Ostende, a Protestant church in a Rhenish village. He was endlessly solicited. Toward the end of his life, anonymously but in memory of his parents, he gave Robert Koch, the discoverer of the tubercle bacillus, a choice plot of

sixteen acres in Berlin and 1 million marks, for the construction
of a new hospital and for the treatment of destitute patients.[16]

Neither Bleichröder's achievements nor his munificence shielded
him from growing attack. On the contrary, his prominence made
him the perfect target. The polemics began in the 1870s, when
Germans first became conscious that they had been engulfed by a
new economic system. Their hostility to the system was personified
by branding the Jews (who did play a major role in promoting
capitalism in Germany) as the culprits of subversion. In the
beginning, Bleichröder was cited as the proof of racist charges: he
was cunning, corrupt, and powerful—and so were all his fellow
Jews. In the turmoil of that first decade after unification, when
exultation over foreign victories gradually gave way to concern
over domestic divisions and depressions, the charges against Jews—
validated as it were by Bleichröder's known role—confirmed what
Barzun has written about racism generally: "it satisfies a need
common in complex societies—the need to give body to vague
hostility, to find excuses for what goes wrong, to fear aliens or
neighbors and curse them, while enjoying self-approval from within
the shelter of one's own group. . . . It satisfies the starved sense
of kinship and it promises a vast supernatural community."[17]
In Germany, this combined anti-Semitism and anti-capitalism remained a powerful subterranean current, ready to
burst forth when the dams of social order and moral restraint
weakened.

The life of Bleichröder exemplifies the many faces of capitalism
in nineteenth-century Germany and the many interconnections
between realms that historians all too often keep in separate
compartments. To speak of "the triumph of capitalism in Germany"
is much too simple—and yet among economic historians the
principal debate focuses on when this putative event took place.[18]
Bleichröder should be a reminder that the triumph was but partial,
that the animus of economically, socially, and psychologically
aggrieved groups against the new economic order remained strong,
as did the nostalgia for a precapitalistic and pre-industrial world.
For many decades, anti-capitalism was a sentiment that informed
both the Right and the Left, though it could be argued that until
recently it was a stronger force on the Right than on the Left.

Balance sheets of capitalism beyond market fluctations, production rates and cost-accounting are subject matter for a book that still needs to be written; the culture of capitalism remains a subject worthy of study and reflection.[19]

Capitalism is too serious a subject to be left to the economic historians alone. It is too subtle and elusive a subject to be captured by the rigorous specialist in the laws of the market or in the stages of economic growth; it does not yield to statistics. Put differently, capitalism is so much more than economics, so much more than collusion with government or class conflict. It expresses itself in changing attitudes and sentiments, in different self-perceptions and masks, in dress and painting and furniture, in a spreading rationality and a recoiling from it—in short, in all the aspects of a culture. The cultural historian, often so heedless of the transformations wrought by material changes, needs to rescue a subject which cuts so deeply into modern history, which tells us so much about human motives and achievement, about social reality and thought. "Nothing but the fullest and clearest—which is not the same as the simplest—view of our cultural past and present should satisfy us," wrote Jacques Barzun nearly twenty years ago, and the injunction has become even more timely.[20]

Capitalism has ever been suspect. In our own day, when the corruptibilty of capitalism appears as an everyday headline, and when the traditional justification for capitalism—its successful functioning—seems once more threatened, we might do well to ponder the paradox that one of the most valuable and insidious consequences of capitalism is anti-capitalism: valuable because of its reformist impulse, and insidious because beneath it often lurks a Utopian illusion that social evil springs from capitalism and that some, often nebulous, alternative would usher in a period of human brotherhood and goodness. As with all great themes of past and present, the study of capitalism is at once a command of our craft and a dictate of our social existence. Capitalism has brought misery and degradation; it has also brought freedom, mobility and rationality. It is a subject worthy of study, for it involves not only the functioning of a worldwide market but the minds and habits of men. In an age that speaks of late capitalism or post-capitalist society, perhaps we need to ponder as well the likely consequences of a withering of capitalism. To paraphrase the title of an essay that Jacques Barzun long ago recognized as portentous, we may need to think of "The Moral Equivalent of Capitalism," for the Faustian impulse will reassert itself—in our understanding of the past and in the shaping of some future.

Notes

INTRODUCTION

1. One of the most prominent of younger historians, Michael Stürmer, entitled his history of pre-1914 Germany *Das Ruhelose Reich* (Berlin, 1984). Stürmer is a meticulous historian; as a publicist he represents a new national assertiveness.
2. See, for example, the admirable book by S. S. Prawer, *Karl Marx and World Literature* (Oxford, 1976), especially Chapter 3.
3. On Goethe's *Tagebuch*, see Hans Rudolf Vaget, *Goethe: Der Mann von 60 Jahren* (Königstein, 1982), *passim*.
4. In 1982, I gave a lecture at the Goethe House in New York on "talent and genius in Bismarck's Germany." The lecture was a mere beginning and has no place here. But it is a topic worth pursuing; a recent survey is Jochen Schmidt, *Die Geschichte des Genie-Gedankens 1750–1945*, vol. 2, *Von der Romantik bis zum Ende des Dritten Reichs* (Darmstadt, 1985). On the special place of poets, see Wolf Lepenies, *Die Drei Kulturen: Soziologie zwischen Literatur und Wissenschaft* (Munich, Vienna, 1985), especially pp. 245–247.
5. Quoted in *Gold and Iron* (New York, 1977), p. 230.
6. On Wolfgang Köhler in particular and on German psychotherapists and psychologists under the Nazis in general, see my "Fink Shrinks," *New York Review of Books*, December 5, 1985.
7. See, for example, Eberhard Jäckel, *Hitler in History* (Hanover, N.H., 1984), *passim*.
8. Wolf Lepenies, *Die Drei Kulturen*, p. 245.
9. See Ralf Dahrendorf, *Society and Democracy in Germany* (New York, 1967), pp. 435–450 and *passim*.
10. A leading German political scientist, Hans-Peter Schwarz, notes that

Germans have lost all interest in power, all knowledge of what power represents; many of them simply distrust "power." See *Die gezähmten Deutschen: Von der Machtbesessenheit zur Machtvergessenheit* (Stuttgart, 1985), *passim*.

11. Foreigners voiced their unease at this new restlessness. Brigitte Sauzay, a French authority steeped in German life, wrote about her apprehensions in *Die rätselhaften Deutschen: Die Bundesrepublik von aussen gesehen* (Stuttgart, 1986).

12. For the English version of Weizsäcker's speech, see Geoffrey H. Hartman, ed., *Bitburg in Moral and Political Perspective* (Bloomington, Ind., 1986), pp. 262–273. See *Das Parlament* 36, no. 20–21 (17/24 May 1986); my particular references are to the articles by Michael Stürmer and Hans-Ulrich Wehler.

13. In the spring and summer of 1986 began a great and acrimonious debate among German historians and scholars; Jürgen Habermas and some historians attacked efforts at "relativizing" Nazi crimes, at trying to revive a nationalistic version of the past. The debate, ill-focused though it was, constitutes the most searching examination of the place of the past in German life. On one level it seemed to me to echo the implicit difference between Weizsäcker and Helmut Kohl, between the former's forthrightness and the latter's effort to dissolve the past into gestures of reconciliation, such as the Bitburg visit. See also Christian Meier, "Kein Schlusswort: Zum Streit um die NS-Vergangenheit," *Frankfurter Allgemeine Zeitung*, Oct. 1986.

14. See, for example, the eloquent farewell speech of Helmut Schmidt before the German Parliament, warning an endangered nation not to forswear the dictates of practical reason. *Das Parlament* 36, no. 39, (27 Sept. 1986).

CHAPTER 1 : *Einstein's Germany*

1. Quoted in Banesh Hoffmann, with the collaboration of Helen Dukas, *Albert Einstein: Creator and Rebel* (New York, 1972), p. 139.

2. Lionel Trilling, *Mind in the Modern World* (New York, 1973), pp. 13–14.

3. Richard Hofstadter, "History and the Social Sciences," in Fritz Stern, ed., *The Varieties of History*, 2d ed. (New York, 1972), p. 369.

4. Max Weber, *Gesammelte politische Schriften* (Munich, 1921), p. 29.

5. Theodor Mommsen, *Reden und Aufsätze* (Berlin, 1905), pp. 5–8.

6. Martin J. Klein, *Paul Ehrenfest* (Amsterdam, 1970), p. 77.

7. Erik H. Erikson, *Childhood and Society*, 2d and enl. ed. (New York, 1963), p. 337.

8. Copy in Einstein Papers, Boston; see also *Gedächtnisausstellung zum 100. Geburtstag von Albert Einstein, Otto Hahn, Max von Laue, and Lise Meitner*, Staatsbibliothek Preussischer Kulturbesitz, 1979, pp. 63–64.

On Nicolai's "Manifesto to Europeans," see Bernhard vom Brocke, " 'Wissenschaft und Militarismus!' Der Aufruf der 93 'An die Kulturwelt!' und der Zusammenbruch der internationalen Gelehrtenrepublik im Ersten Weltkrieg," in *Wilamowitz nach 50 Jahren*, ed. William M. Calder III, et al. (Darmstadt, 1985), pp. 649–719.

9. See also a forthcoming essay of mine, "Haber und Einstein: Freunde im Widerspruch," in *Forschung im Spannungsfeld von Politik und Gesellschaft: Zum 75. jährigen Bestehen der Kaiser-Wilhelm/Max-Planck-Gesellschaft 1911–1986*, ed. Rudolf Vierhaus and Bernhard vom Brocke (Stuttgart, 1987).

10. Otto Nathan and Heinz Norden, eds., *Einstein on Peace* (New York, 1960), p. 25.

11. Noel Annan, " 'Our Age': Reflections on Three Generations in England," *Daedalus* (Fall 1978), p. 83.

12. Einstein to Max von Laue, 26 May 1933; Laue to Einstein, 31 May 1933; Einstein Papers, Boston.

13. Albert Einstein, *Ideas and Opinions* (based on *Mein Weltbild*, ed. Carl Seelig), new trans. and rev. by Sonja Bargmann (New York, 1954), p. 11.

14. *Ibid.*, p. 4.

15. Gerald Holton, *The Scientific Imagination: Case Studies* (Cambridge, Mass.,1978), p. 279.

16. Nathan, Norden, *Einstein on Peace*, pp. 111–112.

17. Albert Einstein and Sigmund Freud, *Why War?* (Paris, 1933), p. 12.

18. The *Times* (London), 8 November 1919.

19. Albert Einstein to Chaim Weizmann, 29 November 1929, and December [n.d.] 1929. The Weizmann Archives, Yad Chaim Weizmann, Rehovoth.

20. Weizmann to Albert Einstein, 30 November 1929; the Weizmann Archives, Yad Chaim Weizmann, Rehovoth.

21. Weizmann to Felix Warburg, Einstein Papers, Boston.

22. Robert Oppenheimer, "On Albert Einstein," *New York Review of Books*, 17 March 1966.

23. Albert Einstein to Max Wertheimer, 26 September 1940; Albert Einstein to Dr. Julius Schwalbe, 18 July 1924. Both in Einstein Papers, Boston.

24. Einstein to Paul Ehrenfest, quoted in Martin J. Klein, *Paul Ehrenfest*, p. 312. Letters in the Einstein Papers, Boston.

25. Max Born, ed., *Albert Einstein–Hedwig und Max Born Briefwechsel 1916–1955* (Munich, 1969), p. 55.

26. Richard Willstätter, *Aus Meinem Leben* (Weinheim, 1949), pp. 235, 342–351.

27. Max Born, *My Life and My Views* (New York, 1968), p. 38.

28. Letter in the Einstein Archives, Boston.

29. Erwin Panofsky, *Meaning in the Visual Arts* (New York, 1955), p. 322.

30. See James Franck to Einstein, 11 December 1945 and Einstein to Franck, 3 April 1946, James Franck Papers, The University of Chicago Library.

31. Einstein, *Ideas and Opinions*, pp. 12–13.

A NOTE ON SOURCES

It seems superfluous to list the standard works on and by Albert Einstein. For purposes of this essay I found *Ideas and Opinions* and *Einstein on Peace* particularly pertinent. I was also fortunate enough to be allowed to use the Albert Einstein Archive at the Institute for Advanced Study in Princeton, N.J., a treasure made still more valuable by the ever helpful advice and recollections of Helen Dukas, who is in charge of it. I also read the unpublished correspondence of James Franck and Albert Einstein, deposited at The University of Chicago Library. In addition to the books cited in the preceding notes, I found the following particularly useful: Allan D. Beyerchen, *Scientists under Hitler: Politics and the Physics Community in the Third Reich* (New Haven, Conn., 1977); Gerald Holton, *The Scientific Imagination: Case Studies* (Cambridge, Mass., 1978); Richard Willstätter, *Aus Meinem Leben* (Weinheim, 1949); Harriet Zuckerman, *Scientific Elites: Nobel Laureates in the United States* (New York, 1977).

I benefited from conversations with Marshall Clagett, Felix Gilbert, Gerald Holton, Martin Klein, I. I. Rabi, and Malvin Ruderman. It was in long and frequent talks with Otto Stern that I first sensed how extraordinary those early days in Zurich must have been.

CHAPTER 2 : *Fritz Haber: The Scientist in Power and in Exile*

1. Fritz Haber, "Gedächtnisrede auf Justus von Liebig," *Zeitschrift für angewandte Chemie*, 41, no. 33 (18 August 1928): 892.
2. *Ibid.*, p. 893.
3. Unfortunately, I obtained a copy of J. L. Heilbron, *The Dilemmas of an Upright Man: Max Planck as Spokesman for German Science* (Berkeley, Cal., 1986), only after I completed the revision of this lecture.
4. Richard Willstätter, *Aus Meinem Leben: Von Arbeit, Musse und Freunden* (Weinheim, 1949), p. 247.
5. See Willstätter, *Aus Meinem Leben*, p. 243, and his entire chapter on Haber, pp. 241–271. For a more recent account of Haber's life and work, see Paul Günther, "Fritz Haber—ein Mann der Jahrhundertwende," in *Fridericiana: Zeitschrift der Universität Karlsruhe*, no. 4 (May 1969): 3–26. See also the articles by Johannes and Walther Jaenicke and Lothar Suhling on Haber in *Fridericiana*, no. 35 (Dec. 1984).
6. J. E. Coates, "The Haber Memorial Lecture," delivered before the Chemical Society on April 29, 1937, *Journal of the Chemical Society*, Nov. 1939: 1645, also 1642–1672, *passim*.
7. From Karl Friedrich Bonhoeffer's obituary notice, "Fritz Haber," *Chemiker Zeitung*, 58, no. 20 (March 10, 1934). It was an act of courage to publish an obituary about a Jewish chemist, an act characteristic of Bonhoeffer and of his entire family, which behaved so heroically and suffered so cruelly under the Nazis.
8. F. Haber, "Über Hochschulunterricht und elektrochemische Technik in den Vereinigten Staaten," *Zeitschrift für Elektrochemie*, 9, no. 16 (April 16, 1903): 291–303, and 9, no. 18 (April 30, 1903): 347–348, and 9, no. 45 (5 November 1903): 893–898.
9. See an essay of mine on Haber and Einstein in a forthcoming volume on the seventy-fifth anniversary of the founding of the Kaiser Wilhelm Gesellschaft, Rudolf Vierhaus and Bernhard vom Brocke, eds., *Forschung im Spannungsfeld von Politik und Gesellschaft* (Stuttgart, 1987).

10. Michelle Besso–Albert Einstein, *Correspondence 1903–1955* (Paris, 1972), pp. 139–140.
11. L. F. Haber, *The Poisonous Cloud: Chemical Warfare in the First World War* (Oxford, 1936), p. 27 and *passim*.
12. Letter from Haber to Rudolf von Valentini, 2 February 1916, Max Planck Archive.
13. Quoted in L. F. Haber, *The Poisonous Cloud*, p. 292.
14. Haber to Valentini, 2 January 1916, Max Planck Archive.
15. Moellendorff to Haber, Sept. 5, 1916, Moellendorff Papers, Bundesarchiv, Koblenz; see also Gerald D. Feldman's excellent *Army Industry and Labor in Germany 1914–1918* (Princeton, N.J., 1966), pp. 170–173 and *passim*.
16. Scheüch to Haber, 27 November 1918, Max Planck Archive.
17. See Rudolf A. Stern, "Fritz Haber: Personal Recollections," *Leo Baeck Institute Yearbook*, vol. 8 (London, 1963), pp. 75–76.
18. Haber to Moellendorff, 9 December 1918, Bundesarchiv, Koblenz; on Moellendorff, see also Ralph H. Bowen, *German Theories of the Corporative State, with Special Reference to the Period 1870–1919* (New York, 1947), pp. 182–195.
19. Fritz Haber, *Aus Leben und Beruf: Aufsätze Reden Vorträge* (Berlin, 1927), p. 20.
20. Haber to Einstein, 30 August 1920, Einstein Papers, Boston.
21. Haber to Willstätter, June 1924, Max Planck Archive.
22. Erwin Chargaff, *Heraclitean Fire: Sketches from a Life before Nature* (New York, 1978), pp. 51 and 50; Coates, "The Haber Memorial Lecture," p. 1664. Willstätter, *Aus Meinem Leben*, p. 258.
23. The German original can be found in Stern, "Fritz Haber," pp. 96–97.
24. James Franck to Haber, 15 April 1933, Max Planck Archive.
25. Haber to Willstätter, no date, but almost certainly from early May 1933, Max Planck Archive.
26. K. D. Bonhoeffer to Haber, 5 May 1933, Max Planck Archive.
27. Einstein to Haber, 19 May 1933, Einstein Papers, Boston.
28. Haber to Einstein, 7 or 8 August 1933, Max Planck Archive.
29. Haber to Willstätter, January 1934, Max Planck Archive; Haber to Rudolf Stern, January 1934, Max Planck Archive.
30. James Franck to Hermann and Marga Haber, 6 February 1934, Max Planck Archive.
31. Fritz Haber, "Justus von Liebig," p. 897.

CHAPTER 3 : *Ernst Reuter*

1. Wolfgang J. Mommsen, *Max Weber und die deutsche Politik 1890–1920*, 2d ed. (Tübingen, 1974), p. 185.
2. Karl-Dietrich Erdmann, ed., *Kurt Riezler. Tagebücher, Aufsätze, Dokumente. Deutsche Geschichtsquellen des 19. und 20. Jahrhunderts.* vol. 48 of Bayerische Akademie der Wissenschaften (Göttingen, 1972), pp. 270, 288.
3. Alexis de Tocqueville, *Democracy in America*, vol. 1 (New York, 1945), pp. 200–202.

4. *The Complete Poems of Heinrich Heine, A Modern English Version*, trans. and ed. Hal Draper (Boston, 1982), pp. 514–515.
5. Max Weber, *Gesammelte Politische Schriften*, 3d ed. (Tübingen, 1971), p. 332.
6. Max Weber, *Gesammelte Aufsätze zur Soziologie und Sozialpolitik* (Tübingen, 1924), p. 414.
7. Sigmund Freud, *Civilization and Its Discontents*, trans. and ed. James Strachey (New York, 1961), pp. 62–63.
8. *Ernst Reuter: Schriften Reden*, ed. Hans E. Hirschfeldt and Hans J. Reichhardt, vol. 1 (Berlin, 1972), pp. 203, 205.
9. *Ibid.*, pp. 207, 209, 211–212.
10. Theodor Fontane, *Der Stechlin* (Berlin, 1905), p. 270.
11. *Reuter: Schriften Reden*, Hirschfeldt, vol. 1, pp. 273, 275.
12. *Ibid.*, pp. 351–393.
13. David W. Morgan, *The Socialist Left and the German Revolution: A History of the German Independent Social Democratic Party, 1917–1922* (Ithaca, N.Y., and London, 1975), p. 101.
14. *Ernst Reuter: Schriften Reden*, vol. 2, eds. Hans E. Hirschfeldt and Hans J. Reichhardt (Berlin, 1973), p. 62.
15. *Ibid.*, pp. 66–67.
16. *Ibid.*, pp. 68, 83.
17. *Ernst Reuter: Schriften Reden*, vol. 3, ed. Hans E. Hirschfeldt and Hans J. Reichhardt (Berlin, 1974), p. 380.
18. *Reuter: Schriften Reden*, Hirschfeldt, vol. 2, p. 56.
19. *Ibid.*, p. 88.
20. *Reuter: Schriften Reden*, Hirschfeldt, vol. 3, p. 132.
21. *Reuter: Schriften Reden*, Hirschfeldt, vol. 2, p. 129.
22. *Reuter: Schriften Reden*, Hirschfeldt, vol. 1, pp. 335–336.
23. *Reuter: Schriften Reden*, Hirschfeldt, vol. 2, pp. 354–355.
24. *Reuter: Schriften Reden*, Hirschfeldt, vol. 3, p. 176.
25. *Ibid.*, p. 155. I am grateful to David Morgan for giving me the full text of Hilferding's letter.
26. *Reuter: Schriften Reden*, Hirschfeldt, vol. 2, p. 253.
27. *Reuter: Schriften Reden*, Hirschfeldt, vol. 3, p. 100.
28. *Ibid.*, p. 120.
29. *Konrad Adenauer: Reden 1917–1967*, ed. Hans-Peter Schwarz (Stuttgart, 1975), p. 83.

CHAPTER 4: *The Burden of Success*

1. Lionel Trilling, *The Liberal Imagination: Essays on Literature and Society* (London, 1951), p. 188.
2. Gerson D. Cohen, "German Jewry as Mirror of Modernity: Introduction to the Twentieth Volume," *Leo Baeck Institute Yearbook*, vol. 20 (London, 1975), p. xi.
3. An outstanding example of this new approach is Ismar Schorsch, *Jewish Reactions to German Anti-Semitism 1870–1914* (New York, 1972); this present essay does not mean to deal with the new literature, and I would refer the reader to the more general discussion and comprehensive bibliographical references in my *Gold and Iron: Bis-*

marck, Bleichröder, and the Building of the German Empire (New York, 1977).

4. Lionel Trilling, *Sincerity and Authenticity* (Cambridge, Mass., 1972), pp. 24–25.

5. See Jacob Katz's important work, *Out of the Ghetto: The Social Background of Jewish Emancipation, 1770–1870* (Cambridge, Mass., 1973).

6. Trilling, *The Liberal Imagination*, pp. 209–210.

7. Sigmund Freud, *The Standard Edition of the Complete Psychological Works*, ed. James Strachey, et al., vol. 19 (London, 1959), pp. 273–274. (I owe this reference to my friend Peter Loewenberg.)

CHAPTER 5 : *Germany 1933*

1. Gordon A. Craig, *Germany 1866–1945* (Oxford, 1978), p. 544.

2. Franz Neumann, "Anxiety and Politics," *The Democratic and the Authoritarian State* (Glencoe, Ill., 1957), pp. 270–300.

3. Richard F. Hamilton, *Who Voted for Hitler?* (Princeton, N.J., 1982). For an excellent survey of the new findings, see James J. Sheehan, "National Socialism and German Society: Reflections on Recent Research," *Theory and Society*, 13 (1984): 851–867.

4. Francis L. Carsten, *Reichswehr und Politik, 1918–1933* (Cologne and Berlin, 1964), p. 377.

5. Quoted in MacGregor Knox, "Conquest, Foreign and Domestic, in Fascist Italy and Nazi Germany," *Journal of Modern History*, 56, no. 1 (March 1984): 37.

6. Reinhard Neebe, *Grossindustrie, Staat und NSDAP 1930–1933: Paul Silverberg und der Reichsverband der Deutschen Industrie in der Krise der Weimarer Republik* (Göttingen, 1981), *passim*, esp. pp. 159–174.

7. Georg H. Kleine, "Adelsgenossenschaft und Nationalsozialismus," *Vierteljahrshefte für Zeitgeschichte*, 26, no. 1 (January 1978): 116 and 100–143 *passim*.

8. Thomas Mann, *Sorge um Deutschland: Sechs Essays* (Frankfurt am Main, 1957), pp. 18, 20.

9. Friedrich Heer, *Der Glaube des Adolf Hitler: Anatomie einer politschen Religiosität* (Munich, 1968), pp. 252–253.

10. Raymond Aron, *Mémoires: 50 ans de réflexion politique* (Paris, 1983), pp. 79–80, 76.

11. To Henry Pachter, quoted in Hamilton, *Who Voted?*, p. 647. See also David R. Lipton, *Ernst Cassirer: The Dilemma of a Liberal Intellectual in Germany, 1914–1933* (Toronto, Buffalo, London, 1978), esp. pp. 171–172.

12. Phillip W. Fabry, *Mutmassungen über Hitler: Urteile von Zeitgenossen* (Düsseldorf, 1969), p. 130.

13. Heinrich August Winkler, "Warum die Macht an Hitler fiel—zur 50. Wiederkehr des 30. Januar 1933," published in *Mahnendes Gedenken*, University of Freiburg, 1983, p. 35.

14. Quoted in Uriel Tal, "Nazism as a 'Political Faith,'" *The Jerusalem Quarterly* no. 15 (Spring 1980): 71.

15. *Adenauer: Briefe 1945–1947*, in Adenauer, *Rhöndorfer Ausgabe*, ed. Rudolf Morsey and Hans-Peter Schwarz (Berlin, 1983), p. 172.

16. For a recent reassertion by a leading German historian of the importance of these preexisting sentiments, see Hans Mommsen "Vom Versagen der deutschen Eliten," *Merkur*, 38, no. 1 (January, 1984): 97–102, who cites my *The Politics of Cultural Despair* (Berkeley, Cal., 1961) as a valid analysis of the pervasiveness of these sentiments.

17. Herbert A. Strauss, "Jewish Emigration from Germany—Nazi Policies and Jewish Responses (I)," *Leo Baeck Institute Yearbook*, vol. 25 (London, 1980), pp. 313–361.

18. Jacob Boas, "Germany or Diaspora? German Jewry's Shifting Perceptions in the Nazi Era (1933–1938)," *Baeck Yearbook*, vol. 27 (London, 1982), pp. 109–126.

19. Friedrich Nietzsche, *Die fröhliche Wissenschaft, Werke in drei Bänden*, vol. 2, ed. Karl Schlechta (Munich, 1955), p. 127.

20. J. V. L. Casserley, *The Retreat from Christianity in the Modern World* (London, 1952), and C. S. Lewis, *De Descriptione Temporum. An Inaugural Lecture* (Cambridge, England, 1955), p. 7.

21. Owen Chadwick, *The Secularization of the European Mind in the Nineteenth Century* (Cambridge, England, 1975), p. 239.

22. *Ibid.*, p. 49.

23. Klaus Scholder, *Die Kirchen und das Dritte Reich*, vol. 1, *Vorgeschichte und Zeit der Illusionen 1918–1934* (Frankfurt am Main, 1977), p. 20 and chapters 1 and 2 *passim*.

24. For this brief summary I have relied on Fritz Fischer's "Der Deutsche Protestantismus und die Politik im 19. Jahrhundert," *Historische Zeitschrift*, 171 (May 1951): 473–518, and Klaus Scholder, *Kirchen*. See also Werner K. Blessing, *Staat und Kirche in der Gesellschaft: Institutionelle Autorität und mentaler Wandel in Bayern während des 19. Jahrhunderts* (Göttingen, 1982), esp. pp. 250–264.

25. Albrecht Mendelssohn Bartholdy, *The War and German Society: The Testament of a Liberal* (New Haven, Conn., 1937), p. 291.

26. That is how Charles de Gaulle saw Germany from the vantage point of his years as war prisoner; see his remarkable *La discorde chez l'ennemi*, 2d ed. (Paris, 1944).

27. *Hitlers Machtergreifung*, ed. Josef and Ruth Becker (Munich, 1983), pp. 36–38.

28. *Berlin Alert: The Memoirs and Reports of Truman Smith*, ed. Robert Hessen (Stanford, Cal., 1984), p. 102.

29. Detlev Grieswelle, *Propaganda der Friedlosigkeit: Eine Studie zu Hitlers Rhetorik 1920–1933* (Stuttgart, 1972), pp. 190, 183–195 *passim*. Kenneth Burke, "The Rhetoric of Hitler's Battle," in *The Philosophy of Literary Form: Studies in Symbolic Action* (Berkeley, Cal., 1941, 1973), pp. 191–220.

30. Manfred Franz, *Die Erlanger Studentenschaft 1918–1945* (Würzburg, 1972), p. 179.

31. Nadezhda Mandelstam, *Hope Against Hope: A Memoir* (New York, 1976), p. 43.

CHAPTER 6: *National Socialism as Temptation*

1. Theodor Heuss, *Hitlers Weg: Eine Schrift aus dem Jahre 1932*, ed. Eberhard Jäckel (Tübingen, 1968), p. 11.
2. Joachim C. Fest, *Hitler: Eine Biographie* (Frankfurt am Main, 1973), p. 579.
3. Theodor Heuss, *Erinnerungen 1905–1933* (Tübingen, 1963), pp. 413, 436.
4. Friedrich Nietzsche, *Also Sprach Zarathustra: Werke in drei Bänden*, vol. 2, ed. Karl Schlechta (Munich, 1955), p. 298.
5. *Deutsches Geistesleben und Nationalsozialismus: Eine Vortragsreihe der Universität Tübingen*, ed. Andreas Flitner (Tübingen, 1965), p. 117.
6. Joachim C. Fest, *Hitler*, p. 514.
7. The literature about most aspects of the Third Reich is vast. It is impossible to list even the most relevant works. Yet even in what may be the best-plowed field of twentieth-century history, there remain important gaps. A useful study of popular opinion and the Hitler cult is Ian Kershaw, *Der Hitler-Mythos: Volksmeinung und Propaganda im Dritten Reich* (Stuttgart, 1980).
8. For an exemplary study of the reciprocal relation between historic events and unconscious wishes, see Peter Loewenberg, "The Psychohistorical Origins of the Nazi Youth Cohort," in *Decoding the Past: The Psychohistorical Approach* (New York, 1983), pp. 240–283.
9. Berhard Schulz, "Die Gleichschaltung des öffentlichen Lebens," in *Deutschland 1933*, ed. Wolfgang Treue and Jürgen Schmädeke (Berlin, 1984), p. 71.
10. This was obviously a long-term historical process, affecting most of Europe. For a recent discussion, see Thomas Nipperdey, *Deutsche Geschichte 1800–1866: Bürgerwelt und starker Staat* (Munich, 1983), pp. 300ff.
11. Fritz Stern, *The Politics of Cultural Despair: A Study in the Rise of the Germanic Ideology* (Berkeley, Cal., 1961). Recently, too: Geoffrey G. Field, *Evangelist of Race: The Germanic Vision of Houston Stewart Chamberlain* (New York, 1981).
12. See Zeev Sternhell, *La droite révolutionnaire 1885–1914: Les origines françaises du fascisme* (Paris, 1978).
13. Hugo von Hofmannsthal, *Das Schrifttum als geistiger Raum der Nation* (Munich, 1927), p. 27.
14. Friedrich Nietzsche, *Morgenröte: Werke in drei Bänden*, vol. 1, ed. Karl Schlechta (Munich, 1955), p. 1145.
15. Edgar J. Jung, "Neubelebung von Weimar? Verkehrung der Fronten," *Deutsche Rundschau*, 231 (June 1932): 154, 159. Joachim Fest, *Hitler*, p. 631. Outstanding on this subject as well as on National Socialism in general is Karl Dietrich Bracher, *The German Dictatorship: The Origins, Structure, and Effects of National Socialism* (New York and Washington, D.C., 1972).
16. There is an excellent doctoral dissertation by Jerry Zucker Muller, "Radical Conservatism and Social Theory: Hans Freyer and the Other God That Failed," Ph.D. Diss., Columbia University, 1984.

17. Thomas Mann, *Tagebücher 1933–1934*, ed. Peter de Mendelssohn (Frankfurt am Main, 1977), p. 458.

18. Karl Löwith, *Mein Leben in Deutschland vor und nach 1933: Ein Bericht*, with a preface by Reinhart Koselleck (Stuttgart, 1986), pp. 48, 71.

19. See Peter Loewenberg, "Psychohistorical Origins," p. 251.

20. Konrad Heiden, *Geschichte des Nationalsozialismus: Die Karriere einer Idee* (Berlin, 1932), p. 295.

21. Flitner, *Deutsches Geistesleben und Nationalsozialismus*, pp. 34, 36.

22. Uwe Dietrich Adam, *Hochschule und Nationalsozialismus: Die Universität Tübingen im Dritten Reich* (Tübingen, 1977), pp. 23, 40. See also Geoffrey J. Giles, *Students and National Socialism in Germany* (Princeton, N.J., 1985).

23. Kurt Nowak, *Evangelische Kirche und Weimarer Republik: Zum politischen Weg des deutschen Protestantismus zwischen 1918 und 1932* (Göttingen, 1981), pp. 315–316.

24. *Ibid.*, p. 326.

25. Klaus Scholder, *Die Kirchen und das Dritte Reich*, vol. 1, *Vorgeschichte und Zeit der Illusionen 1918–1934* (Frankfurt am Main, 1977), pp. 174, 179.

26. Christoph Strom, "Der Widerstandskreis um Dietrich Bonhoeffer und Hans von Dohnanyi," in *Der Widerstand gegen den Nationalsozialismus: Die deutsche Gesellschaft und der Widerstand gegen Hitler*, eds. Jürgen Schmädeke and Peter Steinbach (Munich and Zurich, 1985), pp. 303–304.

27. Gerhard Ritter, *Carl Goerdeler und die deutsche Widerstandsbewegung* (Stuttgart, 1954), pp. 43–64 *passim*. See, too, in connection with Ritter's biography, the critical remarks on it in Christian Müller, *Oberst i. G. Stauffenberg: Eine Biographie* (Duesseldorf, n.d.), pp. 12–23 *passim*.

28. *Die Mittwochs-Gesellschaft: Protokolle aus dem geistigen Deutschland 1932 bis 1944*, ed. Klaus Scholder (Berlin, 1982), pp. 66–69.

29. Hans Mommsen, *Beamtentum im Dritten Reich: Mit ausgewählten Quellen zur nationalsozialistischen Beamtenpolitik* (Stuttgart, 1966), p. 21.

30. Klaus-Jürgen Müller, *General Ludwig Beck: Studien und Dokumente zur politisch-militärischen Vorstellungswelt und Tätigkeit des Generalstabschefs des deutschen Heeres 1933–1938* (Boppard am Rhein, 1980), p. 64.

31. Albert Krebs, *Fritz-Dietlof Graf von der Schulenburg: Zwischen Staatsraison und Hochverrat* (Hamburg, 1964), p. 92, and Hans Mommsen, "Fritz-Dietlof von der Schulenburg und die preussische Tradition," *Vierteljahrshefte für Zeitgeschichte*, 32, no. 2 (1984): 213–239, esp. p. 224.

32. Karl Löwith, *Mein Leben*, p. 58.

33. Sigmund Freud, "Thoughts for the Time of War and Death," in the *Standard Edition*, vol. 14, ed. James Strachey et al. (London, 1957), p. 287.

34. See p. 291, note 6.

35. I am grateful to Dr. Otto Pfleiderer, Weber's last assistant, for this reminiscence. Letter to me, 9 May 1985.

36. Peter Hoffmann, *Widerstand Staatsstreich Attentat: Der Kampf der Opposition gegen Hitler* (Munich, 1969), p. 36.

37. Reinhard Neebe, *Grossindustrie, Staat und NSDAP 1930–1933: Paul Silverberg und der Reichsverband der Deutschen Industrie in der Krise der Weimar Republik* (Göttingen, 1981), p. 194.

38. *Max Planck in Selbstzeugnissen und Bilddokumenten*, ed. Armin Hermann (Reinbek bei Hamburg, 1973), p. 89.

39. Bruno Walter, *Theme and Variations: An Autobiography* (New York, 1946), p. 299.

40. Klaus Schwabe and Rolf Reichardt, eds., *Gerhard Ritter, Ein politischer Historiker in seinen Briefen* (Boppard am Rhein, 1984), pp. 279, 283, 312–314.

41. Erich Ebermayer, *Denn heute gehört uns Deutschland: Persönliches und politisches Tagebuch, von der Machtergreifung bis zum 31: Dezember 1935* (Hamburg and Vienna, 1959).

42. *Ibid.*, p. 471.

43. On *Vulgäridealismus*, see Fritz Stern, *The Failure of Illiberalism: Essays on the Political Culture of Modern Germany* (New York, 1972), p. xxxvii and *passim*.

44. Karl Löwith, *Mein Leben*, p. 58.

45. Quoted in Eckhart Grünewald, *Ernst Kantorowicz und Stefan George: Beiträge zur Biographie des Historikers bis zum Jahre 1938 und zu seinem Jugendwerk 'Kaiser Friedrich der Zweite,' " Frankfurter Historische Abhandlungen*, 25 (Wiesbaden, 1982): 123.

46. Thomas Mann to Ernst Bertram. *Briefe aus den Jahren 1910–1955*, ed. Inge Jens (Pfullingen, 1960), p. 178.

47. Thomas Mann, *Tagebücher*, p. 38.

48. Prof. Dr. C. F. Freiherr von Weizsäcker to the author, 24 March, 1982. See also his *Der Garten des Menschlichen: Beiträge zur geschichtlichen Anthropologie* (Munich and Vienna, 1977), pp. 563–570.

49. Thomas Mann, *Tagebücher*, p. 174.

50. Erich Ebermayer, *Denn heute gehört uns Deutschland*, p. 249.

51. Friedrich Meinecke, *Ausgewählter Briefwechsel*, ed. Ludwig Dehio and Peter Classen (Stuttgart, 1962), pp. 346, 348, 363–364.

52. Quoted in Eberhard Zeller, *Geist der Freiheit: Der Zwanzigste Juli*, (Munich, 1963), p. 242.

53. Thomas Mann, *Sorge um Deutschland: Sechs Essays* (Frankfurt am Main, 1957), pp. 18, 20.

54. *Ibid.*, p. 63.

55. Thomas Mann, *Tagebücher*, pp. 7–8, 32, 171.

56. *Ibid.*, p. 355.

57. *Ibid.*, p. 83.

58. *Ibid.*, p. 46.

59. *Ibid.*, p. 54.

60. *Ibid.*, p. 130.

61. *Ibid.*, p. 132.

62. Thomas Mann to Ernst Bertram, Jens, *Briefe*, p. 179.

63. Erika Mann, *Briefe und Antworten*, vol. 1, *1922–1950*, ed. by Zanco Prestel (Munich, 1984), pp. 72–89.

64. Thomas Mann, *Tagebücher*, p. 243.

65. *Ibid.*, p. 463.

66. *Ibid.*, p. 472.

67. For Bultmann and Bonhoeffer, see the texts in Günter van Norden, *Der deutsche Protestantismus im Jahr der nationalsozialistischen Machtergreifung* (Gütersloh, 1979), pp. 339–341 and 351–356. For the students' pronouncement, see Karl Löwith, *Mein Leben*, pp. 74–75. See also Richard Gutteridge, *Open Thy Mouth for the Dumb!: The German Evangelical Church and the Jews 1879–1950* (Oxford, 1976).

68. For a deeply moving account of the thoughts and apprehensions of some of the youngest members of the Confessional Church, see the partly autobiographical reflections by Eberhard Bethge, "Zwischen Bekenntnis und Widerstand: Erfahrungen in der Altpreussischen Union," in *Der Widerstand gegen den Nationalsozialismus*, pp. 281–294.

69. See the recent book by John F. Pollard, *The Vatican and Italian Fascism, 1919–1932* (New York, 1985).

70. Heinz Hürten, "Selbstbehauptung und Widerstand der katholischen Kirche," *Der Widerstand gegen den Nationalsozialismus*, p. 243.

71. Klaus Scholder, "Politischer Widerstand oder Selbstbehauptung als Problem der Kirchenleitungen," in *Der Widerstand gegen den Nationalsozialismus*, p. 256. Scholder was the leading scholar in the field of church history in the time of National Socialism, and his early death in 1985 was a great loss.

CHAPTER 7 : *Germany in a Semi-Gaullist Europe*

1. On this issue, see Michael Howard's profound and disturbing essay, "The Forgotten Dimensions of Strategy," *Foreign Affairs*, 57, no. 5, 1979: 975–986.

2. In a public opinion poll in 1978, 35 percent of Germans asked thought that the Warsaw Pact had a greater military potential; 14 percent saw NATO ahead; 47 percent saw them as equal. See "The American Shield: How Others See It Today," *Public Opinion*, March–May 1979, pp. 10, 17.

3. Richard Hofstadter and Michael Wallace, eds., *American Violence*, (New York, 1970), p. 43.

4. Stanley Hoffmann, "Fragments Floating in the Here and Now," *Daedalus*, Winter 1979, pp. 1–26.

5. For one prescient discussion of the change, see David Watt, "The European Initiative," "America and the World 1978," *Foreign Affairs*, 57, no. 3 (1979): 573, 587–88.

6. Take as but one example the *New York Times* account of the 1979 meeting of the IMF and the World Bank: "But the West Germans also came with a message, which they were not too discreet in stating, that they represented, at least financially, the strongest power in Europe and that the rest of the world, particularly the United States, should accept the kind of discipline that had brought them their success." Clyde H. Farnsworth, "A Message from Germany," *The New York Times*, October 7, 1979.

7. Henry Kissinger, *White House Years* (Boston, 1979), p. 422.

CHAPTER 8: *Germany and the United States*

1. Marion Gräfin Dönhoff, *Amerikanische Wechselbäder: Beobachtungen und Kommentare aus vier Jahrzehnten* (Stuttgart, 1983), p. 77.
2. Richard Hofstadter, *The American Political Tradition and the Men Who Made It* (New York, 1948), p. x.
3. *The Economist*, September 25, 1982.
4. Carl Friedrich von Weizsäcker, *Der bedrohte Friede: Politische Aufsätze, 1945–1981* (Munich, 1981), p. 595.
5. Part of the Soviet response to the new American missiles was the stationing of new and modern Soviet missiles on GDR territory—to be paid for by the GDR—which is a perpetual debtor to the FRG. In a curious way, these twin developments made some Germans on both sides of the divide feel as if the nation had been put in double jeopardy, both sides equally endangered by their respective super-powers. But it also enhanced their consciousness of common danger, common fate.
6. It is perhaps worth noting that our language has changed as well. It was customary to speak of West Germany; we now usually speak of Germany or of German, when we mean the FRG. A tacit upgrading of the FRG, a belated denial of the existence of the other Germany, or an unacknowledged wish expression? There is an analogous process, annoying to many Europeans, whereby people on both sides of the Atlantic speak of Europe when they mean Western Europe. These rhetorical nuances and the responses to them have their own political importance.
7. Richard von Weizsäcker, *Die Deutsche Geschichte geht weiter* (Berlin, 1983), p. 7.
8. Such a view of the GDR can be gleaned from Günter Gaus, *Wo Deutschland liegt: Eine Ortsbestimmung* (Hamburg, 1983), a one-time best-seller in the FRG. Gaus is the former head of Bonn's Permanent Mission in East Berlin.
9. Helmut Schmidt, "Fürchtet Euch Nicht," *Die Zeit* (North American ed.), December 30, 1983.
10. Hans-Dietrich Genscher, Bundestag Debate, November 21, 1983, in *Statements and Speeches*, vol. 4, no. 19 (November 25, 1983), published by German Information Center, New York.
11. *The Complete Poems of Heinrich Heine: A Modern English Version*, ed. and trans. Hal Draper (Boston, 1982), p. 514.
12. *The New York Times*, September 30, 1983.
13. *Ibid.*, December 9, 1983.
14. Weizsäcker, *Der bedrohte Friede*, p. 11.
15. I recently heard a leading FRG official, charged with special respon-sibility for German-German relations, remark: "The German dy-namic will not stop until reunification has been achieved." An honest and honorable avowal—and yet how to convince the other powers of Europe, East and West, that the dynamic will stop *then?*
16. John Dos Passos, "The Use of the Past," in *The Ground We Stand On: Some Examples From the History of a Political Creed* (Boston, 1941), p. 3.

CHAPTER 9: *Americans and the German Past*

I wish to thank Felix Gilbert, Christoph Kimmich, and David Rothman, who at one stage or another read my manuscript and made most useful comments and suggestions. I also wish to acknowledge the help of Michael Fitzsimmons, Thomas L. Hughes, John Lukacs, R. R. Palmer, and G. Thomas Tanselle. I am grateful to two successive assistants, Adam Bellow and Arthur Brenner, for their aid in my research.

1. Richard Hofstadter, *The Progressive Historians: Turner, Beard, Parrington* (New York, 1968), p. 7; *America at 1750: A Social Portrait* (New York, 1971), p. ii.
2. Leonard Krieger, "European History in America," in John Higham, with Leonard Krieger and Felix Gilbert, *History*, The Princeton Studies of Humanistic Scholarship in America (Englewood Cliffs, N.J., 1965), p. 243.
3. Jurgen Herbst, *The German Historical School in American Scholarship: A Study in the Transfer of Culture* (Ithaca, N.Y., 1965), p. 1.
4. Hofstadter, *The Progressive Historians*, p. 35.
5. Raymond J. Cunningham, "The German Historical World of Herbert Baxter Adams: 1874–1876," *Journal of American History* 68, no. 2 (Sept. 1981): 268; on Droysen, see also Fritz Stern, ed., *The Varieties of History* (New York, 1956, 1972), pp. 120–121 and 137–144.
6. Cunningham, "Adams," p. 261.
7. George Bancroft to Leopold von Ranke, 5 Sept. 1885. In *Papers of the American Historical Association* , no. 6, Report of the Proceedings, Second Annual Meeting, Saratoga, 8–10 Sept. 1885, by Herbert B. Adams (New York and London, 1886), p. 63, n. 1.
8. Hofstadter, *The Progressive Historians*, p. xiii.
9. The text of Judge Dubbin's speech can be found in the archives of the Johns Hopkins University and was quoted in an unpublished speech by Felix Gilbert on the occasion of the Centenary Celebration of the university in 1976.
10. Nicholas Murray Butler realized the dream of creating a major research university. Like many other presidents of American colleges and universities, Butler had studied in Germany and remembered that his time in Berlin had "left an ineffaceable impression of what scholarship meant, of what a university was and of what a long road higher education in America had to travel before it could hope to reach a place of equal elevation." Quoted in Richard Hofstadter and Walter Metzger, *The Development of Academic Freedom in the United States* (New York, 1955), p. 375; see the excellent section "The German Influence," pp. 367–412.
11. John W. Burgess, "Germany and the United States," address before the Germanistic Society of America on 24 Jan. 1908. In The Germanistic Society of America, *Publications*, 1909, no. 1: pp. 6–7, 8.
12. Charles Kendall Adams's *Manual of Historical Literature*, first published in 1882, makes clear that there was almost no German history being

written in America. Adams was a man of very decided taste. Of Carlyle's *Frederick* he wrote: "A work of superlative genius . . . the best history of Frederick the Great in any language." He also thought "there is, perhaps, no more brilliant historical writing in any language than some of the writing of Michelet." 3d ed. (New York, 1889), pp. 292, 328.

13. Albert Bushnell Hart, quoted in Higham, Krieger, and Gilbert, *History*, p. 161.

14. "A Study of History in Schools, Being the Report to the American Historical Association of the Committee of Seven (1898)." In AHA, *Annual Report 1898* (Washington, D.C., 1899), pp. 434–435, 521, 529–530.

15. Hartmut Lehmann, "Deutsche Geschichtswissenschaft als Vorbild," *Aus Reichsgeschichte und nordischer Geschichte*, ed. Horst Fuhrmann, et al. Kieler Historische Studien, vol. 16 (Stuttgart, 1972): 384–396. National Commission on Excellence in Education, *A Nation at Risk: The Imperative for Educational Reform: A Report to the Nation and to the Secretary of Education, U.S. Department of Education* (Washington, D.C., 1983).

16. William James, *The Letters of William James*, ed. Henry James vol. 1, 2d ed. (Boston, 1926), pp. 110–111.

17. Quoted in Herbst, *German Historical School*, p. 17.

18. On Dodd, see Robert Dallek, *Democrat and Diplomat: The Life of William E. Dodd* (New York, 1968), pp. 20–21, 80.

19. Quoted in Hofstadter, *The Progressive Historians*, p. 121.

20. It was a time when Americans became aware of the growing differences between American and German practices; in 1901, the Association of American Universities declared that doctoral exams in the United States "in nearly all cases . . . were more rigorous than the examinations held at the University of Berlin." Association of American Universities, *Journal of Proceedings and Addressess* (1901), pp. 11, 38. Quoted in Herbst, *German Historical School*, p. 9. In a different context but at the same time, Henry Adams expressed his frustration at teaching history at Harvard: "The rather pretentious name of historical method was sometimes given to this process of instruction, but the name smacked of German pedagogy. . . . Nothing is easier than to teach historical method, but, when learned, it has little use." *The Education of Henry Adams*, ed. Ernest Samuels (Boston, 1918, 1973), p. 302.

21. See Fritz Stern, ed., *The Varieties of History*, "A 'New History' in America: Robinson and Beard," pp. 256–266. On the German connection and the New History, see Louise Schorn-Schütte, *Karl Lamprecht: Kulturgeschichtsschreibung zwischen Wissenschaft und Politik*, Schriftenreihe der Historischen Kommission bei der Bayerischen Akademie der Wissenschaften (Göttingen, 1984), pp. 287–309.

22. James Harvey Robinson, "The Study of the Lutheran Revolt," *American Historical Review* 8, no. 2 (Jan. 1903): 207.

23. Hartmut Lehmann, "Martin Luther in the American Imagination,"

typescript p. 435. I am grateful to Professor Lehmann for allowing me to see and cite his excellent manuscript, even before its publication.

24. Bernadotte Schmitt, "Germany and International Peace," letter to the editor, *The Nation* 92, no. 2392 (4 May 1911): 444.

25. Thorstein Veblen, *Imperial Germany and the Industrial Revolution* (New York and London, 1915), pp. 238, 70, xii–xiii.

26. Talcott Parsons, "Democracy and Social Structure in Pre-Nazi Germany," *Essays in Sociological Theory*, rev. ed. (Glencoe, Ill., 1954), pp. 104–123.

27. Bernadotte Schmitt, "Made in Germany," letter to the editor, *The Nation* 99, no. 2565 (27 Aug. 1914): 251–252.

28. Lovejoy had probably seen an early copy of "The Manifesto of the Ninety-three," which was formally published in early October 1914 and in which the leading men of German science and public life sought to rebut Allied charges that Germany had begun the war, had criminally violated Belgian neutrality, and had committed atrocities in Belgium. The manifesto also insisted that German militarism and German culture were identical, while Allied writers—in deference to German culture—had insisted that the two were distinct. The manifesto had the most profound and lasting effect in creating an anti-German mood, especially among Allied academics. On this, see Bernhard vom Brocke's authoritative article " 'Wissenschaft und Militarismus,' " in *Wilamowitz nach 50 Jahren*, ed. William M. Calder III, et al. (Darmstadt, 1985), pp. 649–719, which appeared after I delivered this talk. See also my essay "Einstein's Germany," chap. 1 of the present volume.

29. Arthur O. Lovejoy, "German Scholars and 'Truth About Germany,' " letter to the editor, *The Nation* 99, no. 2569 (24 Sept. 1914): 376.

30. Quoted in Hofstadter, *The Progressive Historians*, p. 286.

31. Quoted in Carol S. Gruber, *Mars and Minerva: World War I and the Uses of Higher Learning in America* (Baton Rouge, La., 1975), p. 70.

32. Albert Bushnell Hart and Arthur O. Lovejoy, eds., *A Handbook of the War for Readers, Speakers and Teachers* (New York, 1917), pp. 70, 85.

33. Charles H. Haskins, "European History and American Scholarship," Presidential Address delivered before the AHA on 27 Dec. 1922. In *AHR* 27, no. 2 (Jan. 1923): 217.

34. Carlton J. H. Hayes, *A Political and Cultural History of Modern Europe* (New York, 1936), p. vii. Quoted in Higham, Krieger, and Gilbert, *History*, p. 278.

35. *Year Book*, Carnegie Endowment for International Peace (Washington, D.C., 1928), p. 170. See also James T. Shotwell, *Autobiography* (New York and Indianapolis, 1961), pp. 134–155.

36. See Chapter 6 of George A. Finch, "History of the Carnegie Endowment for International Peace, 1910–1946" (Carnegie Endowment, Washington, D.C., mimeographed, n.d.).

37. Haskins, "European History," p. 226.

38. David H. Pinkney, "American Historians and the European Past," *AHR* 86, no. 1 (Feb. 1981): 2; AHA *Annual Report 1926* (Washington, D.C., 1930), p. 68; William H. McNeill, "A Birthday Note," *Journal*

of Modern History 51, no. 1 (Mar. 1979): 1. In 1931 a replacement for Charles Kendall Adams's *Manual* was published: George Matthew Dutcher et al., eds., *A Guide to Historical Literature* (New York, 1931, reprinted 1949), with S. B. Fay covering a still quite thin section on Germany, Austria, and Switzerland; see pp. 695–728.

39. John Lukacs, *Decline and Rise of Europe* (Garden City, N.Y., 1965), p. 267, n. 12.

40. Hofstadter *The Progressive Historians*, p. 442.

41. These figures are culled from the Reports of the President and the Treasurer of the John Simon Guggenheim Memorial Foundation (1979), p. xxxii. I am grateful to G. Thomas Tanselle, vice-president of the Guggenheim Foundation, for his help in this matter.

42. Philip Mason Burnett, *Reparation at the Paris Peace Conference*, vol. 1, (New York, 1965), p. 66.

43. William L. Langer, *Gas and Flame in World War I* (New York, 1965), p. xi.

44. Robert K. Merton, "The Fallacy of the Latest Word: The Case of 'Pietism and Science,' " *American Journal of Sociology* 89, no. 5 (March 1984): 1093.

45. Eugene N. Anderson, "Recent Works on German Unification," review article in *JMH* 7, no. 1 (March 1935): 198.

46. In Eckart Kehr, *Economic Interest, Militarism, and Foreign Policy: Essays on German History*, ed. Gordon A. Craig (Berkeley, Cal., 1977), p. ix.

47. I do not mean to suggest that there was any kind of unanimity of view or quality among historians. Some émigré historians, often reluctant departers, could not shed their conservative nationalist views, such as Hans Rothfels. Some younger American scholars could not resist the temptation to reinterpret the past in a conveniently simplistic fashion, as if Hitler really were the culmination of all German traditions. Peter Viereck, *Metapolitics: From the Romantics to Hitler* (New York, 1941), is one such example, distinguished at least by style and learning. After I finished the revision of this paper, Karen J. Greenberg kindly sent me "The Search for Silver Lining: The American Academic Establishment and the 'Aryanization' of German Scholarship," *Simon Wiesenthal Center Annual* 2 (White Plains, N.Y., 1985), pp. 115–137, in which she documents the continued pro-German attitude of some leading American academics and university presidents in the years 1933 to 1938.

48. In Higham, Krieger, and Gilbert, *History*, p. 291.

49. "From the Editors," *Central European History* 1, no. 1 (March 1968): 3. William H. McNeill, "Modern European History," in *The Past Before Us: Contemporary Historical Writing in the United States*, ed. for the AHA by Michael Kammen (Ithaca, N.Y., and London, 1982), p. 97.

50. Gordon A. Craig, *The Politics of the Prussian Army, 1640–1945* (New York, 1955), p. xiii.

51. Hajo Holborn, *Germany and Europe: Historical Essays* (Garden City. N.Y., 1970), p. 1.

52. Hajo Holborn, *A History of Modern Germany: The Reformation* (New York, 1959), p. x.

53. Carl E. Schorske, *Fin-de-Siècle Vienna: Politics and Culture*, paperback ed. (New York, 1981), p. xiv.
54. Mack Walker, *German Home Towns: Community, State, and General Estate, 1648–1871* (Ithaca, N.Y., 1971), p. 4.
55. Haskins, "European History," p. 224.
56. McNeill, "Modern European History," pp. 108–109.
57. Haskins, "European History," p. 223.
58. Noel Annan, Introduction to Isaiah Berlin, *Personal Impressions* (London, 1980), p. xiii.
59. On the *Holocaust* audience, see *The New York Times*, 19 Apr. 1978; 21 Apr. 1978. On William L. Shirer, see *Eighty Years of Bestsellers*, ed. Alice Payne Hackett and James Henry Burke (New York, 1977), p. 40. On Bracher, private information from publishers.
60. Fernand Braudel, *On History* (Chicago and London, 1980), pp. 14, 5.
61. Richard von Weizsäcker, *Die deutsche Geschichte geht weiter* (Berlin, 1983).

CHAPTER 10: *Capitalism and the Cultural Historian*

1. I am told that a German social historian has recently "quantified" the results of the *Buddenbrooks;* he studied and found that indeed a large percentage of family enterprises in Germany faltered in the third generation, as happened in the *Buddenbrooks*. Are such "verifications" likely to enhance or impoverish our understanding of either the novel or reality? Perhaps another study can "quantify" how many British armament magnates left their enterprises to foundlings?
2. Jacques Barzun, *Darwin, Marx, Wagner: Critique of a Heritage*, 2d ed. (New York, 1958), p. 154; and *Berlioz and the Romantic Century*, vol. 1 (Boston, 1950), p. 530.
3. David S. Landes, *The Unbound Prometheus: Technological Change and Industrial Development in Western Europe from 1750 to the Present* (London, 1969), frequently reminds the reader that "attitude is more decisive than law or fiat," that "ideology has roots of its own, and the economy is as much its servant as its master," and that "too often it is assumed that non-economic obstacles simply melt in the face of economic opportunity," pp. 129, 541, 550. On this general subject, see also the earlier, rather biased collection, F. A. Hayek, ed., *Capitalism and the Historians* (Chicago, 1954).
4. For details on Bleichröder, see my *Gold and Iron: Bismarck, Bleichröder, and the Building of the German Empire* (New York, 1977).
5. Relevant here are Joseph Schumpeter's remarks about the motivation of entrepreneurs: "First of all, there is the dream and the will to found a private kingdom, usually, though not necessarily, also a dynasty. . . . The sensation of power and independence loses nothing by the fact that both are largely illusions." *The Theory of Economic Development* (New York, 1961), p. 93.
6. Comte Paul Vasili, *La Société de Berlin* (Paris, 1884), p. 158.
7. Police Report, 16 Jan. 1874, in Bismarck Archive, Friedrichsruh.

8. Lionel Trilling, *Sincerity and Authenticity* (Cambridge, Mass., 1972), p. 15.

9. Adam Smith, *The Theory of Moral Sentiments*, vol. 1 (London, 1801), p. 99.

10. Albert O. Hirschman, "An Alternative Explanation of Contemporary Harriedness," *Quarterly Journal of Economics* 87 (Nov. 1973): 634–637. I am grateful to Professor Hirschman for a discussion of "economic man," and for calling my attention to this passage from Adam Smith: "But the principle which prompts to save, is the desire of bettering our condition, a desire which, though generally calm and dispassionate, comes with us from the womb, and never leaves us till we go into the grave. In the whole interval which separates those moments, there is scarce perhaps a single instant in which any man is so perfectly and completely satisfied with his situation, as to be without any wish of alteration or improvement of any kind. An augmentation of fortune is the means by which the greater part of men propose and wish to better their condition." *An Inquiry Into the Nature and Causes of The Wealth of Nations* (New York, 1937), pp. 324–325.

11. I developed this theme in an earlier essay, "Money, Morals, and the Pillars of Society," in *The Failure of Illiberalism: Essays on the Political Culture of Modern Germany* (New York, 1972), and in a lecture, "Der Krach der Werte," at the Berlin Akademie der Künste in September 1974.

12. One of the most striking of contemporary works on German history, Mack Walker's *German Home Towns: Community, State, and General Estate, 1648–1871* (Ithaca, N.Y., 1971), analyzes and evokes the real experience of communitarian life and briefly sketches its transformation into retrospective ideology.

13. Otto von Bismarck, *Die Gesammelten Werke*, vol. 9 (Berlin, 1924–35), p. 476, and Lenbach receipt, August 10, 1882, Bleichröder Archive.

14. Barzun, *Berlioz and the Romantic Century*, vol. 1, p. 538.

15. Reinhold Begas to Bleichröder, Bleichröder Archive.

16. Gossler to Bleichröder, Robert Koch to Bleichröder, and *Norddeutsche Allgemeine Zeitung*, 2 December 1890, Bleichröder Archive.

17. Jacques Barzun, *Race: A Study in Superstition*, rev. ed. (New York, 1965), pp. x, xix.

18. See the very useful summary by Karl W. Hardach, "Some Remarks on German Economic Historiography and Its Understanding of the Industrial Revolution in Germany," *Journal of European Economic History* 1, no. 1 (Spring 1972): 37–99.

19. A quite unsatisfactory beginning was made by two German sociologists, Dieter and Karin Claessens, in *Kapitalismus als Kultur: Entstehung und Grundlagen der Bürgerlichen Gesellschaft* (Düsseldorf, 1973), but it does at least raise the question "whether in Germany 'capitalism' has ever existed," p. 200.

20. Barzun, "Preface to the Second Edition," *Darwin, Marx, Wagner*, p. xvi.

Acknowledgments

Writing is a time of solitude enlivened by support. I am happy to express my thanks for support, intangible and tangible, received from friends, colleagues, and institutions.

Two of the essays here reprinted carried their own acknowledgments, which I have retained. For other essays I benefited from the counsel of James Brennan, Ronald Breslow, William P. Bundy, Eric Kandel, Peter Loewenberg, Hans Mommsen, Jerry Muller, I. I. Rabi, David Rothman, Robert Schulman, Martin Schwarzschild, and John Stachel. I am grateful for the advice and help of Abraham Pais, peerless biographer of Einstein. Bernard vom Brocke and Brigitte Schroeder-Gudehus kindly showed me their unpublished articles on the Kaiser-Wilhelm-Gesellschaft. Dr. Hennig and Dr. Kazemi of the Max Planck Archives in Berlin facilitated my research on Fritz Haber; so did a grant from the Alfred P. Sloan Foundation and the kindness of Eric Wanner. An earlier grant from the Ford Foundation and McGeorge Bundy's encouragement gave me a further impetus to write about contemporary politics.

I am grateful to Diana Barkin, Kristie Macrakis, and Liza Womack for helping me at various stages of research. As a primitive in modern technology and a persistent revisionist in writing, I have had every reason to be thankful for the help of successive, suffering secretaries, Evelyn Ledyard and Dorothea Phares.

My friend Robert K. Webb read a draft of the Introduction, and his fine and practiced eye spotted various infelicities. Christoph Kimmich read many of these essays, some in several versions and languages, and I gratefully acknowledge his help and friendship. My editor, Ashbel Green, worked with me on the translation of the Haber lecture, and his criticisms and suggestions improved this volume, as he improved earlier works.

Marion Countess Dönhoff gave an early German text of "National Socialism as Temptation" a marvelously critical reading. I owe her more than so warmly austere a person would want me to say. My friendship with Ralf Dahrendorf—which began precisely thirty years ago—has had a bearing on everything I have done.

The book is dedicated to Felix Gilbert, who read several of these essays and who in countless, treasured conversations made me see past and present in a much clearer light. His wisdom and his counsel have been invaluable, and his friendship has been a sustaining boon.

March 1987   FRITZ STERN

Index

A NOTE ABOUT THE AUTHOR

A recognized authority on modern Europe, Fritz Stern is Seth Low Professor of History at Columbia University. He was born in Germany in 1926 and he moved to the United States in 1938. Prof. Stern holds three degrees from Columbia, where he has taught for four decades, and served as provost of the University from 1980 to 1983. He has also taught at Cornell, Yale, The Free University of Berlin, and the University of Konstanz in West Germany, and as Élie Halévy Professor at the Fondation Nationale des Sciences Politiques in Paris. He received a D.Litt. degree from Oxford in 1985 and the Leopold-Lucas Prize from the Evangelical-Theological Faculty of the University of Tübingen in 1984. His other books include *Gold and Iron: Bismarck, Bleichröder, and the Building of the German Empire*, which was nominated for a National Book Award; *The Politics of Cultural Despair*; and *The Failure of Illiberalism*. He was also the editor of *The Varieties of History* and co-editor, with Leonard Krieger, of *The Responsibility of Power*. He was a member of the Center for Advanced Study in the Behavioral Sciences at Stanford in 1957–1958, of The Institute for Advanced Study in Princeton in 1969–1970, and of the Netherlands Institute for Advanced Study in 1972–1973. He has been awarded fellowships by the Guggenheim Foundation, the American Council of Learned Societies, and The Ford Foundation. A member of Phi Beta Kappa, he is on the Editorial Advisory Board of *Foreign Affairs* and of The Collected Papers of Albert Einstein. Fritz Stern is currently at work on a book to be titled "Genius and the Germans: Einstein, Haber, and the Passions of Their Time."

A NOTE ON THE TYPE

This book was set on the Linotron 202 in a type face called Baskerville. The face is a facsimile reproduction of types cast from molds made for John Baskerville (1706–1775) from his designs. The punches for the revived Linotype Baskerville were cut under the supervision of the English printer George W. Jones. John Baskerville's original face was one of the forerunners of the type style known to printers as "modern face"—a "modern" of the period A.D. 1800.

Composed by PennSet, Inc.
Bloomsburg, Pennsylvania

Printed and bound by Fairfield Graphics
Fairfield, Pennsylvania

Book design by Marysarah Quinn